Praise for *Strategic Innovation*

"This book makes an important contribution to new thinking about products and markets that do not yet exist. We know that strategies that worked in the previous industry transformation rarely work in the next one. This book shows the companies and strategies that will build the future."

—**Jouko Ahvenainen**, Chairman and Founder, Grow VC Group

"Anyone can spot a winner with hindsight. As readers of business literature we eagerly follow the mainstream in digesting retrospective tales of excellence from proven performers. This book attempts to beat the crowd in turning to accounts of promising outliers in the midst of white heat emergence where performance outcomes are still undefined. That's interesting! It is delivered through a varied set of rich cases, written from multiple vantage points with also external commentators. The prose that binds it all together is fresh, witty, and full of zest. Yeah! Wow! Oomph!"

—**Professor Arne Carlsen**, BI Norwegian Business School

"Getting past the conventional wisdom is critical and this important new work shows how to use strategic novelty to challenge your thinking."

—**Bill Guns**, CEO, Strategic Business Insights

"From Silicon Valley to Scandinavia and practically everywhere in between, Liisa Välikangas is a pioneer in the realm of studying, supporting, and identifying early-stage innovations across sectors. The collection of authors that she has gathered here represents an incredible cross-section of perspectives on innovation around the world, and offer an illuminating view into the frequently misunderstood world of innovations in both technology and social practice."

—**David Evan Harris**, Research Director, Institute for the Future

"Competitive environment is increasingly not only complicated but complex. Linear, accepted, strategies of the past, which might have worked in complicated-only competition, no longer work. This book gives vanguard thoughts on how to build strategic novelty to paddle the chaotic flow of the new-complex-environment."

—**Jussi Jaakonaho**, Software Integrity Group, Synopsys Inc.; Toolcrypt Group and Former Chief Advisor, Enterprise Risk and Security for Nokia.

"This book reveals the importance of spotting outliers while their radically creative business models and practices represent opportunities, before they become mainstream when everyone, including your competitors, is copying them."

—**Soren Kaplan**, best-selling author of *Leapfrogging*, and founder of InnovationPoint

"An intriguing selection of companies that may help shape the future."

—**Roland Kupers**, University of Oxford and co-author of *Complexity and the Art of Public Policy*

"This book addresses an important topic—the study of outliers—that is long due."

—**Professor Arie Lewin**, Duke University

"*Strategic Innovation* is a thought-provoking book about the quiddity of outlier organizations. The authors have a razor-sharp eye for the hidden markers that reveal strategic novelty as it unfolds. In this book, the authors introduce a methodology that unravels the concept of prediction outliers: how uniquely different companies with unconventional business models have lingering, staggering, and industry-wide effects. As in her previous writings, Ms Välikangas once again contributes a nuanced and insightful outlook for understanding effective business innovation."

—**Claudia Medina**, Consultant in learning technologies

"Learning from outliers is THE challenge of the 21st century. Not because today is more complex than yesterday or tomorrow, but because right now we want to embrace diversity, anchor resilience in diversification, and find ways to align our capabilities to our aspirations for freedom. As the authors of this important book argue, the capacity to appreciate strategic novelty requires sense making that goes beyond the search for averages and the aggregation of common denominator statistics that obscure and ignore outliers. Getting better at learning from outliers is essential if humanity wants to take advantage of the richness of complex emergence."

—**Riel Miller**, former Head of Foresight, UNESCO

"In a world of accelerating change and opportunity, innovation matters more than ever. Yet the greatest potential for disruption lies not in new products and services, but in models that challenge how business is done. That's why learning from outliers to build strategic novelty is the next big management methodology—and mindset."

—**Nancy R. Murphy**, Director of Experience Design and Communications, Worldview Stanford

"*Strategic Innovation* delivers on three important promises: a fresh view of innovation 'before' it is obvious, a deep focus on organizations and business model innovation as the key focus, and a series of actionable steps to identify and implement on such 'strategic novelty' in your firm or agency. Great insights, excellent and varied case examples, and realistic 'what to do now'."

—**Marc J Ventresca**, Strategy and Innovation faculty, University of Oxford and Wolfson College

"A refreshing new look at how you can learn from the outliers who are pushing envelope on new business models. Read this book and you will never look at strategy the same way again!"

—**Peter Williamson**, Professor, International Management, University of Cambridge

STRATEGIC
INNOVATION

To all outliers who wow us:
With a relentless search for strategic novelty,
you lay the foundations for an awesome future.

STRATEGIC INNOVATION

The Definitive Guide to Outlier Strategies

LIISA VÄLIKANGAS
MICHAEL GIBBERT
WITH LAKSHMI B. NAIR,
MARKUS PAUKKU, AND INÊS PEIXOTO

Publisher: Paul Boger
Editor-in-Chief: Amy Neidlinger
Executive Editor: Jeanne Glasser Levine
Development Editor: Natasha Wolmers
Cover Designer: Alan Clements
Managing Editor: Kristy Hart
Project Editor: Andy Beaster
Copy Editor: Cenveo® Publisher Services
Proofreader: Cenveo Publisher Services
Indexer: Cenveo Publisher Services
Compositor: Cenveo Publisher Services
Manufacturing Buyer: Dan Uhrig

For information about buying this title in bulk quantities, or for special sales opportunities (which may include electronic versions; custom cover designs; and content particular to your business, training goals, marketing focus, or branding interests), please contact our corporate sales department at corpsales@pearsoned.com or (800) 382-3419.

For government sales inquiries, please contact governmentsales@pearsoned.com.

For questions about sales outside the U.S., please contact international@pearsoned.com.

Company and product names mentioned herein are the trademarks or registered trademarks of their respective owners.

First Printing September 2015

ISBN-10: 0-13-398944-5
ISBN-13: 978-0-13-398944-1

Pearson Education LTD.
Pearson Education Australia PTY, Limited
Pearson Education Singapore, Pte. Ltd.
Pearson Education Asia, Ltd.
Pearson Education Canada, Ltd.
Pearson Educación de Mexico, S.A. de C.V.
Pearson Education—Japan
Pearson Education Malaysia, Pte. Ltd.

Library of Congress Control Number: 2015944609

Contents

1

Introduction

For the Strategists Reading This Book

Johann Sebastian Bach composed *The Well-Tempered Clavier* for a keyboard instrument, or Clavier, without knowledge of the newly invented piano in Italy.[1] Since then, many leading artists have recorded his famous piece on piano. Leonardo da Vinci invented the flying machine long before airplanes ever came to exist. Arpanet—the predecessor to the Internet—came to exist before e-mail, Skype, or social media were even conceived of.

This book is about such inventions, which have great impact before they have actually happened; it is a book about what we call "strategic novelty." Strategic novelty may seem like a truism—after all, isn't all strategy novel and shouldn't all novelty (at least in business management) be strategic? It should. However, all too often it is not. We will be talking about instruments, machines, and Internet applications, but in particular we expose what is potentially impactful out there in a number of pioneering companies; many of which you might have never heard of, and yet, they are already making a difference.

Because these companies are ahead of their time, we term them "outliers," meaning that they are vanguards, they are off the beaten track. Whether or not they will be trailblazers, e.g., pioneers off-track, isn't so clear (yet). They may sell and produce novel products and services too, but the most compelling story is about their business models. These vanguard outliers embody strategic novelty as they

---

[1]http://www.britannica.com/EBchecked/topic/639313/The-Well-Tempered-Clavier-BWV-846-893.

reimagine and show the ways in which business will be conducted and impacted around the world in years to come.

You may dismiss these outliers as still unproven one offs. They may fail. Yet by the time either these companies or their imitators demonstrate their economic value by conventional metrics, beyond doubt and replicated many times over, their strategic novelty has become mainstream for all to see. They thus no longer provide a potential source of competitive advantage.

The time to learn about them is now. We remember Bach, Leonardo da Vinci, and Tim Berners-Lee for being pioneers, ahead of their time. They were courageous and brilliant in their vision. The rest of us—fast and smart learners—can at least follow the vanguards and outliers working on tomorrow before everyone else does so too.

Introduction

Strategists, both academics and managers alike, search for novelty, foresight, and what's next. When novelty becomes ubiquitous, what is "really" new? Boilerplate strategy is being challenged as theories of momentary competitive advantage are being disrupted by industry shifts and the strategic innovation that organizations, which do not fit established ways of doing things—*outlier* organizations—bring about. Such outlier organizations are often found at the fringes of industries where they are already challenging, uninvited, the prevailing industry or business logic.

Our focus is on *strategic novelty*, where to look for it, how to recognize it, and even how to harness it. We believe that composing music for a "clavier," even before the instrument has been conceived, is useful—both for musicians as well as for creators of instruments. Outliers, and their perspectives at the frontiers of (not-yet-formed or to-be-challenged) industries, can provide valuable lessons for strategists, whether they are in that particular industry or not. We are not advocating generally applicable silver bullets, nor are we focusing on "lessons learnt" in the conventional sense.

Consider two quite opposite approaches for tackling the important task of distilling "generalizable" lessons learned. One is to look back at the historically successful, proven to be relatively stable bloc of incumbent organizations, i.e., those which are said to be driving and often dominating an industry. A second, alternative way, of looking for novelty is to borrow the lens, insights, and visions of the outliers that are driving the not-yet fully formed businesses, or seeking to disrupt established industry models. They are outliers precisely because they lie outside, or at the very edge of, the conventional understanding of industry dynamics and even industry boundaries. By analyzing outliers that lie outside the boundaries of "something," we can also gain more knowledge about that particular "something," in new and important ways. By focusing on outliers, their business models, constraints, and opportunities, we also gain a better understanding of the industry, the incumbents, that the outlier differentiates itself from.

We believe that the second perspective is not only the more exciting, but also the more sustainable, approach. However, it is admittedly more challenging intellectually, cognitively, and even emotionally (more on these aspects of detecting outliers in our toolbox). Yet, it is precisely because such vanguards are underdefined—their outlook is less stable, their vantage points are less clearly defined, and their impact on incumbent structures and emergent markets is more uncertain—that these outliers are an often overlooked invaluable source of strategic novelty.

How to study outliers, then? In management and social science at large, there is a long-standing divide between those believing in quantitative methods, with a focus on large samples to come up with generalizable averages, and those who believe in deep, qualitative insight into idiosyncratic patterns of only a handful of cases. We believe both camps provide meaningful insight. There is a practical snag, though. Outliers by definition are small in number, so a method relying on large sample sizes just isn't feasible. In this book, we therefore use a qualitative analysis, deviant case methodology, to uncover characteristics of outliers as they evolve. The methodology and analysis are less concerned with generalizable, abstract insights—insights already well-known to any experienced student of management. Instead we aim to study examples of those few companies and the business models about to challenge you and the lessons outliers divulge as they do so. This is what Intel's long-standing CEO Andy Grove meant by "only the paranoid survive." The deviant case analysis seeks to expose what is *really* different and novel about a particular company and its strategy. That is our focus here. It is curious to us that so much of strategy research is focused on understanding similarity when being different is at the very core of any strategy worth its name.

We find that outlier companies often exploit digital or industry leading technologies in new ways. However, though technologically savvy, the novelty exhibited by these companies is largely strategic in that they have found new models by which to organize their business. For example, one of our outlier cases, Quirky, a New York-based consumer goods producer rapidly gaining a foothold in the market, is able to harness ideas for new product inventions from an open community of more than a million enthusiasts. Despite its digital innovation and technological and production capabilities, the decision on which ideas to develop and launch is made at a town-hall meeting, via show of hands. It thus brings together digital technology and onsite presence, to launch up to three new consumer products *per week* to the product development pipeline. Quirky is a pioneer in collective innovation.

Recognizing and Acting on Strategic Novelty (Before Everyone Else Does)

The deviant case analysis allows us to identify, track, and ultimately analyze real-time phenomena as they evolve, and in the contexts in which they evolve. This is critical as it helps us address a strange paradox: The emergence of important novelty often goes unnoticed in its early stages, i.e., before "novelty" starts to have an impact. Yet the impact is obvious in retrospect. It is easy to overlook (and dismiss) a company that is still experimenting with its business model, and is far from being able to prove its sustainability along conventional metrics such as business stability. So, one may ask, why should I pay attention to something that may still fail?

These outliers' early commitment to experimental business models opens up the window for new discoveries of strategic importance—learning something others have not yet seen or understood. Subsequently, once this window closes, the impact of the novelty will have manifested itself and become blatantly clear and obvious for everyone to see. Business journals write about it, consultants repeat the story. Heard enough about Apple? It is easy to point at proven success stories and nod in unison. Unfortunately, by the time we are at this "nodding" stage, where any useful information has been masked as a myth, the very aspects that brought about the success are long gone. The sheen has worn off or expired—any instance of strategic novelty is neither strategic nor novel any longer. We might still not be able to easily imitate or learn the source of competitiveness, as its originating contexts would also have changed. Who would not wish to become another Apple today? (Despite many efforts and detailed historic analysis you don't see too many likes of Apple replicating the company's profitability or novelty.) While you wait for the second coming of Steve Jobs, you might as well sit back, relax, and enjoy this book.

The old adage about only searching under the streetlight reminds us to widen our perspective and to peer fearlessly into the dark. The challenge lies in recognizing, tapping into, and experimenting with novelty in a meaningful way, and while it is still relevant to do so, before the novelty becomes the new normal. Yet some courage is required: Novelty is intricately tied to humor, novelty makes you smile, and perhaps therefore is also often ridiculed by those inclined to sarcastic upmanship. Novelty often fails, but in the process of experimentation, you may have learned something very valuable, serendipitously. You may have found something you were not looking for, which is the only free lunch there is! You have met *serendipity*, and *she* is powerful; indeed many if not most valuable things in the world are side effects, unintended consequences, or unexpected discoveries of the pursuits of something else, from love (most likely) to penicillin to Viagra.

Far too seldom do people go out looking to be surprised. Far too seldom are we ready to be WOW-ed, least of all in strategy! We find inspiration thinking of a young chef examining the gifts of Nordic forests and gathering wild ingredients, while also exploring Helsinki's city parks to examine what is growing there naturally, finding *Polypodium* ferns and spruce. A few years later Sasu Laukkonen's Chef and Sommelier restaurant gains its first Michelin star.

Surprise, while often seen as negative and dismissed as a failure of strategy, outliers have been clinically shown to have tremendous impact in terms of learning. Neuroscientists have found that young learners learn best when expectations are defied (Stahl and Feigenson, 2015). However, in order to process all that we see efficiently, we need to look through serendipity and surprise and ask ourselves the infamous question, SO WHAT? We need to systematically interrogate the significance of what we see for ourselves, for our companies. Indeed, learning happens when existing predictions and patterns are found to be wrong and windows of opportunity open in which we are challenged to try to figure out how the world really works, or could work. Unfortunately many companies that rely on uncertainty minimizing corporate strategy have developed a tin ear for surprise and serendipitous discovery. Instead, they favor and reward the familiar using established, safe, and proven metrics, to which, they together with their competition, have decided to limit their strategy. Receptivity to surprise requires a certain degree of vulnerability. Like Odysseus, we have to hear the sirens' song in order to know when to tie ourselves to the mast. This means accepting the risk of a possibly painful unsettlement of one's beliefs, with the attendant need to rework one's expectations and redirect one's conduct (Scheffler, 2010). The outlier companies featured in this book seek to reawaken this natural curiosity for novelty and bring it back into strategy.

Being a strategic novelty hunter may be a lonely undertaking. This book keeps you company: It offers guidance on how and who to learn from, ahead of others, but also addresses the risks related to strategic novelty. In other words, we invite you to learn from things that have not yet happened. Are you ready?

Vignette 1: Why to Learn from Outliers

"There is no use trying," said Alice, "one can't believe impossible things."

"I dare say you haven't had much practice," said the Queen. "When I was your age I did it for half an hour a day. Why, sometimes I've believed as many as six impossible things before breakfast."

—Lewis Carroll

There is ample reason to focus on outliers that are ahead of their time, precisely because they are ahead. First, there is a paucity of theories, methodologies, and perspectives in the strategy literature that support the study of the novel, unique and uniquely novel. To begin with, methodologically, the study of the "unique" has been eclipsed by a rife infatuation with the "general." What is unique and idiosyncratic is often dismissed as insufficiently rigorous, in terms of scientific evidence, as it does not generalize to a larger population.

So why study outliers in management?

Consider a provocative analogy from medicine: Why study the handful of smokers worldwide who turned out to live to a hundred, when most others (smoker or non-smoker) die well before? While the very reason for strategic management is to provide the insights by which to achieve the difference—the long life—the field has by and large concentrated on the replication of typical causal models and average outcomes. But consider the strategic (or plainly, the managerial) relevance of such research findings. What's the value of learning from yesterday's average outcomes and the typical? These insights are by their very nature not strategic, since they perpetuate known, average (rather than outlying, surprising) performance. We submit that it is more fruitful (and interesting) to focus on those couple of centenarians and learn about their psychology, way of living, genetic make-up, and uncover unknown factors by actively searching for possible explanations that have not yet been shared— discover the novelty that is strategic.

Second, even industries that have been thus far the exclusive domain of large corporations or tried-and-tested business models are now being entered by small start-ups and other would-be innovators aiming at disrupting wide sectors. Indeed, we are currently living through a veritable Cambrian Explosion of new organizational forms. Just as during the Paleozoic Era long ago, not all experiments in diversity will survive. However, the ones that do— such as the more advanced multicellular organisms of the Cambrian times—may indeed have a profound and disruptive effect out competing those less evolved.

Technology is allowing for the rapid emergence of, and experimentation with, different ways of organizing complex processes that were, until now, only possible to efficiently transact within the boundaries of a large corporation. Web-based and mobile technologies are connecting individuals at negligible costs. This enables architectures of contribution whereby hitherto unimaginable numbers of individuals could efficiently participate in these unbundled yet sophisticated processes. Piecemeal consulting projects, global social biomedical research or crowdsourced consumer goods design have quickly become commonplace resources supporting innovative strategies. The spaces from which these outlier organizations, business models, or social movements emerge can be the source of considerable knowledge on strategic novelty. The great variation (and lack of common denominators—or generalizable strategies which can easily be applied and replicated across the board) can either be seen as strategic novelty to learn from or something dangerous and disruptive, depending on how one is prepared to deal with outliers. With this book, we encourage you to attune to the former perspective: learning about strategic novelty through studying cases of outliers. Strategy, after all, is about experimenting with variation. The goal of this Case Book with its careful (and intentionally serendipitous) selection of caselets is precisely to provide you with some examples of these sources of inspiration and variation as well as to guide you on your own journey of discovery.

Learning from Outliers and Benefitting from Their Strategic Novelty

So what does the process of "Learning from things that may not quite have happened yet" look like?

An essential first step is to get over the attitude of dismissal, by embracing what can be learned serendipitously. "You cannot be more wrong than be right, before your time." Dismissal or wariness of the unfamiliar seems hardwired into humans. Indeed, we would have trouble making sense of the world without some resistance or skepticism to every new idea that we come across. However, strategists must, in the process of finding a useful middle ground between all novelty-denying skepticism and all-accepting radical credulity, avoid resorting to strategic management dogmas—denying or overlooking important evidence simply because it does not support existing paradigms or known business models. Instead of epistemic apathy (Scheffler, 2010), the inherent surprise of novelty ought to be capitalized on and investigated further.

Outlier organizations are outliers precisely because they are unique and different. Once they become mainstream, they no longer lie outside the main distribution of organizations on the industry scatterplot. Therefore, unless we open our minds during this fleeting window of opportunity we will miss the strategic novelty and all that can be learned about pioneering new ways of doing business. Think of how to integrate this hypervigilant learning approach into your company's strategy process. Outliers may be potential disruptors to your industry or may indicate a new reference group that you can compete or collaborate with. This vigilance may also be directed inward allowing for learning to be gained and better metrics to be developed that capture the experimentation of overlooked divisions and undervalued subsidiaries within your company. There may be outliers inside your organization to learn from also.

By studying such cases that deviate from the mainstream, especially incumbent companies can draw important serendipitous lessons for inventing the future before it happens.

A Methodology with Tools

Innovators are intuitively interested in what's new. We are intrinsically geared to consider situations that are incongruous to our expectations, recognize that which does not fit in. However, translating this inherent human sensibility to discovery into equally powerful strategic insights is often challenging. While what is incongruous may be interesting, its very incongruity makes it difficult for us to integrate with our existing knowledge. In short, it is difficult to learn from novelty. In seeking out lessons from outliers we reframe strategy from a science of studying the average and minutiae of the already known, to an art of potential serendipity and discovery of that not yet widely known. To provide guideposts along this reorientation toward the novel, we suggest the following tools and methodology to the strategic-novelty hunter: First, identify the WOW (strategic novelty), then, execute the SO WHAT? (decipher the significance for your company). Finally, amplify the OOMPH (leverage learning for outsized impact). The following pages will provide you with a methodology to accompany each step in your journey. The accompanying tools and their instructions can be found in Chapter 3.

1. Identify the WOW

Curiosity is piqued when one comes across an outlier. This reaction may be provoked by any number of reasons but is characteristic when one discovers outliers. We ask you to consider, what intrigues you in the case? Why? It may be the emotion that stems from discovering an unexpectedly diverse group of people creatively advancing biotech or an improbable number of people participating in the R&D process of product development. This initial reaction is highly informative and provides a wealth of insights about the observed outlier phenomenon. The reaction may also be instructive about you as a strategist: What is your attitude toward novelty and surprise? These reactions may well range from wonder to anger to relief depending on your relative vantage point. All too often these reactions are rationalized away and dismissed.

One must note that those engaged in the outlier cases are accustomed to that which may be considered novel and unsettling for you or your industry's established norms and practices. For example, at BioCurious, one of our outlier companies, the citizen scientists working in an open biotech laboratory see their creative workspace open to a diverse community as contributing factor, not a deterrent, to scientific innovation. For the multitudes involved in the R&D processes at Quirky an organizational model benefiting from the perspectives of thousands of peers is the new normal, not a managerial nightmare. For a strategist unfamiliar with these business models these organizations may seem lacking in legitimacy, manageability, and/or credibility. Yet they may thrive.

Outliers provide a natural experiment of ideas and business models that counter industry incumbent groupthink. Incumbents, the dominant or established companies, can learn from paying attention to an organization that attempts something that was thought implausible, improbable, or even impossible. Even if the outlier fails, one is better off knowing exactly why the idea did not succeed. If it succeeds you are paying attention to the emergence of novelty. Dismissing failed companies like Napster may mean turning a blind eye to the iTunes and Spotifys that follow.

If you dismiss these cases one must ask, why? The reaction and potential resistance to the outlier cases you come across in this book and elsewhere are highly informative of the strategic mind-set you inhabit, and the boundaries or limitations of your perspective. To emphasize this point, outliers lie "outside" the boundaries of the usual and commonplace. Thus, by their very nature, they also point to the boundaries within which companies pursue the already known and potentially average. In a nutshell: Take this as an opportunity for a personal discovery. What kind of resistance does the case instantly evoke in your mind (e.g., it will never work because . . .)? Is the outlier company too small to be competing in an industry dominated by large incumbent companies? Do the outliers lack the formal qualifications and methods generally deemed necessary to participate in the advancement of science, development of products, or diffusion of ideas? Is their business model unproven, open, and inclusive, when the industry norm is closed and proprietary? What are the strategic implications for you if your industry's practices are outdated, these outliers are onto something, or even succeed?

As the Harvard philosopher of education Scheffler pointed out, "Surprise is, after all, unsettling; it risks the distress of disorientation and the potential pain of relearning" (2010).

2. Execute the SO WHAT

Take the next step. What can incumbent firms and strategists learn from these outliers? After all, many start-ups and new companies are incapable of maintaining their innovativeness for extended periods of time. Many more simply disappear without a trace. Indeed, it is because outlier companies are fleeting windows into the leading edge of ideas and new industries that they provide an opportunity to imagine and develop novelty of strategic importance. When studying outlier companies one does not benefit from the certainty of comparing one's relative position to a known industry average, benchmark, or best practice. Instead one aims to gain from the outliers' perspectives— vantage points at the leading edge. In contrast, the average companies with which strategic management texts are generally concerned are relatively stable and well-known, and thus information sources of limited strategic value in terms of novelty.

Being receptive to new ideas is not enough. Knowing what ideas can enrich your organization is where novelty benefits strategy. This is where the "SO WHAT?" begins. The outliers that provoke the most resistance often demonstrate the kind of novelty that either the industry as a whole, or perhaps only your company, is least receptive to. As the future is not distributed evenly across organizations—it only converges on the average as the industry matures—we argue that strategists' idiosyncratic reactions to outliers can guide this process.

What if established companies experimented with radical business models? Industry incumbents often have the benefit of resources, complementary knowledge and know-how, industry presence, legitimacy, and, of course, examples of prototypes of outliers that serve as trailblazers. The largest hurdle for many companies is to instill an internal cultural sense of curiosity, receptiveness to surprise, and strategic experimentation that would allow for renewal and transformative learning. You may ask, how can your company experiment with novelty in a controlled yet meaningful way? While outlier companies are fully committed to a single experimental business model, you can experiment with strategic novelty on a project or a business unit basis. To further lower the perceived threat of newness leaders must remember that strategic novelty need not be something never before tested. Outlier companies are often able to create the new by transposing existing tools and organizational ideas into original contexts. For example, BioCurious looked to the maker movement and open innovation culture prevalent in Silicon Valley, and the well-known TechShop working spaces as inspiration for its biotech laboratory rather than incumbent university or closely guarded corporate laboratories. By following outliers one can develop portfolios of different strategic options that can then be deployed across the organization in strategically novel ways which scale up impact.

How to de-risk discovery and experimentation in your company? Experimentation, deploying red teams, and exposing strategic plans to contrarians, internal or external, can test existing business models with little or no risk. Industry incumbents have secured their position by developing valuable networks and platforms by which they do business. Outliers have typically had to build versions of these from scratch or have had to develop business models that innovate around these resources. Strategists in established companies can benefit from their position while exercising the option of partnering with strategically novel organizations. Making small, early investments into such relationships could better leverage or optimize existing networks and platform assets, and at the very least, keep your company informed and externally oriented.

The biggest risk is not to try. Many of the established organizations that are following the industry logic are underperforming or failing. Politically, conventional mediocrity is safer than experimenting with novelty. Strategically however, it is not.

3. *Amplify the OOMPH*

The strategic novelty employed by the outlier companies identified in this book, as well as those that you will discover hereafter, serves to amplify the results of the business model. Outliers do not seek to innovate new practices and challenge established strategies simply to be different or for the sake of being novel. They experiment in order to better achieve impact. How can your company gain from these lessons in impact or scale ("OOMPH")?

To leverage strategic novelty your company needs cultural leadership that empowers a receptive audience. An organization that does not want to be surprised will often miss, if not readily dismiss, innovation and opportunities for serendipitous learning. Will you act as an example of being open to novelty that others dare follow? Outliers only seem odd because incumbents have developed practices and methods that are so similar to each other. We argue that group consensus, while warm and fuzzy, is strategically unsustainable and should be avoided at your own competitive peril.

Here are some ideas on how to achieve impact both inside your organization, and externally in the marketplace. They are also addressed in the tools provided.

How to Create OOMPH Internally:

1. ***Leadership.*** How might you show an example that others can follow? How might you de-risk experimentation for others so

that they dare to join you? How might you communicate that the mission is important enough for it to be worth the risk?

2. **Resource Leverage.** How would you gain outsized benefits with a small, early investment? How would you secure a portfolio of real options that you can learn from? How might you move faster than your competitors based on these early resource commitments? How might you commit the absolutely best global resources to your venture?

How to Create OOMPH in the Marketplace:

3. **Multiplying.** How would you make the impact of novelty scale in your markets? How would you make it in others' interest to join you? (e.g., "issue spreading" so that others support the cause; "product enhancing" so that others develop complementary products or services; "agenda shaping" so that others buy into a strategy of experimentation; "niche creating" so that there is a particular market that is being co-created) (Alexy et al, 2013).

4. **Scaling/Combining.** How might you scale this up, either by scaling the experiment or combining many different experiments together? (Try enlarging or integrating.)

5. **Network/Platform Effects.** What kind of strategy would give your company a large role in the unfolding of novelty, or how would you punch above your weight? Whom could you partner with? What would give you a decisive competitive advantage (e.g., cost, timing, lock-in, speed, distracting competition/ strategic signaling)?

Table 1.1 provides a summary of why to learn from outliers in the context of the methodology. The WOW! is a reminder of the nature of outliers as momentary windows into the future. The SO WHAT? invites interested intrapreneurs to experiment with the meaning of novelty and contribute toward the company's strategic renewal. The third step of OOMPH! calls for impact. Strategic novelty can be leveraged to determine or build the future—develop "next" practices or define the "new" normal. Thus, there is competitive value that can be captured via learning from outliers before novelty fades. Ideas and outliers often regress to the mean over time and by then, the leading edge of novelty would have moved on.

Table 1.1 How to Learn from Outliers: A Methodology

Nature of Outliers		Nature of Learning	Nature of Strategy
Outliers offer a fleeting window to strategic novelty that guides trailblazers.	**WOW!**	Learning is at its most effective when expectations are deliberated, defeated, or defied.	Research on strategic management tends to eliminate outliers, i.e., data that is very different from the average performance.
Outliers experiment with different business models and thus expand the horizons on what is possible, plausible, or profitable.	**SO WHAT. . .?**	Emotional responses— such as dismissal— indicate important limits to learning, worth exploring and potentially expanding.	Any decent strategy is about breaking new ground, being different, not the same as other organizations.
The experimental novelty can be amplified (or scaled)— and possibly even become mainstream.	**OOMPH!**	Such serendipitous learning is the only free lunch there is, i.e., you find something you were not looking for.	By the time strategic novelty has become mainstream, it has likely lost its capacity to be a source of strategic learning or offer a source of competitive advantage.

Punching Above One's Weight: Strategy Amplification

In the pages that follow, we describe how the outlier companies not only experiment with novelty but punch above their weight, or create outsized impact. How do companies amplify their strategy, and for example, achieve a significant impact despite limited resources? This is something that large companies need also to learn—how to use resource scarcity as a lever for innovation, not merely a limitation (Gibbert et al, 2007).

Rather than scaling up their strategy with large investments, vanguard outliers smartly and cost-consciously amplify their strategy and its global or inventive impact. We selected our case companies for their potential insights into such strategy amplification.[2] Some,

---

[2]*A Note to Incumbents:* All the companies we examine use resource scarcity as a lever for innovation: rethinking their business models at a much lower cost points to deliver value. This is not only a starting point, or a necessity for survival for many start-ups, but also a useful technique for incumbent companies seeking to contain costs. Rather than cutting costs with 10 percent, try cutting 90 percent and experiment on the emergent solutions.

like Quirky, reached out to a community of inventors and thus used massive search for ideas through *inclusiveness* as an amplifier. Grow VC Group, a pioneer in finance, is another example where building *a novel contributor architecture* enables disproportionate potential competitive advantage. Taking modularity to the extreme of *plug and play* provides amplification for Shapeways in rapid design and manufacturing of industrial products. And of course, doing something so radical that *the costs plummet*, like in the case of Organovo and its revolutionary contribution to clinical drug trials (providing 3D-printed cell tissue replacing the need for testing on living animals or humans), is a tried and true amplification strategy applied first by outliers in ways not conceivable before. An organizational design fostering *generativity* for problem solving could be an amplifier when used skillfully to invite people to address the issue from different angles and then to build on these multiple perspectives and adjacent ideas. Robin Hood Minor Asset Management Coop is generative in its approach for redefining, and democratizing access to equity.[3] Kaggle is highly generative in inviting leading scientists and amateurs to compete on big data problem solving and develop new solution approaches.

Vignette 2: Strategy Amplification, or "Punching Above One's Weight"

The strategic capacity of a resource-constrained organization may be potentially transformative in its competitive environment, for example, by

- Building an architecture for contribution that draws a large number of voluntary actors via inclusiveness and/or enabling modularity through plug and play like Quirky or Shapeways
- Radically reducing cost in a particular industrial activity like Organovo
- Being highly generative in problem solving/opportunity identification like Kaggle

---

[3]*Disclosure*: One of the authors is in the board of the Robin Hood organization and another is a minor asset investor.

In Chapter 2, we introduce the theoretical and methodological perspectives that support our study. In Chapter 3, we offer the Workbook which includes tools for facilitating learning from the cases and, broadly speaking, from novelty and outlier organizations. Then, in the chapters that follow, the cases, some with commentaries from the CEOs, founders or analysts, and participants in organizational activities, are presented in the order of their strategic novelty, or how far out we deem their business model innovation to be from the current mainstream. We start with Fondia, a new kind of a legal firm, and end with Robin Hood Minor Asset Management Cooperative that is in the process of launching its own synthetic finance instruments based on Blockchain technology (an emergent Internet technology for transacting records). Bang & Olufsen, a 90-year old high-tech, high-design sound system veteran, provides a final incumbent perspective on strategic renewal. We conclude with a reference summary of the cases and an outlook for the strategist.

2

Outliers from a Theoretical and Methodological Perspective

Before we introduce the cases, allow us two brief vignettes on the more scientific and technical aspects of outliers. In particular, we describe the methodology and logic behind different types of outliers. If you are not interested in research methodology and the academe of outliers, simply skip the following section.

Outliers from a Theoretical Perspective

Outliers are intuitively interesting organizations from a theoretical perspective in that they both challenge and build upon existing knowledge structures (Murray and O'Mahoney, 2007; Bogers and West, 2012). However, in academic research it is unclear how these outside or fringe sources of knowledge interact with other organizations in order to achieve the major impact they have the potential for. Outliers—whether individuals, movements, or companies—are a potential source of new practices and knowledge. Due to this very difference that defines them, outliers (cf. Hill and Rothaermel, 2003) are credited with being able to disrupt technology, innovate business models, rethink organizational structures, and cross industry boundaries. While often small in size or short on history, such outliers may embody big ideas (Välikangas and Sevón, 2010), and hence exercise more influence than their often humble, or occasionally brash, appearance would at first suggest.

However, outside of the realm of technological innovation and competitive dynamics, the interaction between outliers and incumbents is less well understood, particularly from a knowledge creation and transfer perspective (e.g., Lyytinen and Damsgaard, 2001; Birkinshaw et al, 2008; Abrahamson, 1991; Carlile and Lakhami, 2011). Even within an industry the conditions that enable an innovator to build upon the work of others are not fully understood (Murray and O'Mahoney, 2007). As innovators often rise out of very different types of organizations and contexts (Owen-Smith and Powell, 2003; Padgett and Powell, 2012; Schumpeter, 1942), it is unclear how some, of the many, outliers acting on, and beyond, the fringes of industries manage to leverage their difference to drive system-wide change (cf. Andriani and McKelvey, 2009)—after all difference in and of itself does not equal voice or impact.

As a basis for our empirical research we first assess how outliers have been treated by the strategic management literature, a field with a stated goal of explaining difference and heterogeneity (Felin and Foss, 2004), through an analysis of the scholarship. After noting the implications of omitting outliers we suggest how strategic management research could develop methods and concepts by which to better understand the mechanisms of knowledge creation and transfer.

Outliers and Management Research

We note, in line with Hawkins (1980), that outliers are a potentially heterogeneous subgroup relative to a larger group of mainstream organizations. They can even deviate so much from the other observations as to arouse suspicion that they were generated by a different mechanism. They are noted as potentially important by definition, and their practices make up a significantly different subgroup from the rest of the population (Massini et al, 2005). These subgroups of outlier organizations are not often far from permanent. Instead, such difference in environments and systems has been found to suffer from a regression to the mean (Upton and Cook, 2006) whereby even once exceptional organizations become increasingly average over time. Thus, this difference should be recognized in strategic management research while it exists as firm heterogeneity has been described as the very *raison d'être* of strategic management, and thus contributes to the very essence of competitive advantage (Felin and Foss, 2004).

We conducted a keyword search for "outliers" in the complete electronic archives of a number of the leading management research journals that exhibit empirical studies. Our analysis yielded 198 articles that showed that 74 percent of the studies noted the presence of outliers in their data yet proceeded to utilize methods by which to eliminate or control outliers with the objective of cleaning up the dataset or simply "to keep the graph nicely scaled" (Fuentelsaz et al, 2012). Established methods, including winsorizing the top and bottom of datasets are regularly evoked. Regressions are conducted in order to "counter the bias introduced by potential outliers . . ." (Roper et al, 2008) and justify the manipulation of datasets. (See the U.S. Commerce Department's *National Institute for Standards and Technology Statistics* handbook for a full discussion.)

While outliers were summarily dismissed in most articles in the sample our analysis showed that 17 percent of studies still noted the presence and significance of outliers as indicative or something potentially more than an error term. For example, Fagerberg and Srholec recognized that "[s]imply excluding the outliers from the sample may not be the best solution, as we then may lose important evidence" or that they "do not want to dismiss [data points] as outliers, but on the contrary we believe it would be worthwhile to study them in some detail" (2008). Indeed, of the analyzed articles that recognized outliers in the first place, only 8 percent explained, or sought to explain, why outliers were present or what they may signify.

This is not surprising, given the fact that other studies in management and organizational science have also noted that the potential of outliers is vastly neglected. The study by Gibbert, Nair, Weiss, and Hoegl (2014) identifies that during two decades (1993–2012), only 318 papers (less than 5 percent of the papers published in the top six Management journals[1]) explicitly reported the detection of outliers. Of these 318 papers, only six papers actually perused a further examination of the deviant cases, and only two of them moved on to actual deviant case analysis.

With the noted exceptions, our analysis of the strategic management literature found that most studies did not consider the different explanatory mechanisms, or the potential knowledge they may signal, that caused outliers to be found in datasets. Together with other researchers (such as Daft and Lewin, 1990; Siggelkow, 2007) we are concerned about the methodological sleight of hand that leaves outliers out of studies. Being very different points to a knowledge source that, by the researcher's methodological choice, is left unstudied. We argue that sweeping potentially important knowledge under the proverbial carpet of data-model fit is unlikely to drive progress

---

[1]Strategic Management Journal, Academy of Management Journal, Administrative Science Quarterly, Journal of Management, Organization Science, Management Science and Research Policy.

in management research or practice. This is noteworthy, we feel: As according to Karl Popper, scientific progress comes directly from observations that do *not fit* expectations. Finding that one black swan in a sample collected on the presumption (a.k.a. hypothesis) that all swans are white raises a lot of questions about reasons for this dismissed "unexplained noise" as methodologists prefer to call it.

With this book, we try to show that this unwelcome "noise" in the data can actually be turned into novel questions in the hands of an intellectually curious and methodologically informed researcher. Why is this swan black? Is it actually a swan? Were all the white creatures we believed to be swans perhaps just large seagulls? What makes us see things in black and white in the first place? What else is out there? Where are the other colors?

Toward an Outlier Inclusive Understanding of Knowledge

In order to both understand the conditions under which such very different knowledge can be developed and transferred, the study of outliers must be reconceptualized from a framework where they are simply error terms that do not fit the mean to research on knowledge that can potentially change the mean, redistribute the curve, or establish a new normal (Paukku and Välikangas, 2012). While there are outliers that arise due to measurement or data collection error we argue for the study of the other type of outliers. These are the "interesting outliers" (Aguinis et al, 2013), which hold immense potential for constructive and in-depth understanding of empirical phenomenon (Gibbert et al, 2014). Such outliers are often characterized as the frontrunners of business model innovation, the first adopters of breakthrough technologies and manifestations of future trends (see e.g., www.iftf.org). However, the myriad versions of the future suggested by these frontrunners do not represent the leading edge of a predetermined linear future. Instead the variation they bring about presents real or additional options of next practices, business models, and technologies.

Thus we argue that outliers represent alternative, often competing technologies, knowledge perspectives, or trajectories and challenging models, organizations, and knowledge bases. Difference can, of course, mean failure as well as success (March et al, 1991). Yet omitting outliers comes at a great cost to the comprehensiveness of research (Siggelkow, 2007; Daft and Lewin, 1990; McKelvey and Adriani, 2005). Understanding industry transitions and systemic change requires a study of all of the deviating organizations that, despite, and especially due to their low probability and distance from the mean, may have an impact on the system. We suggest that by reframing the scope of enquiry to include outliers may provoke some interesting theoretical and empirical research findings of the mechanisms by which novelty is created and transferred.

What is the significance of outliers and the novelty they bring to a population? Strategic novelty brought about by outliers can introduce or renew existing practices within an industry. The ideas generated by outliers drive the boundaries by which mainstream organizations eventually perceive, acquire, and process knowledge, and subsequently, process the world. Outliers experiment with business models in various contexts, blurring boundaries and generating more diversity, making the overall system more resilient. For example, the nonprofit sector, led by such organizations as the Bill and Melinda Gates Foundation, has for long adapted best practices from business. Today, some of these organizations are cited as sources of innovation for business organizations tackling complex or wicked problems. In the study of systems, instances of such positive deviance have proved vital when the "positively deviant" have survived otherwise failing systems or when their knowledge has been leveraged to find local solutions to global complex problems (Pascale et al, 2010).

The delineation between the creation of knowledge and the transfer thereof becomes blurred. For innovation to occur, ideas must be widely accessible (Murray and O'Mahoney, 2007) yet different at the same time. We posit that often it is these interactions and knowledge creation and transfer mechanisms that occasionally drive transformation achieving far reaching, and outsized impact. In line with this framing of outliers and incumbents that we seek to understand the mechanisms that can move the goalposts—delimit the context, drive transformational change, and create and transfer knowledge from the margins to the mainstream.

Outliers from a Methodological Perspective

To understand differences between different types of outliers, let's start by looking at a number of recent topical books.

Malcolm Gladwell's New York Time's best seller "*Outliers: The Story of Success*" comes to mind first. The author picks various persons as outliers and examines the factors that contribute to their outstanding success. Other authors, have looked at outliers, too, albeit less explicitly. For instance, W. Chan Kim and Renée Mauborgne (*"Blue Ocean Strategy: How to Create Uncontested Market Space and Make Competition Irrelevant"*) and James C. Collins (*"Good to Great: Why Some Companies Make the Leap . . . and Others Don't"*) have investigated outlier companies and the complex phenomena contributing to their success. Kim and Mauborgne examined companies such as Cirque du Soleil, which succeeded by creating new, unchallenged, uncontested market space, also known as "Blue Oceans," instead of competing in an established market. Collins studied outlier companies that evolved sustainably from "good" to "great" (above average) in terms of financial performance. However, a follow-up analysis of the same set of companies showed that later they actually underperformed the S&P 500. Steven Levitt, author of *Freakonomics*, suggested that a backward-looking, historic analysis of the reasons for success of outstanding performers would not be helpful in providing principles for future success. Professor Rita McGrath, on the other hand, studied outliers that achieved steady growth for 10 consecutive years. She found a small set of 10 companies out of a sample of 5000 publicly traded firms listed on stock exchanges with market capitalization of over 1 billion USD. The 10 companies are very different from the others, though they shared certain common traits combining stability with dynamism, which McGrath identified and explained.

It would appear that the common denominator underlying these studies is their direct focus on higher-than-average performance, success, and competitive advantage, typically measured in stock price or growth rate in comparison to industry peers or market average over a specific period of time. To be sure, there is nothing wrong with extremely good performance, understanding where it comes from, and how it can be replicated. However, this book, and in particular its cases, deviate from this route. We believe that there are expiry dates to the strategies that support these cases of superb performance. Even the most compelling strategy decays over time. Therefore novelty, and the business models that can push the next great performance frontier, might be worth investigating.

Outliers Versus Deviant Case: Why Extreme Performance Isn't Enough

What differentiates the present study from other similar studies is the *type* of outliers we focus on. Rather than using performance as a measure to sample and select outliers, we searched for *deviant* companies that depart significantly from established industry practices. What makes deviant cases different from performance-based outliers?

A recent study by Aguinis and colleagues (2013) suggested a three-pronged classification of outliers: *construct outliers, model-fit outliers, and prediction outliers*. Construct outliers are the outliers that display extreme values on a variable of interest (dependent or independent variable/X or Y), for instance, the small number of people who are exceptionally tall relative to the rest of the population. Model-fit outliers, meanwhile, are observations with extreme values on the predictor variable, and correspondingly extreme values on the outcome. That is, they are observations that have an independent variable or causal condition similar to the typical cases, but have an extreme value on the dependent variable (same X, extreme Y). For instance, if we assume that a theoretical model predicts that tall parents have tall children, we may observe an outlier case in which exceptionally tall parents' children are exceptionally tall (X-height of parents, Y-height of children). Then we come to the final type of outliers, the prediction outliers. These outliers have large, so-called model residuals (only), or large model residuals in addition to having extreme values on the focal variables (similar to model-fit outliers underlying the infatuation with extreme performance we discussed earlier). In simple terms, these are outliers that are significantly "different," i.e., they deviate from the existing phenomenon of interest. They are not (just) extreme values, they are (also) deviant (same X, different Y or same X, different and extreme Y). Keeping with the previous examples, prediction outliers would be cases of people who have tall or extremely tall parents, but are quite short themselves (or are very tall despite having short parents). Thus, the "residuals" in the model are the (unconsidered or unknown) factors that cause unexpectedly (from the perspective of the theoretical model) short body height, despite the tall parents. Figures 2.1 to 2.3 illustrate these three types of outliers.

In terms of this classification, then, Gladwell focuses on construct outliers, whereas Kim and Mauborgne, and Collins study model-fit outliers. In fact, most of the outlier books of the last four decades invariably focus on extreme performance, and try to explain what brought it about. *By contrast, we focus on prediction outliers, i.e., outlier companies which deviate from the industry norms with their uncharacteristic business models* and, despite their different approach and a dearth of the assumed requisite relative resources and experience, *are able to be impactful*. In short, these cases have large "residuals," i.e., differ in amplification with performance

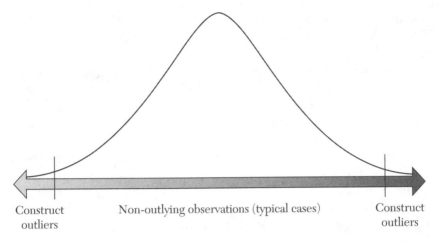

Construct
outliers

Non-outlying observations (typical cases)

Construct
outliers

Figure 2.1　Construct outliers

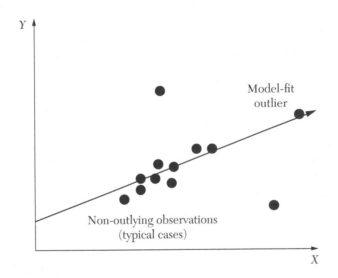

Figure 2.2　Model-fit outlier

implications. Figure 2.4 shows one such example. In this example, the company "BioCurious" is the prediction outlier with a highly innovative business model. The typical cases in this case's field are the incumbents, i.e., traditional university research centers and pharmaceutical companies. The main factor that sets BioCurious apart from its incumbents is its open and inclusive model. Unlike traditional companies, BioCurious makes science accessible and affordable to all. BioCurious calls them citizen scientists. It allows diverse people to engage with biotech for a range of purposes and

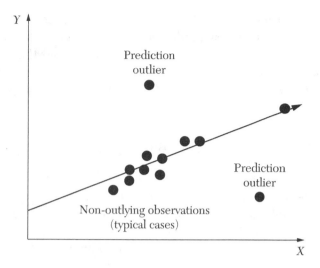

Figure 2.3 Prediction outlier

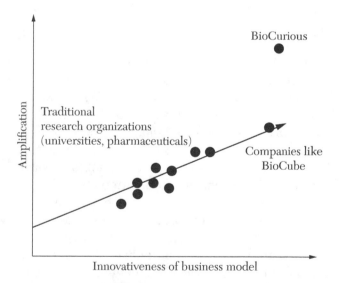

Figure 2.4 BioCurious: illustrative example of an outlier company in comparison with its incumbents

goals, such as experimenting to improve one's work performance, and thus not only pursue academic or corporate biotech objectives.

We believe that an analysis of these prediction outlier companies may shed new light on the inconsistencies emerging whilst trying to reconcile theoretical predictions (industry norms) with real-world observations (Lieberson, 1992). By pointing out a new causal factor (uncharacteristic business model), which has been so far neglected, the analysis of these companies could actually improve the correspondence between what we knew so far (industry norms) and what we now observe (strategic novelty).

Sampling Approach and Research Design

How did we find the outlier companies? We identified broad fields currently undergoing major transformations, in particular due to unique combinations arising from the use of digital technologies and open collaborative practices. It appealed to us that digitization and inclusiveness were major drivers of potential transformation. So, we looked out for outliers in industries and competitive spaces where these drivers were making a unique impact. Despite this systematic method for hunting outliers and their strategic novelty, we tried wherever possible to practice what we preach by being consciously open to serendipitous discoveries and surprise. We found companies like BUG through this openness.

Our mind-set was one of discovery, so we cast a wide net in an effort to search for any company that did not fit norms and/or deviated from what could be loosely termed its peers. We followed a research method akin to grounded theory (Strauss and Corbin, 1990), a systematic discovery-driven method that is suited for exploratory research of phenomena that have been understudied. Thus, for over 3 years we followed closely printed and digital media (publications and blogs) in the fields of business, technology, and entrepreneurship. True to the grounded theory approach, we used a variety of sources, from interviews, archival data, and even participant observation, triangulating wherever possible and relevant the various sources as a means for ensuring the construct validity of our findings. Analysis involved travelling back and forth between data and emerging propositions (with the occasional surprise in between). We also used respondent validation, e.g., by sending emerging and final drafts of the cases to the founders to elicit feedback and commentary. We also extensively draw on external commentary (published in this book) by industry and academic experts both as a kind of peer-review valuation as well as a source of insights in its own right (procured commentaries are published with the cases). We were on high alert looking to uncover novelty at conferences, meetings, and workshops. From several discussions, we followed leads that snowballed into new conversations. In addition, we created opportunities to engage in discussions about outliers with researchers and industry leaders as well. We discussed outliers in the Opening Plenary of the Strategic Management Society's Lake Geneva Conference and presented some company examples, together with their leaders, to the Global Drucker Forum in Wien in 2013. We engaged in a "Talkoot" workshop on non-profit outliers with the Institute for the Future in Palo Alto, California, in 2012 (http://www.iftf.org/future-now /article-detail/at-talkoot-small-makes-for-big-changes-in-the-future/). Throughout this period, we stored and organized, in a systematic way, data collected from company materials and notes from observations and discussions so that we were able to continuously analyze the growing set of data and point to potential cases of novelty. Finally, we considered companies which deviate from incumbent companies in the same arena and demonstrated the ability to create business models that amplify their impact, either by transforming existing strategies or by creating whole new strategies. Despite all this, we have still missed many outliers worth noting and must limit ourselves to the edition presented here.

The majority of the cases we have selected utilize open business models or models, which are more open or inclusive than the industry norm. Many of these involve crowdsourcing (via cloud labor, crowdfunding, crowd-creativity, collective intelligence, co-creation, open innovation, micro-tasking, crowd-contests, etc.). These companies have found ways to address either some unmet customer needs (e.g., Scoopshot, Gengo), new needs (e.g., Kaggle) or unarticulated needs (e.g., BioCurious, Spire), or existing needs through novel means (e.g., Grow VC Group). They use digital technologies in novel ways to accommodate participation and make contribution modular and as easy as possible. They build inviting architectures for contribution that appeal to their target group.

Overall, our goal was to make the outliers' amplification strategies more visible, tangible, and perhaps even replicable. Augier, March, and Marshall (2015) revealed that the creation of the infamously productive RAND Corporation was perceived by some as a "happy accident." Following their in-depth study of the history of RAND, they came to the conclusion that such ventures are unpredictable in their emergence, broadly impactful and distinctive only for a short period of time. (For readers who are interested in studying our outlier companies further deeply, please refer to Box 2.1.)

So why study outliers if they are rare and short-lived? The relevance of the outliers we present in this book lies precisely in this

Box 2.1 How to Look at Prediction Outlier Companies When You See Them: A Methodological Manifesto

For our readers who are interested in going deeper into prediction outlier companies, we suggest a new approach, which comes from organizational research methods and is about theory building from unexpected events. We called this the "deviant case analysis" or "DCM" (Gibbert, Nair, Weiss, and Hoegl, 2014; see also Yin, 2003; Eisenhardt and Graebner, 2007). The most basic DCM technique involves the in-depth analysis of a single prediction outlier, as we have done in subsequent chapters. To further enhance your learning experience from outlier companies, we suggest two more sophisticated DCM designs: replication DCM and full range DCM. See the figure below.

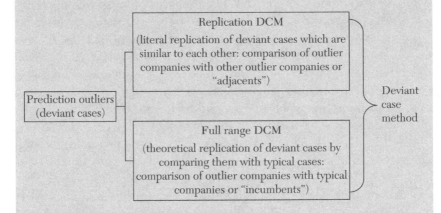

Replication DCM: After the first step, i.e., the single deviant case analysis, a comparison of the business models and subsequent amplification of the outlier companies with those of the "adjacents" or other outlier companies in the space can be done (i.e., comparison of outliers with other similar outliers in the same domain), e.g., comparing *Gengo* with *Conyac*, its Tokyo-based competitor. Expect to learn about the differences between outliers—what does the variation at the leading edge look like?

Full Range DCM: A more sophisticated comparative analysis of the outlier companies can be done by comparing the business models and subsequent amplification of the outlier companies with those of the "incumbents" or the industry's typical companies (i.e., comparison of dissimilar cases in the same domain, with each other), for example, comparing *Gengo* with traditional manual/human translation services. Expect to learn about the differences between what is established, tried, and tested, and what is currently being experimented. What does novelty look like in contrast to the establishment?

very currency. The insights their business models offer have potential beyond the companies themselves. As we discussed in the introduction, appreciating strategic novelty comes at the price of openness to risk and uncertainty. Companies who have already proven their success (even extreme success) are no longer novel in the strategic sense that this book espouses. As their distinctiveness might be short-lived, and even if they persist they are hard to imitate, studying outliers becomes a unique opportunity to tease out potentially transformative yet fleeting strategies. However, we stress the point that this study is not by any means an exhaustive study of all the outlier companies in a particular area. Rather, it is a hopefully eye-opening "fishing trip" to find novelty in deviance—to explore novelty that can expand the boundaries of our current thinking about strategic innovation.

3

Workbook: The Strategic Novelty Tools and How to Use Them for Innovating and Amplifying Strategy

To make the journey more productive and perhaps less self-conscious, we have named the tools in such a way that their purpose can easily be remembered and are intuitive to connect with. Humor is a ready accompaniment to strategic novelty, yet it is important to maintain the boundary between a productive laugh and a cynical put-down. Indeed, those who poke fun at novelty are likely to be right in the short-term as, after all, most new ideas fail—at first anyway. However, this short-sighted perspective, more often than not, comes with a fatal limitation of not being open to learning. In the long term such cynicism carries the accountability for shortchanging the organization's, and hence our society's, potential for renewal (see Table 3.1).

To guide your journey of discovery, this book develops tools to organize your thinking when faced with outliers and novelty. However, these tools are far from boilerplate strategies and serve as mere guideposts by which to bring back the lessons learned from the leading edge

Table 3.1 Embracing Strategic Novelty: How to Learn from Outlier Cases

The outlier case:	What's novel?	Why the novelty is potentially strategic?	How to amplify the novelty's strategic impact?
Company	The "WOW"	"SO WHAT?"	"OOMPH!"

of strategy and potential future best practices, back to your organization. These three tools aim to provoke receptivity to discovery, contextualize relevant lessons from outliers and translate strategic novelty into impactful action.

You may also consult the "Reference Summary on Outliers" for inspiration (you will find it toward the end of this book).

A METHODOLOGY WITH TOOLS*

YOU MAY PROCEED TOWARD YOUR CONCLUSION AS FOLLOWS:

1.

IDENTIFY THE WOW
(strategic novelty)

2.

EXECUTE THE SO WHAT
(significance to your company)

3.

AMPLIFY THE OOMPH
(create outsized impact)

*The visual image of the tools was designed by Johanna Etelävirta.

1. WOW!

Are you often surprised these days? If not, we suggest you reboot your perspective. The world has not have stopped innovating even if you or your organization has. In the past, breakthroughs may have come out of closed laboratories or hard to find Silicon Valley garages. However, today through the connectivity of the Internet and an increasingly open culture of innovation, many novel business plans are hiding in plain sight. The relevant question thus becomes what kind of perspective does your organization have toward next strategies and future best practices?

How to develop this perspective? The first step is open up to surprises at the fringes of what you consider the boundaries of your industry. Developing a sensitivity toward noticing the unfamiliar may require a process of becoming attuned to the diversity of organizations typically not captured by generic strategic management tools. The strength of most strategic management tools is the capacity to distill heterogeneous and complex organizations into limited quantitative characteristics in order to homogenize companies making comparative, cross-organizational analysis possible. Outliers, new practices, and strategic novelty often do not fare well in this kind of analysis. Think different, not similar. Rather than focusing on the similar, such as performance indicators and revenue, much can be learned from how companies organize themselves and the business plans hiding behind the numbers.

There are countless ways by which outlier companies can provoke a reaction. If you think that they are too different and their business model will not work, ask yourself Why? Is their business model open and inclusive when the industry norm is closed and proprietary? Is the outlier company too small to be competing in an industry dominated by large incumbent companies? Do the outliers lack the formal qualifications and methods generally deemed necessary to participate in the advancement of science, development of products, or diffusion of ideas? What are the strategic implications for you if these outliers are onto something, or even succeed? How could your organization do something surprising?

2. So What?

Strategic novelty need not be something the world has never seen before. Many instances of invention and novelty have come about through the application of old tools for new purposes or in new or not-yet contexts. While open innovation, new technologies, and inclusive business models are not radically new in and of themselves, they are increasingly being applied in unexpected industries and contexts, with strategic consequence.

Outliers often blend organizational models across industries. For example, social media has emerged as a new industry that has impacted the way humans communicate and interact. Genomera has boldly asked how this technology can be used in a radically different context, medical research. Enabled by technology and spurred on by broad participation, open and inclusive business models are showing up in unexpected places. These same characteristics, technology and openness, are also making these business models visible to those who pay attention. These visible natural business model experiments conducted by Genomera, BioCurious, Organovo, and other outlier companies are a wealth of information, both confirming and challenging existing organizational models as well as the boundaries of relevant industry strategies.

After identifying something unexpected, something outlying, something strategically novel, ask yourself if this outlier organization, or the business model that it is experimenting with, may possibly challenge your company. Particularly if you decide that this particular company is not the one to challenge you, one must ask how your company's foresight and strategic sensitivity compare with that of your existing competition. For years, Google never thought of Facebook as a competitor. After all, Facebook is in social networking, and Google isn't—right?

3. OOMPH!

Resistance is one of the signals of potential for OOMPH! "If an innovation does not create a lot of internal resistance, it is not really an innovation" according to a senior executive in one industry-leading company. The founders of a major crowdfunding group note that many incumbent financial firms have moved from fiercely dismissing the potential to wanting to collaborate. Look for points of resistance and keep asking (yourself, to start off with) why those holding onto established practices are so impassionate, dismissive, or perhaps fearful.

To punch above your weight, look first for internal amplifiers. Can you show leadership and thus provide an example for others to follow, like Fondia is doing? Are there resources that can be smartly

1.

CONSIDER AN OUTLIER CASE

IDENTIFY THE WOW:

This section helps you identify the strategic novelty. You may think about what intrigues or surprises you in the outlier case and why, or why you feel a particular emotion—a joy, relief, anger, frustration, and so on. You may also experience resistance thinking, "this will never work" or "sure, but not for us."

EMOTIONAL:
Feel joy, relief, anger?

_____

_____

INTUITION:
Intrigued/Surprised/Excited?

_____

_____

RATIONAL (RESISTANCE):
"It will never work …?"

_____

_____

**IN NONSENSE/IRRATIONAL
ACTION/FADDISH:**
"This will not have any
impact…"…"Too far out…" …

_____

_____

REJECTION:
"We definitely should not do
anything like that."…"Over my
dead body…"

_____

_____

**THREATENED/
POWERLESS/UNPREPARED:**
"That is great but we cannot do it"….
"too risky"…"I wish…"

_____

_____

2.

EXECUTE THE SO WHAT:

INTRIGUED/SURPRISED/EXCITED:
If you were intrigued or surprised, address the following in your organization:

Goals/Renewal:
How is the intrigue, or the novelty, potentially transformative to your company and industry or geography you operate in?
How should the novelty impact your company goals/lift ambition?
How far into the future do you set your goals?
How much opportunity creation is built into your goals?
How might a competitor take advantage of the novelty to outcompete your company?
Who in the industry is best positioned to benefit from such novelty?
What is your worst nightmare of a competitor?

RATIONAL:
If you felt dismissive, then address the following in your organization:

Culture of action/Rapid learning:
How might you experiment on the novelty in a small way?
How can you use the novelty to improve the culture of action in your company and move from wait-and-see to learning about it?
How can you use the novelty to encourage experimentation?
What would your customers like you to learn?
How do you learn about what customers are likely to want in the future?
What is your internal tolerance for experimentation?

EMOTIONAL:
If you felt joy, relief or anger, or other strong emotion, think about:

Ability to engage:
What does the emotion suggest about your relationship with issues surrounding the novelty?
Does the emotion help you lead or does it slow you down?
How might you be able to turn the emotion into a personal strength and source of growth?

THREATENED/POWERLESS/UNPREPARED:
If you didn't know what action to take after this feeling,
then address following in your organization:

Culture of action/Derisking:

How might you minimize the risks of implementation of
novelty in your business?

For example: Develop red teams/act as a devils advocate/
hire contrarians to test the incumbent business models/
cultivate loyal opposition/avoid group consensus at your
own peril.

How quickly would you be able to turn new information into
actionable experimentation?

How might you experiment on the novelty in short term (2-6
months) in a small team (4-5 people) with a small or no budget?
Build a prototype/engage with lead users/make a trial internally/
launch a temporary start-up/ask for passionate volunteers/learn
from others.

IN NONSENSE/IRRATIONAL ACTION/FADDISH:
Address the issue of creativity by attaching a
performance measure that is aligned with your
organization, now and going forward.

Accountability for results/Growth:

How might you use the novelty as a new growth platform?
Who could take charge of the new venture in your organization?
Can you use the new venture to engage intrapreneurs or
internal outliers in your organization? Include a measure of
"opportunities lost" in the balance sheet?

How would you identify early mover advantage and catalyze
small scale experimentation?

How might you benefit from ongoing innovation "despite the
system"?

REJECTION:
If you rejected the novelty out of hand, then consider
the following:

Who in your organization can renew the company?
Where do your ideas come from? How inclusive are your
processes? What is your exposure to new ideas?

How receptive are you to new ideas as an organization?
Where do disruptive ideas come from in your business?
What is your reference group?

What is the pace of your internal renewal? What is your
interface with the unknown?

Do you lead or follow?

How viable is your strategy?

(Measures of strategy decay: replicated, supplanted,
exhausted, eviscerated, faded away)

3.

AMPLIFY THE OOMPH:

If you decided to invest in the culture of action and amplify renewal in your organization, then consider the following. If you rejected the novelty, then start from the beginning with another Outlier case.

HOW TO CREATE OOMPH INTERNALLY:

1. LEADERSHIP:

How might you show example for others to follow?

How might you derisk the following for others (e.g., by showing example) so that they dare to join you?

How might you make the mission important enough to be worth taking the risk?

2. RESOURCE LEVERAGE:

How would you gain outsized benefits with a small, early investment?

How might you create real options to learn from?

How might you move faster than your competitors based on an early resource commitment?

How might you commit the absolutely best global resources to your venture?

HOW TO CREATE OOMPH IN THE MARKETPLACE:

3. MULTIPLY:

How would you make the impact of novelty manyfold in your markets?

How would you make it in others' interest to join you? (e.g., issue spreading, product enhancing, agenda shaping, niche creating)

4. SCALING/COMBINING:

How might you scale this up, either by enlarging the experiment or combining many different experiments together? (enlarge/integrate)

5. NETWORK/PLATFORM EFFECTS:

What kind of strategy would give your company a large role in the unfolding of the novelty, or how would you punch above your weight?

Whom could you partner with? What would give you a decisive competitive advantage? (e.g., cost, timing, lock-in, speed, distracting competition/ signaling...)

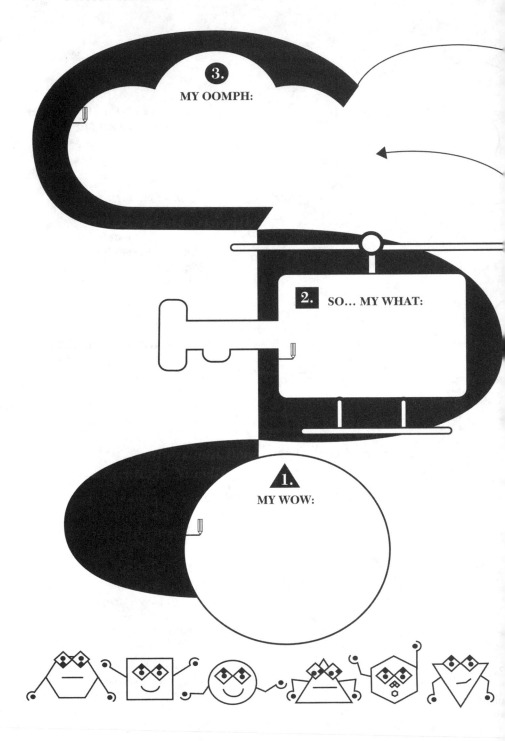

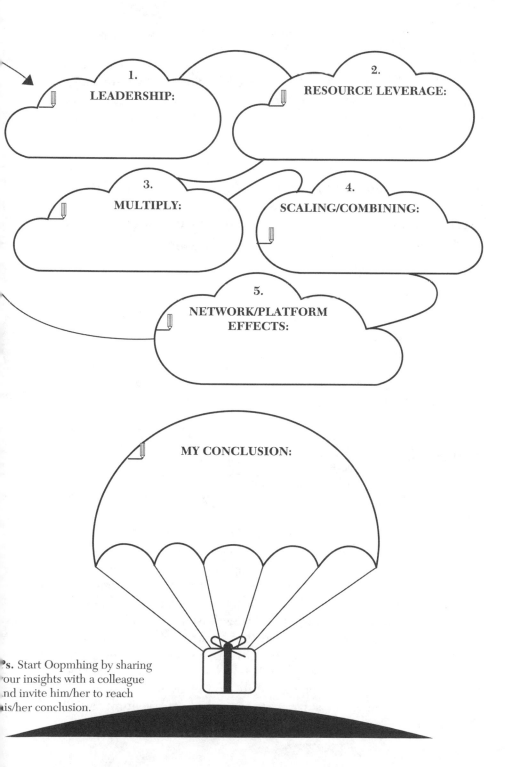

1.
LEADERSHIP:

2.
RESOURCE LEVERAGE:

3.
MULTIPLY:

4.
SCALING/COMBINING:

5.
NETWORK/PLATFORM
EFFECTS:

MY CONCLUSION:

's. Start Oopmhing by sharing
our insights with a colleague
nd invite him/her to reach
is/her conclusion.

leveraged, like in Kaggle? Is there a group of internal outliers you could partner with?

Look to the marketplace. Are there possible external amplifiers such as platform or network effects, like Shapeways? Are there available experiments you can learn from and combine for scale, like Quirky? Can you build an architecture where the global *apassionata* for the cause will join you, like a Robin Hood?

Amplifying may mean that you follow the approach by a senior venture mentor who described his work with start-ups: "I help the founding team to expand their vision 100-fold." Vision may be one amplifier. There are many others as suggested in the tool accompanying Step 3, in learning from outliers and making their lessons matter for your organization and the world.

How to OOMPH? Use Amplification Strategies!

How do outliers punch above their weight, or achieve outsized impact that is far beyond their size, legitimacy, and resources? They use a number of amplification strategies.

Inclusiveness/Openness

The transition from closed, contained innovation systems toward open ecosystems (Chesbrough, 2003) results in an expanding and wider inclusiveness that can reach increasingly distant outliers (Hoegl et al, 2011). As a consequence, closed platforms will lose hierarchical control over the knowledge that is kept within their systems as well as that which is to be kept out. While open platforms allow many to contribute to open systems they do not mandate participation—just because everyone can contribute doesn't mean that everyone will. The implications for competition between business models will thus entail structuring organizations and their interactions in a way that is conducive to contribution, further driving openness and inclusiveness. For example, peer-to-peer and commons models are leveraged to transfer and generate knowledge in, and of outliers, in contexts ranging from open source software to the targeting of venture capital investment.

Radical Cost Reductions

Traditionally even the most willing consumers have been excluded from the development process of products simply due to the prohibitive cost of manufacturing technologies. However, the recent radical cost reduction of prototyping machinery (Chua et al, 2010) and even clinical laboratory experiments will have far-reaching implications for the creation and diffusion of knowledge. 3D printing, life-hacking, and reverse innovation, for example, have shifted the knowledge work of engineering and life-science laboratory experimentation from the corporate lab to the Internet and hacker garage, and back—while democratizing the process of innovation (von Hippel, 2005).

Modularization

The value of manufactured products is composed of the integration of the collective parts. However, the increasingly rapid commodification of components is enabling the modularization of products. When combined with the digitization of physical goods through technologies such as 3D printing, the arena becomes open to consumers to develop and refine products. In doing so the control over the knowledge built into consumer products is being increasingly diffused and becomes open to contribution. Furthermore, drawing on the plug and play characteristics of the software and mobile industry, many emerging platform-based business models are becoming reliant on increasingly diverse organizations. Thus, even outliers with specific or narrow knowledge are able to contribute to highly complex ecosystem of modularized products, previously the domain of closed manufacturing.

Massive Search Strategies

Innovation is often a complex problem-solving process that needs to take into account multiple (often conflicting) aspects such as technological and commercial feasibility, design, aesthetics, degree of novelty, and sustainability. How do companies find ideas for growth and renewal? Facing complex settings and high search costs, such organizational search behavior (Katila and Ahuja, 2002; Simon, 1947) will often end in the selection of the closest satisficing option instead of continuing the search for a more distant but more impactful or beneficial solution—where outliers are often found. Indeed, successful innovation efforts frequently depend on the interplay of many organizations across different industries requiring search beyond close industry counterparts.

The digitization of social and work relationships together with affordable, open-source manufacturing hardware (e.g., desktop 3D printers) and organizational experimentation (e.g., funding through Kickstarter) enable massive search. A current example of the emerging social product development (e.g., Quirky) makes use of the diffused skills and creativity widespread across the globe to bring about products that consumers really want and need, equipped with features that solve many of the problems and weak aspects of existing products. Massive search allows users to engage in very low-cost global search, with direct implication for the nexus of knowledge creation and transfer mechanisms.

(Re)Combination of Adjacent Ideas

Innovations are often the result of the cross-pollination and interaction of knowledge from different industries and fields. Historically this hub of innovation has been the city with its dense overlapping urban networks. The virtualization of these interactions through the digitization of information initially brought together similar communities across geography. However, the second and current stage of this evolution has enabled the virtual cultivation of physical hotspots and building of heterogeneous communities around unifying themes. The diversity of these communities often fosters innovation with even greater impact (Fleming and Sorenson, 2003). For instance, the distributed concept of biomimicry brings together actors from architecture, biology, computer science, design, etc., to create knowledge by exchanging and recombining ideas that can be then transferred back to each incumbents' respective field.

The Courage to Experiment and Learn

We are in the outliers' debt as experimenters of the new. We are in their debt for broadening our horizons and expanding our opportunities as consumers, citizens, and inventors. The society we live in benefits from the exploration of the new. Interpret their boldness like a reference book on strategic novelty—what is novel and out there right now. The courage to experiment is the means and also the message. It is up to you to make sense of what it might mean for your organization.

Be mindful that novelty in the world moves so fast that by the time you have finished reading this book, some of the case companies may have ceased to exist. They may have failed as commercial enterprises. Yet their footprints remain, pointing the direction, beating a path for others to follow (Välikangas, 2007). There are likely to be a dozen other companies on their heels trying out variations of strategies along the same path. For many, or even for most of them, the timing will be not right. They may not be able to overcome the obstacles in their way. However, one of these experiments will eventually break through, with consequence. One of them may well be the future Google, Apple, Facebook, or GE.

Expect to be surprised. Being cognizant of some of the experiments being conducted at the leading edges of your industry will surely expand the scope of strategies for you to consider or compete with, and better attune your organization to the future being built.

One of the surprises we encountered while writing this book was that learning from outliers is very personal and organization-specific. There is no generalizable theory that says what any specific person or organization should focus on learning, although many people are more than eager to assert such pretense. Indeed, such generic approaches of learning could never keep up with the moving target that is strategic novelty. In fact, generalizable averages are the very antithesis of idiosyncrasy and competitive advantage. In other words, learn something others don't. You have a competitive advantage only as long as you are different from, and not the same as, everybody else. For example, Quirky may either teach us that opening up the product development to a community of inventors accelerates the organization's ability to launch new products, or it may teach you the very opposite, that you may wish to hold the function very close to the organization in order to protect your intellectual property. Both are defensible positions. Indeed, if you wish to learn the first option, Quirky is a great case to study implementation and impact of open innovation processes. However, whatever decision is made, the strategy process is more rigorous and better informed after the consideration of a wider range of strategic options. Quirky has experimented with various options at hand. The company leadership understands now that, in order to remain a community-powered invention machine, the company has to become an enabling platform for inventions that leverage others' resources. So, Quirky has partnered with larger established brands such as Mattel and GE. It is important to note that outlier companies are constantly seeking to expand this set of feasible strategies by experimenting with organizational forms, technology, and business models.

Much of the strategic novelty that we discuss in this book is found in organizations or companies that are new, small, and nimble. Peter Leyden, the CEO of Reinventors in California, has found that in his career as well as throughout Silicon Valley, many of the creative people leave following an acquisition. Peter Leyden said in an interview with one of the authors: *"There is something about being small and nimble. Flexibility is important. Innovative people do not do well in large organizations."* Newcomers are unburdened by the legacy practices of incumbent companies and fixed costs of past technological investments. However, outlier companies are often also limited by a paucity of resources and, being vanguards, lack mainstream legitimacy.

We look forward to updating this reference book for strategic novelty every couple of years. The set of strategy options at the leading edge will continue to evolve, as will the outliers that will be pushing this innovation. From our experience in learning from the cases of outliers and their strategies, we note that the prevailing trend points to a veritable explosion in strategic novelty—unexpected organizational forms and business models that are blending across industries and leveraging technologies and creating communities. Right now, we offer a unique tabulation to draw on when designing your own strategy and considering its impact. By familiarizing yourself with this sampling of novelty, your organization will be able to accelerate and expand its change agenda and draw on some great, vanguard ideas currently being experimented on as documented in the outlier cases of this book. Read on.

CASES

4

Fondia: "We Law Your Business"

As the elevator door opens toward the entrance of law firm Fondia's office, we wonder whether we mistakenly pushed the button to a creative company's floor. A few leaflets that read "make law, not war" and "we law your business" assure us that we are in the right place but a distinct feeling of surprise remains. The scent of good coffee blends in with the feel of a unique and inspiring work environment. It is no wonder that Fondia has been awarded as "a best place to work." More than 10 years ago, its founders realized that to follow their intent of rewriting the legal industry they had to break the taken-for-granted rules of their own profession. Could they turn legal counsels into business managers' best friends?

Fondia is a law firm dedicated to business law, established in 2004 and headquartered in Helsinki, Finland, with offices in Sweden and Estonia. The firm operates with over 60 legal experts with knowledge of several industries. Its bold approach to legal services granted visibility to its practice through the award of most innovative law firm in corporate strategy in 2013 by the annual Financial Times Innovative Lawyers Report which is regarded as being among the best researched in the market and the top legal rankings in Europe.

Fondia rewrites the legal industry by taking a proactive approach to law and breaking with the culture of traditional law firms. The company designed a portfolio of services that is strongly customer-oriented and favors efficiency, effectiveness, and flexibility. It includes fixed fee services, standardized and free digital legal support, virtual tools to manage critical documents, and expert case-based counseling. Thus, the core of Fondia's innovative service is its proactive approach to law that is substantiated mainly in an outsourced legal service model, based on a predefined fee, which is used by well over 100 companies.

Furthermore, legal services that can be standardized, such as advisory on contract models, are offered in a one-stop shop mode at low fees. This is useful for start-ups and entrepreneurs that benefit from getting off on the right foot by addressing their risks early, but have limited resources and cannot afford expensive legal counseling. After all, the management of legal affairs underlies a company's business and its growth. Neglecting it might result in major liabilities and poor business performance. Fondia's service model makes costs with legal compliance lower and predictable for clients.

Entrepreneurs and corporations deal with multiple demands concerning legal issues, which require distinct levels of expertise and work. There is routine work around contracts, expert in-depth work to deal with tough situations and litigation, and specialized work by which to deal with industry-specific issues that require know-how and skill. Whereas having an in-house legal department may prove inefficient for many companies, external legal counselors may be ineffective in dealing with critical problems and may lack substantial knowledge of an industry and the client at hand. Therefore, Fondia's model creates conditions for its lawyers to focus on developing expertise, in order to offer tailored counseling for their clients when needed, by enabling efficient management of time and resources within the firm. Clients appreciate running their business without worrying about legal matters, provided that legal support is present in the background, first and foremost when clients are not aware of needing it.

WOW: From Hourly Billing to the Fixed Fee

Traditionally, external legal service is billed by the hour, regardless of whether it is a "Jaguar" or a "Mini" type of work. In this model, law firms have made substantial revenues by charging high hourly fees for work that was routine, repetitive, and highly standardized, carried out by junior associates who were paid much less than experts and partners. Although clients might have complained about expensive legal bills, this model remains the same until today. However, fixed fee billing models have been discussed more and more in the industry, partly because new entrants have introduced them and economic downturns have forced companies to cut operational costs, including reducing their budget for legal services.

Fondia's outsourced legal service model consists of a fixed fee service that covers continuous legal support for the period agreed with the client. The fixed fee includes an initial legal analysis, a plan tailored to the client, the formation of a team of lawyers with the adequate competences for the client's business needs, and continuous service for daily legal matters.

Fondia gets acquainted with their clients' company and business model facilitating close collaboration and effective support for non-standardized legal work. Getting acquainted involves interviewing executives and managers to learn about the business in order to get an overall picture. This helps Fondia to build a suitable team of legal experts to work with the client. It is also a basis for discussing the necessary amount of work and the fixed price of the service. Furthermore, the client has access to the resources and know-how of the whole pool of experts if necessary. Close collaboration and a comprehensive understanding of the business help Fondia anticipate these needs and propose proactive approaches to address them.

> *The overall benefits for General Counsel are that he/she will not be surprised by the bill and thus it will also be easier to make the legal unit's budget. Most important of all is the trust in the local lawyer who takes care of all important legal aspects of the business and the legal risks are minimized. The local business managers can concentrate on the business.*

> —Maire Laitinen, Legal Counsel/Sales
> Team Leader for Fondia's blog

Furthermore, Fondia offers a special fixed fee service tailored for young gaming companies, which was developed in cooperation with these companies. The service includes a risk analysis that delivers the legal issues to which the company should pay attention, phone support with an assigned lawyer who is available during office hours for an unrestricted number of phone calls, and access to an online legal database that stores answers to legal questions compiled by lawyers, contract templates and online tools for managing legal matters. The service has a fixed setup fee of €300 and a monthly fee of €150. Otherwise, legal support for specific matters is agreed separately with

Fondia and billed hourly or with a fixed price. The fixed fee service benefits start-up companies, especially in the high-risk gaming business, by providing legal support at a low cost.

OOMPH: Virtual Tools for Legal Support

Fondia developed virtual tools to support basic legal services and make available safe information storage for the combination of a fixed setup fee and a fixed monthly fee regardless of the amount of users or content managed. For clients, using the online tools is more cost-efficient than requesting work directly from a lawyer.

The *VirtualLawyer* tool is a free legal databank compiled by Fondia's lawyers which functions as an information source for a company's personnel working in a wide range of functional areas, including HR and corporate governance, as well as for entrepreneurs. VirtualLawyer was developed for non-lawyers, cutting all the jargon that characterizes legal documents and is difficult to understand by lay people. The online tool was designed to be a 24/7 self-help tool for businesses that need to find answers to straightforward legal questions, covering the typical issues encountered by companies in their daily business. It is accessible by anyone by registering on the website a mobile phone number to which an access code is sent. VirtualLawyer can be complemented by a document model package, including over 150 contract templates and implementation guidelines, for a fixed annual fee (€240), updated by legal experts free of charge.

> *I don't see how anybody [in the legal sector] could think they can survive without innovation, or rely on traditional ways of doing things—there is no longer such a thing as traditional.*
>
> —Jorma Vartia, former Managing Director, in a comment for the *Financial Times* in 2013

The transaction services offered by Fondia, which include mergers and acquisitions, are very much supported by virtual tools. They systematize procedures, streamline standardized processes, and help clients manage their information pool and follow the legal counseling projects. Thus, these services facilitate Fondia's approach of having the same lawyer managing the whole transaction project. Information blackouts are avoided and electronic tools to manage and process documents increase effectiveness and safety in the due diligence process.

Avoiding Disputes and Legal Risks: the "Make Law Not War"

Law firms are popularly seen as doing business that lives off litigation and dispute resulting from problems raised in their clients' business. In a traditional professional service industry, such as the law, which has not been transformed yet by the digitization and commodification of services, change has been slow. Although other professions that also deal with business risks, such as accounting and finance, have adopted risk management strategies, corporate law firms maintain a model of dispute resolution and reactive problem solving rather than anticipatory and proactive risk management for their clients. Not surprisingly, reacting to legal issues and litigating on a case-by-case basis is deemed the primary operating model in the industry.

Fondia proposes a distinct approach in which it proactively develops anticipatory suggestions to its clients, based on long-term cooperation, to support the business and secure the company's legal base. The proactive law approach decreases potential costs by laying down legal strategies to anticipate and manage future risks.

Open Culture and Shareholding Structure

Traditionally, law firms have a pyramid organizational structure with a few partners on top and many junior associates at the bottom, which is generally reflected in the kind of legal work each type of legal counsel does, their engagement in the firm, and their monthly pay. The *Financial Times* reported in 2013 that this structure was increasingly threatened. Indeed, Fondia had anticipated this expected change. Fondia was founded as a shareholding structure without partners and is not registered as a member of the country's bar association so that all employees can be shareholders. According to professional rules, only lawyers can be partners in registered member firms. The more open ownership model challenges the established boundaries of the professional practice in an industry where normative codes define the credibility and reputation of a firm.

This decision also speaks to another mold-breaking trend in the legal business, in which non-lawyer staff is playing noteworthy roles in creating valuable services for law firms. For instance, at Allen & Overy, another innovative law firm based in Europe, a non-lawyer developed online legal risk management services that are used by more than 160 institutions and 6000 users. Riverview Law is a new entrant in the law industry that also offers fixed-fee services and recruits people for non-usual functions such as project manager and data analysts.

The open culture of Fondia is reflected beyond its internal work practices toward clients and stakeholders. The firm organizes training seminars in its Fondia Academy in the spirit of "developing expertise by engaging in productive dialogue." The training is arranged six times a year to develop legal skills and continuous monitoring processes. On Fondia's blog, internal legal experts discuss various issues related to innovative practices and industry-specific issues and post practical advice for clients and potentially interest parties from a legal perspective. For instance, in the blog, a legal counsel presents general tips for successful crowdfunding rounds and discusses in broad terms how start-ups are valued and how to proceed when start-ups seek financing.

In recent years, Fondia organized training seminars dedicated to different themes relevant to the gaming industry and posted those videos online for public view. For instance, one of Fondia's legal counsels and experts in the gaming business discussed legal approaches to freemium games, what is involved in meeting national and international legislation, and the implications for compliance with consumer law and advertising to children. The seminars illustrate how Fondia has developed specific services for the gaming industry, which has recently become increasingly important in the Finnish and Swedish business landscapes.

Outlook

Fondia's approach to legal services is completely unconventional and innovative for industry standards. Indeed, the company is rewriting the legal industry using lean services with fixed fees, digital infrastructures, and a proactive approach to law, which reduces its clients' costs with legal affairs. In traditional industries, the mold is so thick and solid it makes it tough to break. Only a pioneer with a bold spirit and an inspiring vision like Fondia could do that. Well beyond changing pricing practices, the company has carved a place at the heart of business. Will this pioneering approach be amplified to make legal matters not a nuisance and afterthought for business but a foundation for strategy?

At Fondia, anticipating risks and standardizing procedures has proven to be a key element for generating credibility and reputation for the mold-breaking legal pioneer. The company commoditized routine and highly standardized work, so that limited human and capital resources can be applied to develop bespoke, creative, and strategic solutions to support legal compliance and growth. Many of these lean and low cost-operating processes can be tailored to support growth in young start-ups, for whom expensive legal support is either typically out of reach or prohibitive for a budget-strapped business development. Currently the digitization of work, production, and leisure is not only a fad. Indeed, it brings about various challenges for companies already today, namely already known legal issues (e.g., property rights, data protection) but also new ones that come about as new markets and new industries emerge. The pioneering approach of Fondia might well be what companies need to help them break the mold of their own industries.

From the Perspective of Dr. Liisa Välikangas, Professor-in-Residence at Fondia

On Work, Resilience, and Legal Environment[1]

You have work to do you don't have time for? Ask TaskRabbit, a US-based company that provides task performers called "Rabbits" on demand. Through their online platform, 4 million USD worth tasks are offered each month, and the demand for their Rabbits, including an Elite service, is growing fast.

Task performance is increasingly automated, and platforms for ever more sophisticated problem solving are emerging. Kaggle, for example, invites those scientifically inclined to compete on solving tough problems related to ocean health, flight paths, or malware with predictive analytics. Kaggle partners with many leading companies

---

[1]This blog post has been published on March 26, 2015 on Fondia website: http://www.fondia.fi/en/blog/work-resilience-and-intent-changing-legal-environment/. Republished with permission.

to address issues of strategic importance to them. GE Aviation for one, learned how to save millions in engine fuel through a Kaggle competition.

Such innovation is accelerating. For more than 10 years Fondia has been changing legal industry rules and ways of engaging clients. Digital channels (virtual lawyer services) and novel pricing models have been introduced that allow professional law experts to focus on proactively contributing to business decisions.

Inspired by the example set by Fondia, I reflect on some observations that may have bearing on future innovation.

First, as business environments are becoming open in terms of the flow of ideas and innovations, *legal astuteness* is needed. It is not enough to have a lawyer on the other end of the telephone but employees need to be more skilled in continuously coping with sharing and protecting knowledge. In an article with Professor Sirkka Jarvenpaa (California Management Review, Fall 2014), we identified a number of such interactive revealing practices in an opportunity creation network. These sharing and protecting practices allowed the network participants to innovate together. I suggest legal astuteness is of increasing importance as employees work together across company boundaries. Much like quality became "everyone's job" in the 1960, using knowledge to innovate is now "everyone's responsibility" but it will require astuteness to do so: Know what to share and what to protect, and how. Experienced legal professionals may be good teachers of such astuteness.

Second, business risks are harder and harder to manage in any planned way. New strategies are emerging that suggest continuous testing of company defenses to reveal their vulnerabilities. Cyber-attacks exploit such weaknesses. The vulnerabilities are exposed only after someone has managed to breach through. There may be an analog to law here. How *resilient* is the foundation on which the company builds its legal defenses? Similarly as in cybersecurity, constant testing of the foundation may be needed to find the vulnerabilities before someone is able to exploit them. Perhaps lawyers—on your side—increasingly provide the smart evaluation of such potential exposure.

Third, strategy literature knows the term strategic intent that suggests a direction the company is heading. Strategic intent also describes the ambition that the company sets for itself, perhaps a stretch target or a visionary goal. A few decades ago Canon sought to beat Xerox (and did). More recently, Toyota—before (ironically) succumbing to quality problems—became a larger car manufacturer than the-then-world-leader, GM.

I suggest companies would do well to reflect on their *legal intent*. In a competitive business environment that challenges companies to consider their innovation strategies, from open to closed, it seems legal intent, or the company's direction and ambition in terms of sharing and protecting its knowledge base, is important. In business models that build on freemium-pricing or that provide the code free, service on charge, or that include a free product in a package of services, or that uses fluid resources from outside the company to perform work, legal intent may increasingly be the most important component in the company's strategy. How do we enhance our competitive edge while building our ability to continue innovating and engaging customers?

Making the client as an effective co-innovator, partnering with competitors, or outsourcing key tasks means opening the company's knowledge resources and sharing them with others. The legal intent ought to guide those involved in their engagement and ensure that the company is able to innovate faster than its competitors or other-wise protect its future business potential.

In the world where work is splintering and being shared around—TaskRabbits, Kaggle data scientists, and others performing tasks and solving problems and perhaps even finding the soft underbelly for attack—it is easy to lose sight of the big picture.

The big picture starts with

1. Ensure legal astuteness as a widely shared skill among employees;

2. Support resilience by exposing business vulnerabilities before they have been exploited by less than friendly parties; and

3. Develop carefully thought out legal intent for guiding business development and partner engagement.

5

A Quirky Way to Product Innovation

Ben Kaufman started to break rules when he had his parents remortgage their house, just before high-school graduation, so that he could travel to China and find a manufacturer to produce his latest invention—*mophie*, a new type of headphone. Eventually, a quite successful ending for mophie's Shenzen adventure rewarded Kaufman's effort and sparked his enthusiasm for venturing into more products and raising funding from investors, yet, mophie turned out to be also a learning experience for Kaufman. He grasped how hard it is for a single inventor to take an idea for a new product, no matter how good it is, to the shelves of a retail store. Moreover, he learned that something had to be done in order to change that. Kaufman turned to developing a technology that supported collaborative decision-making in product development. The venture turned out to be harder than expected as it was difficult to get validation for the idea. Anyway, that was just the start of something much bigger. Quirky was born.

Quirky is a product development company launched in 2009 that envisions itself as "the Procter & Gamble of the 21st century" according to its founder. What does it mean for Quirky to become the leading consumer products innovator of the future? It promises to "make invention accessible" by welcoming anyone to submit a product idea that solves a problem that people encounter when going about their daily lives. Then Quirky develops these ideas into successful consumer products, taking them to market together with a community of contributors that supports a design-led, collaborative product development platform.

SO WHAT?—Why Should We Care About Quirky?

Quirky's innovation engine is a strategy innovation in product development based on an inclusive business model for consumer products. Quirky brings to market innovative products that otherwise would not see the light of day. Garthen Leslie, a former U.S. Department of Energy executive from Maryland, invented a smart window air conditioner for Quirky.

> "I have often had ideas for products that I kept in a shoe box but did not have the funding to move forward. In my wildest dreams I never thought I'd be looking at a finished product. When they unveiled it, I just had a warm feeling in my stomach that said: it's real."[1]

Jake Zien is the inventor of Pivot Power, a power strip that is "one of the crown jewels of the Quirky empire." Zien came up with the idea as teenager, when a team from NASA visited his high school to hold a contest for creative ideas. He was solving a simple problem—in power strips, some plugs and chargers block available ports next to them. So, Zien made a prototype, won the contest, and was awarded a few goodies for his feat. Ben Kaufman uses Zien's story to illustrate the challenges inventors face. "He could not commercialize, he could not change the way we all consume power with a pat on the back and a t-shirt. Invention was inaccessible to Jake."

Product development involves high upfront costs and various risks for a single person to bear, which discourages even the most enthusiastic inventors with great ideas for new products. Quirky takes on those costs and risks by combining capabilities in design and engineering with community feedback to product development which reveal users' insights on preferred products and features.

WOW: What Is Unique About Quirky's Inclusive Product Innovation

Inviting everyone to meddle is about the blurring of the old boundaries between producers and consumers and "outsourcing" key operational aspects to a wider community. Quirky devised a

---

[1] Quoted from a promotional video for Aros published by Quirky.

distributed innovation process that disaggregates the phases of product development, breaking them into chunks to which it is easy for anyone to contribute. This way, different community members contribute with small increments to selecting the most successful product features.

Quirky receives thousands of idea submissions weekly. Quirky receives a license to use the intellectual property (IP) of each idea submitted, becoming the owner of all IP if the idea develops into a product. Ideas pitched to the community can be anything from a drawing to a working prototype or a patent but they need to solve a problem, be simple and be feasible. Community members who build up on submitted ideas do it for free and may be rewarded eventually for doing so.

Each idea is live on the website for 7 days during which the community reviews it, identifies similar products, and eventually votes on the best. After community curation, Quirky reviews the ideas and decides which should proceed to Eval, a weekly product evaluation ritual broadcasted live from Quirky's headquarters. Quirky's staff and community review, understand and debate each idea during Eval, ultimately voting on whether or not the idea should be green lit for full-blown product development. Those that did not get voted through Eval receive feedback from peers and from Quirky.

Then Quirky reaches out to its community members again. Eval is the kick-off for a community-driven process of iteration of design, engineering, branding, and pricing, supported by product expertise, which has enabled Quirky to launch two to three products weekly. Quirky's staff and community work in parallel and their inputs feed each other's work. Community members know product details, have access to creative directors' notes, suggest design improvements, and influence brand strategy by choosing name, tagline, color, and pricing.

This out-in-the-open process is quick and efficient, taking new products from idea to market in a matter of weeks or even days. Table 5.1 shows product releases until 2014. As the community pool and the product portfolio grow, revenues are growing as well. In 2010, Quirky earned $1.2 million in revenues, which increased to $48 million in 2013 and was expected to reach $100 million in 2014. Growth has been financed by venture capital. By 2014, Quirky had raised $175 million in four rounds of funding from top-shelf venture capital firms, including Andreessen Horowitz, Kleiner Perkins Caufield & Byers, and GE.

Table 5.1   Inventions and Product Line Extensions Launched by Quirky[2]

	2011	2012	2013	2014
Inventions	22	26	30	26
Product line extensions	2	38	68	49

Rewarding Community Engagement

Community engagement is crucial in this process. Quirky fuels it by rewarding community inputs with impact and nurturing a strong sense of purpose and participation. In 6 years, Quirky built a growing product development community of over 1 million people that helped to commercialize over 125 products. Quirky splits a share of the sales revenue with the community by granting royalties to contributors according to their influence in developing a product. To calculate these, Quirky uses a proprietary algorithm for collaborative decision-making, developed by founder Ben Kaufman and others, which quantifies a contributor's influence to the final product features.

Community members earn *influence* points for submitting ideas, curating through voting and rating, developing through research, design, and branding, and committing to buy products in the pre-sales stage. The community receives a portion of all gross sales on a royalty basis, depending on how the product is eventually sold. The inventor gets the largest share (40.5 percent) of this *community pot* and other contributors share the rest according to the algorithm. In 2013, Quirky distributed $3.8 million in royalties to inventors and community influencers.

One of the most successful products is Pivot Power, a bendable power strip that makes it easy to plug in chargers of various sizes. Its inventor Jake Zien, at the time a design student at Rhode Island School of Design, earned $3.39 per direct sale of each item and received around $300,000 in royalties 1 year after product launch. By 2015, he earned over $800,000. Another 1005 people contributed to Pivot Power.

Apart from rewards, Quirky engages its community by putting ideas and inventors under the spotlight, either by extensive discussions of ideas every Thursday at Eval or by placing the inventor's photo in product packaging. Also part of Quirky's community engagement strategy is to play down the role of the CEO and leave the center stage of Quirky's success to inventors and contributors.

---

[2]*Source*: Broadcast of Quirky Town Meeting (17/2/2015) at http://www.ustream.tv/recorded/58936980.

Manufacturing and Retail

Prototyping, testing, and quality assurance are carried out in-house with advanced technology, including 3D printing and packaging tools. After passing the market-testing threshold, most products are manufactured in China. Quirky has permanent staff based in Hong Kong to set up and coordinate production in factories. All products are sold on Quirky's website and through a network of brick-and-mortar and online retail partners that includes Home Depot, Target, Bed, Bath & Beyond, Best Buy, Amazon.com, and Wink.com. Brick-and-mortar sales drove around 85 percent of total sales in 2011. Some of the retail partners have extended partnerships with Quirky. Bed, Bath & Beyond collaborated with Quirky in a fast product development competition for design students to bring ideas to shelves in 6 to 8 weeks. RadioShack challenged the community to come up with ideas for smart toys. Home Depot supported Quirky and GE's co-branded line of connected devices for the home.

Alliance with GE

Since 2013, GE and Quirky have collaborated to develop Internet-enabled home devices to scale in the connected devices market. This entailed a $30 million investment from GE, a minority equity stake in Quirky and in-kind services. In turn, Quirky could tap into GE's knowledge and competence pool to develop products with more advanced features. For instance, Aros, a smart air conditioner, combined GE's air conditioning technology with Quirky's improved design and smartphone interface for remote controlling and energy saving functions. The idea submitter has earned more than $300,000 in royalties as the product became very popular since its launch in summer 2014. Aros took only 3 months to be developed from Eval to product launch. As one staff member explained, in Aros's public development timeline:

> "(the idea) was surfaced from the Quirky archive so we could fast track development for one of our interested partners. For this project, we have foregone Live Eval so we can kick off community research immediately. This is a great idea and a great opportunity that we don't want to miss, so we're excited to press forward so quickly."

Together GE and Quirky set up two complementing initiatives within their partnership—Inspiration Platform and WINK, a smart home platform. GE released 2000 patents for the exclusive use of Quirky's community, to find novel applications of GE's proprietary technologies for home appliances. "The fact that you could use a GE jet turbine technology which is tested in a 777 to make a better ceiling fan, that doesn't hurt GE in any way. It's actually going to make them a little bit more money from royalties and allow that technology to actually prosper," said Ben Kaufman at a press conference in 2014. WINK was developed as a software platform that supported a co-branded line of connected devices for the home that were controlled with web applications.

Within 4 months of their partnership, Quirky and GE had brought to market four new products under the Quirky & GE brand, such as an egg tray that reminds its owner of how many eggs there are and which eggs are the oldest. Yet, in September 2014, GE entered into a deal with Electrolux to sell its Home Appliances business and Quirky lost access to hundreds of patents of the white goods business. In fact, the Inspiration Platform had developed slowly and Quirky had not launched yet any product straight from it. Nonetheless, GE continued its partnership with Quirky in automation, energy, and lighting applications, and Quirky was allowed to continue selling its co-branded products.

WINK as New Stand-Alone Business of Quirky

WINK evolved into an open platform that connects home devices of any brand to the Internet. It was turned into a subsidiary of Quirky with separate development and leadership teams. The technology is equivalent to an open operating system that makes Internet-connected home appliances accessible to manufacturers and consumers. It can handle most wireless communication protocols, including Bluetooth, Zigbee, and Wi-Fi, and is compatible with Nest, General Electric, Schlage, and Chamberlain. WINK acts only as a connecting hub facilitating web-based control of devices. Leading manufacturers create products in line with their own brands and product development expertise with the additional benefit of being WINK compatible provided a license fee is paid. For consumers, WINK Android and iOS apps that control appliances are free.

WINK started off with strong support from leading manufacturing and retailers. Companies like GE, Honeywell, and Philips enabled their products to be compatible with WINK, and Home Depot was a first mover in actively supporting its adoption in retail. WINK being a separate company, Quirky will continue to try and compete with leading manufacturers in the connected devices' business. Kaufman claimed that WINK was better off providing a platform for development of connected devices, rather than fragmenting the market by launching yet another one. The platform is set to comprise more than 1 million users and around 3.5 connected devices by the end of 2015. Continuing to grow, Quirky managed WINK to follow its inclusiveness strategy.

OOMPH: Extending Alliances Through "Powered-by-Quirky"

In early 2015, Quirky adopted a new business model in which it integrated invention partnerships with large brands established in particular categories, building on its previous experience with GE. In mid-2015, the partners of Powered-by-Quirky were GE (lighting), Mattel (toys), Harman (audio), and Amazon's Dash Replenishment Service (kitchenware). In the partnerships, Quirky acts as a platform for product ideation and development that deploys the community's engagement and strengths to create new products for its brand partners. In turn, the partner brands evaluate and accept product submissions, and deploy their manufacturing, marketing, and distribution resources to bring the Powered-by-Quirky products to market. Thus, through the brand partnerships, Quirky moved upstream to being closer to a product development firm of the likes of IDEO. In turn, Quirky maintained in parallel the previous product development model for its own categories of connected home, connected appliances and electronics, in which the company covers the activity chain from ideation to distribution.

Outlook: Quirky's Inclusiveness Strategy

Kaufman's dream for Quirky is ambitious and extraordinary to say the least. Speaking at the European E-commerce Conference in 2012, he ascribed Quirky's success to its focus on execution. "We're great at getting ideas and figuring out what the world wants. But in the end of the day, Quirky is an execution company. We do all the heavy lifting on behalf of all the inventors in the world. (. . .) Some people like to put us in the Kickstarter bucket. I would just say to that,

Kickstarter solves the wrong problem when it comes to invention. It helps people raise money. It's not about the money, it's about the execution and that's why Quirky is incredibly different." Kaufman was able to build an innovation machine where quirky people arrange the nuts and bolts in the background while the inventor takes the spotlight, and all of this inspires people to participate. Quirky's well-oiled execution engine makes any of us able to pop into Quirky's website, choose an interesting idea, and contribute to it in a fun and engaging way. Suddenly, we'll find ourselves staring at a line of products on a shelf in the retail store across the street and thinking, "Hey, I chose the name for this, it's 0.000018 percent mine. It's a pity they didn't go for the boxy version. That looked so much better."

In its 6 years, Quirky's portfolio has evolved from small plastic products into more sophisticated electronics supported by its unique operating model, its partnership with GE, venture capital, and a growing stream of revenues. Quirky achieved this by opening up to the community key operational aspects of product development and by rewarding all impactful contributions with a share of royalties. From the outset, Quirky tapped into the creativity and engagement of thousands to deploy a fast and flexible innovation process that brought three products to market weekly. In a TV commercial of Quirky, Kaufman is pictured as the CEO who rubs the inventors' "regular-guy feet" because inventors are more important than the CEO who "just runs the company."[3] This is just another quirky way of thinking about the future.

From the Perspective of Inês Peixoto, a Member of the Quirky Inventor Community

I had started writing about Quirky already when I decided to walk the talk. So, I became a member of its online community and picked a project to start off. There were a few to choose from and I took the one that was closest to my everyday life—an inductive phone charging battery named Echo. At that point of development, I could choose only its price range and based on that I became an *influencer* of Echo. That was exciting! Yet, being one among other 2545 curious fellows like me, that contribution translated into 0.0032 percent of influence.

---

[3]*Source:* Quirky's promotional video.

Unsure of what that meant, I thought it was not so bad after all for a first take and proceeded with picking projects. This was 11 months ago. As I write, Quirky is tooling up to produce Echo. I suppose I will know what that tiny percentage means on royalties when Echo sits on a store shelf for the first time and starts attracting buyers.

In the following months I kept earning influence on products for my pricing choices, while venturing into proposing names and taglines for items as diverse as outdoor games, educational toys, and kitchen appliances. I also voted on others' names and taglines. Later, I was able to influence style and design, which involved thinking about which proposed design would be both appealing and functional among a few that designers and engineers in the community had suggested in a previous step of the process.

The process is engaging. First, I wished to experiment with how it worked to know what I was writing about. I ended up following products and checking up on notifications, eager to vote, or propose an idea before time was up. Furthermore, the process is fun—it has a certain twist of gaming to it. Will someone vote on the tagline I suggested? How is it ranking now? (What about in an hour?) Am I getting influence points for this concept? Finally, each product has a story that I can read and connect to. That story starts with a person sharing a problem and a solution to it. Each chapter of the story is a product development step on its own with characters that influence its outcome. Reading through the chapters, we get to know about what is brought into the process and by whom, and appreciate different designs. Eventually, we may leave the website wondering why that wonderful tagline of ours only made it to the fifth most voted.

Quirky is appealing for someone like me, a layperson who finds product development fascinating in its most creative angle and who doesn't mind the heresy of intruding in what is the experts' business. For the 16 products I was able to influence, there were on average more than 2350 people doing the same. The interest of each person in this "community" underlies a myriad of diverse products coming to life at Quirky—be it a simple cleverly designed orange squeezer or a sophisticated music streaming system that operates in the not so far universe of the Internet-of-things.

6

Grow VC Group

Jouko Ahvenainen, the founder of Grow VC Group, has always questioned how transactions are organized and how efficient business ecosystems are built. Some years ago, Jouko's lawyer was handling the sale of the rights to a name of a company he had founded, Data Storm, to an American firm with the same name wishing to enter Finland. The company made an offer. The lawyer's advice: "Take it. You'll never get a better offer." Jouko's response: "You're fired." Having got rid of the middleman he then renegotiated the deal himself, adding more than 10 percent more to the sale price.

The Grow VC Group has been systematically questioning the way that business and transactions are organized as it aims to get into new markets early and leverage learning across its ecosystem. By actively experimenting with finance and technology the Group's companies aim to reconfigure business models and create platforms whereby a wide variety of individuals and businesses can both find opportunities for investment or raise funds. The Group has realized that current financial arrangements do not adequately leverage technology but instead rely overwhelmingly on middlemen such as investment banks, who have profited from these inefficient, non-scaling arrangements. Furthermore, after the 2008 financial crisis many in finance looked for new sources of growth and noted that the existing infrastructure was not efficiently connecting supply and demand. For example, many small- and medium-sized firms, as well as accredited and non-accredited investors alike, are potential sources of growth, yet markets underserve both. However, the Grow VC Group sees that there is a demand for improved finance infrastructure and more diverse business ecosystems as the world is increasingly connected through technology and transacting is done through software. The Internet is enabling new retail finance markets of ever-increasing choice and reach, better serving both supply and demand. Grow VC Group is positioning itself in the finance technology space, inclusively, as *"a worldwide pioneer and leader in the crowd investing, peer-to-peer and online investment market."*

The Grow VC Group owns numerous companies built around a core vision to build an ecosystem of technology and infrastructure enabling financial connections in growing, and thus, uncertain markets wherever they may be. According to Markus Lampinen, one of Grow VC's board members and the CEO of the Group's CrowdValley .com, which offers the backbone for investing and lending services: "We can connect investment targets in California, for example, to a family office in Abu Dhabi. We create this market by providing visibility to different types of supply and demand without necessarily exposing either party. We do the matchmaking and negotiation of terms as the parties may not be able to talk to each other directly—they may even be competitors." In providing this platform the Group is seeking to connect latent transactions that would otherwise remain unrealized as they are not on the horizon of the limited network of an investment bank. (The founders of Grow VC Group are well aware that large investment banks have large networks. However, as these are exceedingly reliant on personal connections the investment banks have not been open to leveraging the power of the Internet, the scale that it enables, and the opportunity to develop new ecosystems.)

The Group's vision is ambitious. To not only redefine the possibilities of worldwide transactions by building a new financial ecosystem that can unleash the potential of technology to but to also open these opportunities to many different types of investors and leveraging the scale of crowdfunding. In technology-supported finance ecosystems there is no reason that everyone from $100 supporters to $100 million institutional investors could not participate. Also, by being so radically inclusive the Group extrapolates the logic by which venture capitalists operate. A single VC may be right often, but generally will not outperform a group of VCs, especially once they are connected to the invested crowd through technology. By being exposed to so many opportunities and sources of intelligence throughout their ecosystems the Group gains a competitive advantage relative to incumbents. To maintain an efficient deal flow with such a high volume the Group bundles the various investors' smaller monies into larger transactions using the same logic by which mutual funds gain transactional efficiencies. However, instead of supporting the heavy infrastructure of mutual funds, for example, the Group allows supply and demand to connect directly through technology.

OOMPH: Bigger Money, Bigger Data, Bigger Regulation

The Grow VC Group started in Hong Kong as an experiment in the emerging post-crisis new financial order in 2009. According to the founders, Hong Kong was selected as a home base as experimenting with financial business models. The founders considered the United States to be too risky in terms of regulation at the time while Europe's many financial markets were too fragmented to initially achieve the necessary scale. The company quickly expanded from its early Hong Kong-based membership-based model and sought to leverage scale through increased connectivity. The Group is now operating out of Hong Kong, London, New York, San Francisco, and Sao Paolo. It also has operations in India. The holding company has investments in more than 10 group companies that each operates in different parts of the financial ecosystem from investor side platforms to digital marketplaces to issuer side dashboards as well as the technology and software back office operations. The multi-firm structure is designed, according to Jouko Ahvenainen, the serial entrepreneur behind the Group, to maximize the companies' learning opportunities in each market and to allow for the Group to rapidly enter emerging sectors or verticals well ahead of incumbents. The diversified structure also allows different kinds of competencies to be developed within the individual partner firms while also allowing them to be made available to the Group in support of common goals and the development of a truly digital investing and lending ecosystem. An added benefit of the structure is to provide the experimental new ideas a grounding in Group with credibility as well some stature and history. The Group claims to be the first of its kind in the world. Through this distributed structure the group has been exposed to various opportunities and, indeed, Jouko says that the Group has received thousands of inquiries regarding prospective finance deals. The Group, while growing rapidly, acknowledges that no one company can develop a full, global ecosystem but that partners in local markets as well as internationally are required.

The Group's novel organizational structure has resulted in an ecosystem in which all stakeholders are catered to by dedicated companies supporting both the investors or issuers of lending and finance, those seeking funding and investment, as well as those providing the digital marketplace for the ecosystem. The entire ecosystem in turn is able to leverage the software developed by Crowd Valley. This software platform enables the rapid scaling of financial transactions globally while ensuring efficiency despite high volumes. The global platform of numerous companies has been developed over time, and is well equipped, to address idiosyncratic local regulations such as particular financial requirements regarding creditworthiness checks as well as the detection and avoidance of money laundering, for example. The platform also allows for customization and interoperability with other software platforms through APIs, the code that translates transactions across digital systems and rapidly allows for the platform use to scale across the Group's companies and beyond.

Having developed a technology to enable a finance ecosystem of lending and investing the founders leverage the platform's potential by focusing on increasing the deal flow or volume while reducing fees that middlemen have traditionally been able to charge due to a lack of market transparency. The transparency afforded by Grow VC Group's approach, a business model that catches a wider array of potential investment opportunities both in scale and in scope, does not mean everything becomes public or open. Instead the Group is about being able to, discretely, connect those looking to invest with those needing investment, worldwide. The ecosystem also can benefit investment transactions by bundling demands for services or projects. For example, small activities such as "changing the street lamps in a city to LED lighting"—which by as a stand-alone transaction maybe a small job that affords an individual municipality little bargaining power—can be pooled together to form an interesting proposition that can transform the transaction into a buyers' market.

Having challenged the rules of the finance game by creating a new digital ecosystem for lending and investing the founders' nightmare is for the Group to be seen as a bank. One of the challenges of being categorized as an equivalent to the traditional incumbent financial actors, in addition for avoiding the regulatory burden that would follow, would be the difficulty of maintaining the momentum that allows Grow VC Group to learn quickly and to move rapidly enough to be able to learn and build the necessary presence in different emerging verticals throughout the developing ecosystem. Grow VC Group aims to build its global, an inclusive ecosystem that leverages the full potential of demand and supply for lending and investing. However, as this near-term future ecosystem continues to develop, the Grow VC Group also needs to make their own activities profitable in the short run. In other words, be poised and ready for the new financial order but not to burn through their own position in the process.

7

Scoopshot: Pulling the Scoop on the Trendy Photo Crowdsourcing Platform

Context

This is not the first time that Mr. Petri Rahja, the founder and CEO of Scoopshot, has launched a technology start-up company. Petri has a background in IT, IPR, and mobile technology. As a result, when he was working on a documentary of photographers and their attempts to get themselves into media companies, he was quite surprised by the short-comings of traditional media. The inefficiency of photography was one of them. Rahja found the whole process to be incredibly slow and time-consuming. It didn't take him long to come up with an idea to make the world a better place, through efficient photography.

With the help of a few technology gurus, he developed the first functional app of "Scoopshot," a trendy photo crowdsourcing service. The interest of some angel investors accelerated the development and final concept design. In February 2011, 9 months from the initial date, Petri launched the product. Within the first 6 months of business, Scoopshot had generated €120,000 in revenue. It was a matter of a few months before Scoopshot went international by entering Sweden and Denmark (November 2011) and the Netherlands (January 2012). By then, it had 282,000 photos in its system and a total of about 100,000 photographers who shoot news photography on-scene. Since then, Scoopshot has been opening the doors of press photography to common people[1] in 165 countries. As of November 2013, it had received a funding of $11 million in three rounds from three investors.

---

[1]But laymen are not the only members of Scoopshot. This is discussed later on in the article.

WOW: Photography for Everyone— Everyone's a Photographer

So, what exactly is Scoopshot? Scoopshot is a disruptive technology, which provides a platform for photography. It is an international crowdsourcing facility for photography, which connects media, brands, and news organizations with mobile photographers around the world. The basic idea is to give people an opportunity to make money for a thing they are already doing, i.e., taking pictures using their smartphone's camera.

According to Business Insider, one in every five persons worldwide owns a smartphone. This has led to a phenomenal increase in the number of photographs taken around the globe. Statistics show that in 2013 alone, approximately 400 billion photographs were taken throughout the world. This is where Scoopshot enters.

Scoopshot photographers, known as "Scoopshooters," can upload unique, authenticated photos and video content to the Scoopshot app and send it to the global market in minutes. In today's world where authentication of content is an increasingly big worry, Scoopshot stands out with its app-based solution that verifies the location and camera that the picture was taken with.

The photographers are rewarded for uploading exciting pictures or for responding to "tasks" or photo assignments. These assignments range from product as well as background photos for advertisement campaigns to pictures of current events for newspapers. Currently, 600,000 smartphone users are registered to Scoopshot. Brands, organizations, bloggers, and ad agencies make use of Scoopshot to generate content.

Strategies: SO WHAT Makes Scoopshot Worth a Shot?

Media companies are always on the shoot out for unique content. According to the former CEO Mr. Niko Ruokosuo, Scoopshot feeds this demand as well as developing engagement, all through the same platform at a low price. Scoopshot is free and anyone with a smart phone can download it, create an account, and use it. Through this account they upload their pictures to appropriate categories or assigned tasks. These pictures are browsed and, if found to be newsworthy, purchased by customers (publishers, editors, marketers, strategists, etc.). Scoopshot receives a cut of all sales.

As on July 2013, 100 media publications around the world were using Scoopshot, a figure that has continued to increase quarter over quarter. Scoopshot takes care of all the copyright, payment, image authenticity, and transfer concerns. Additionally, unlike in the case of Facebook or Instagram, Scoopshot does not require the users to grant over the rights to use the photographs anyway they see fit. The platform merely acts as a broker between the photographer and the buyer.

Indeed, Scoopshot stresses that the photographer is still the owner of the picture. Nobody can use a picture without purchasing a license. The members can select either "license to use" or "license to own" for each of the photos they upload. In the case of a "license to own" holder, nobody else can use, publish, sell, or offer to sell the concerned picture without his or her permission. But the "license to own" holder has unlimited, exclusive rights to forward, modify, publish, or use the photo in any media around the globe. Of course, the moral rights of the photographer will stay intact, as they are guaranteed under copyright laws. The sold photos are marked "sold" with the exception of the exclusive pictures, which are marked "exclusive."

Scoopshooters receive both recognition and financial rewards (someone made as much as 25,000 USD by selling his pictures!!) as they give the world a view of the real world in real time. But photographers are not the only ones satisfied with Scoopshot. Marketers and strategists utilize the services of Scoopshot to reduce their reliance stock photography and visual research costs. Brands like Oxfam, Malibu, Fiat, and Vogel's are already using Scoopshot to source photos on demand. In the case of publishers and editors, Scoopshot provides an exclusive set of tools for discovering, assigning, and authenticating relevant pictures, allowing clients to progress from concept to content in a matter of minutes. Unsurprisingly, Scoopshot won the best mobile service award at Grand One and also ended up in Flurry's Top 20 World's Best Apps list in SXSW.

How Is Scoopshot a Positive Outlier?

Scoopshot is a disruptive innovation, which has marked its entry into the $4 billion stock photo business. According to Mr. Ruokosuo, "on-demand photography" will be a game changer for the photo industry. He claims that the majority of stock photography will transition to an "on-demand" model in the next few years. Adapting to these new models requires new ways of monetizing photography.

Furthermore, Scoopshot is quite different from its incumbents and a pioneer in the field with regards to its strategy. For example, consider Getty Images, the incumbent company that caters to photography needs of media and companies, just like Scoopshot. The difference between the two models lies in the fact that Getty Images creates a pool of images expecting to match a demand (i.e., an offer-first marketplace). This is a difficult, expensive model, which requires substantial infrastructure. Scoopshot, on the other hand, caters to the quick and easy demand-first marketplace for photographs. Here customers reach out to photographers who could satisfy their specific photography needs. This second model requires substantially less infrastructure. The success of Scoopshot is so remarkable that even incumbent companies are testing the demand-first model. In February 2014, Getty Images beta tested an app called Moment, quite similar to Scoopshot.

Even when compared to other disruptive innovators in the field (e.g., Foap), Scoopshot stands out as the only company with a patented authentication technology to verify the photos. The embedded GPS data provides additional verification of the location of the photograph. In this way, Scoopshot eliminates the possibility of manipulated or filtered images masquerading as fresh and newsworthy content. This is quite significant as this saves the staff-time companies spend on trying to authenticate a photo or video. In some cases, even after such efforts, it would lead to embarrassing results. An example being the newspaper El Pais (Caracas, Venezuela), which published a fake photo of President Hugo Chavez undergoing medical treatment in Cuba. This earned the company a lot of criticism and resulted in monetary losses.

The Scoopshot app also has instant payment and rights management capabilities which none of its rivals have. Foap, for instance, has yet to come up with an airtight copyright policy like Scoopshot's. Scoopshot is also one of the pioneer agencies that work with smartphone-owning amateurs who happen to be at the right place at the right time, in contrast to other agencies that cater to only professional photographers. In an interview with the senior writer for Gigaom, David Meyer, Scoopshot CEO asserted

> "Nobody has the features that we do to do this correctly . . . and the way we keep track of our users—we can send assignments that are location-based and immediate—[this] provides results more effectively than anybody else can do."

Nonetheless, this does not mean Scoopshot overlooks professional photographers. Scoopshot Pro is a new service offered exclusively for professional photographers. It helps professionals receive photo assignments from the media based on their location. Consequently it provides more work opportunities, more demanding assignments, and more visibility to photographers, while taking care of contracts and payments too.

Challenges

Scoopshot marks the birth of on-demand photography and facilitates convenient transactions between buyers and makers of user-submitted photos. However, this also includes a risk factor. According to Scoopshot's terms of service, as long as the photo is in the service of Scoopshot, it controls all given rights to the photo. It maintains "exclusive rights" to the photographs for 48 hours, and if not purchased within that period of time, some of the rights are returned to the photographer. It does not, however, take care of the photographer's long-term rights to the photos.

Another noteworthy aspect is the tax consequences of the revenue made by the Scoopshooters. For Finnish users, Scoopshot withholds appropriate taxes for tax documentation. However, for users from other countries, the company does not provide any assistance. Then again, this is typically a problem for professional photographers or people who earn large amounts of money. For casual photographers who make small amounts, this may not be an issue until earnings increase.

Outlook

The fact that neither the founder of Scoopshot nor its original collaborators had any media experience is a classic example of how detached, outside thinking and vision could lead to innovations. The key idea behind Scoopshot is quite simple. The brilliance of this simplicity might be what encouraged Scoopshot to disrupt a field dominated by "old fashioned minds." By creating a convergence of photography, technology, and leveraging customers to pay for the content, Scoopshot is achieving the scale needed to compete with incumbents like Getty. As Mr. Ruokosuo and founder Petri Rahja, the current CEO, envision, Scoopshot might indeed turn out to be known as the iTunes of the photo industry one day.

From the Perspective of Lakshmi B. Nair, a Scoopshooter

From a User's Perspective

As a person whose favorite hobby is taking snapshots of anything and everything around, it was inevitable that I would become a member of Scoopshot the moment I heard about it. I have been one since September 2014. And I have to say, the experience is really worth a shot. It is quite simple, you download the app, register yourself, and start (or resume) clicking! The beauty of the whole concept (apart from the prospect of a potential customer finding your masterpiece worth buying) is its simplicity. It helps you make money out of something you are already doing, by creating an online marketplace which brings together potential customers (newspapers, companies, whoever is interested in paying for a genuine, exclusive first-hand photograph) and Scoopshooters.

As a user, there are several aspects that I like about Scoopshot. It is easy to use and efficient. So you take a picture or a video with your phone and upload it with a description on the website, using the app. You can fix your own price for your work (who knows better than you?!) and keep waiting for the offers to arrive. Alternatively, you upload content which corresponds to customer assignments (photos, videos, eyewitness reports) and let the customers take their pick. In this case, the customers fix the price, and you can decide whether the offered fee is appealing enough for you. What's more, Scoopshot also has several photo contests, where users can post pictures, and the winners are selected based on the number of votes each picture receives. In all these scenarios, after you post your picture or video, there is nothing more you have to worry about. Scoopshot takes care of everything, and that includes the legal arrangements of the posted content. For each sold image, Scoopshot receives a 30 percent share, which is considerably lower than the commission charged by other services.

As a customer, when you post an assignment or campaign online, you know that you will get the best value. You get a vast assortment of content to choose from, and the authentication technology ensures the pictures or videos you get are genuine, unique, and "fresh." This makes sure that companies and brands have access to time-sensitive and location-specific content, without having to avail of the services of a photographer.

From an External Commenter's Perspective

I find the company quite an "outlier" in terms of its strategic novelty, impact, amplification, etc. Unlike traditional stock photography platforms, Scoopshot is strategically novel with its demand-specific, crowdsourcing business model, which connects photographers with buyers (especially, media). It innovates the stock photography industry by providing "on-demand" services to its customers. This would change the photography industry as well as cause huge ripple effects such as innovation in multiple industries like journalism, advertising, etc.

In today's economy, when companies are trying to cut costs, Scoopshot offers an alternative for media where they can purchase the desired content without actually having to send someone out there to get it. Spatial and temporal constraints won't matter anymore. You will get what you need faster, and you get multiple options to choose from. This could be how the future will look like.

8

Made in the Future[1]: Shapeways' Manufacturing Model

What is common among a father making a replacement for a broken part in his kid's stroller, a woman starting a co-created toys' business, a neuroscientist turning a magnetic resonance imaging (MRI) brain scan into an earring and Victoria's Secret garment design team? They are all customers of Shapeways. Peter Weijmarshausen, co-founder and CEO of Shapeways, figured out the potential of 3D printing for manufacturing and pitched it to Philips' Lifestyle Incubator back in 2009. The technology already existed, as well as creative people skilled in computer-aided design who could leverage it, so Shapeways set out to build what was missing: the scaffold for a marketplace. The company moved from Eindhoven to New York in search for a risk-taking, tech-savvy, and creative environment to build a factory that launches products made in the future. Shapeways lives off of daring designers who only need to allow themselves break the rules about who decides what kind of products should be made and how they should be manufactured.

Shapeways is simultaneously a manufacturing service and a marketplace. It combines a digital platform and a 3D printing manufacturing hub, which enable anyone to turn a digital tridimensional model into a real product. In the digital platform, users can upload designs, order 3D-printed objects, and set up shops. Shapeways' marketplace brings together designers and customers. A constellation of independent designers takes advantage of the company's manufacturing and customer service capabilities that serve thousands of online designer shops hosted in the platform. Buyers can also customize the shape

---

[1]Made in Future is the tagline featured in Shapeways' packaging of delivered goods.

and size of products at the moment of purchase and have them manufactured on demand. Fuelled by 3D printing, Shapeways' "Made in the Future" stands for on-demand manufacturing, zero inventory, customization, and design flexibility.

3D printing is fairly accessible nowadays. It is suitable for producing simple objects but mostly for manufacturing complex and sophisticated designs that are out of reach for injection mold-based traditional manufacturing. Early on in Shapeways, uploaded designs consisted of very basic shapes that populated the bestselling product categories including jewelry, smartphone cases, and miniatures. These relatively simple forms evolved toward sophisticated models that can be manipulated through complex algorithms. For instance, designer team Nervous System created jewelry pieces inspired by Nature, using software that recreates the growth of components of plants. The underwear brand Victoria's Secret commissioned Shapeways to help create a 3D-printed garment for its popular annual runway show. The designer made an algorithm that generated a wearable piece made of textile-like flexible structures that were custom-made to the model's body.

Shapeways started in 2009 in Eindhoven, Netherlands as a spin-off of Philips' Lifestyle Incubator. Co-founder Peter Weijmarshausen had helped launch Blender, the first free 3D modeling software, which helped him realize the latent potential in 3D printing when a friend from Philips introduced it to him in 2006. At the time 3D printing was used for rapid prototyping, but not for producing real consumer products. Shapeways took off in 2007 with seed funding from Philips, founded by Weijmarshausen, Marleen Vogelaar, and Robert Schouwenburg. In 2010 Shapeways spun off as an independent company and established offices and manufacturing hubs in Eindhoven and New York, the latter becoming its "creative epicenter" close to important financing networks from which it raised venture capital. Nowadays, Shapeways operates with more than 140 employees from offices in New York and Seattle, and manufacturing hubs in Eindhoven and Long Island City, New York equipped with high-end industrial 3D printers.

Shapeways' strategy is to offer a manufacturing service enabled by additive manufacturing technologies, powered by the creativity of its community of designers and supported by customers' appeal for unique, customized products. The company's assumption is that people are more likely to adopt 3D printing if they can avoid investment in machines and learning to work with the technology. In addition, Shapeways provides access to industrial machines—prohibitively expensive for the common user—to their high-quality printing and to varied range of materials. Since 3D modeling software is available for free in versions simplified for the laymen, 3D design and printing services became accessible to an increasing number of people. The distinctive features of Shapeways manufacturing model are an affordable service for manufacturing on demand, shorter time to market from concept to customer order, flexibility for iterating products, customization, and the lowering of barriers for small businesses.

WOW: Affordable Manufacturing on Demand

Professional expertise in 3D printing and sophisticated equipment work the magic behind the few button clicks that the customer needs to make on the website in order to bring a digital file to life. Shapeways offers around 50 different materials and finishes, including plastic, food-safe ceramics, and gold. After a 3D design is uploaded or selected, Shapeways checks its printability, manufactures the product, and ships it worldwide. Everyday a team of engineers collects newly uploaded models and checks them for printability, which includes optimizing the printers' chamber to fit as many items as possible, reduce operational costs, and achieve the lowest price possible. Later, a few employees finish up each 3D-printed product by hand using different finishing methods.

An illustrative and rather surprising outcome of customization and on-demand manufacturing is people using Shapeways to create unique, bespoke engagement, and wedding rings. Jewellery is a top selling category and popular among designers.

"Jewelers also love that they don't have to spend money on expensive machines or inventory. They can focus on their designs and let Shapeways take care of the rest."

—Justine Trubey, VP of Supply Chain
at Shapeways[2]

Shapeways offers the most common metals in jewelry, such as silver, gold, and platinum, and non-traditional materials such as flexible

---

[2]Shapeways' press release, July 26, 2014.

plastic and acrylic. According to the company, the quality of pieces is comparable to what is found in high-end jewelry shops at affordable prices. Metal jewelry is produced through a wax casting process in which the model is 3D printed in wax to create a cast that is filled with the metal, after which the final piece is hand-polished.

The price of products is calculated according to labor, materials, and use of machine space, to which Shapeways adds 3.5 percent to cover administrative costs. Designers add a mark-up over Shapeways' price on their curated shops. For one-off products, the price is calculated at the time of order, while for products sold at the designers' shops price is quoted ahead of order and remains fixed. Machine space contributes to over 50 percent of the average cost of products. It is challenging to calculate it for each piece because there is a diverse set of pieces of various sizes and geometries in every print run. Despite the variation across print runs, machine space component is based on the average space occupied by a product in the print chamber regardless of what else is printed at the same time.

In 2014 Shapeways reviewed its pricing structure after realizing it was losing money. After analyzing over 2.6 million parts manufactured over 9 months, it came up with a more reliable model that was also aligned with the degree of complexity of the whole production process. This gave an incentive to designers to make products as simple as possible for manufacturing, which would lower product costs. The new pricing structure resulted in lower prices to the majority of products made in a regular plastic and in steel.

SO WHAT: Shorter Time to Market, Iteration on-the-Fly, and Customization

The digital manufacturing platform supports both individual creative projects and entrepreneurial professional use. In 2013, according to an internal survey, half of Shapeways' shop owners were self-taught in 3D modeling. Having the goal of making 3D printing accessible, the company stimulates autodidacts by providing tutorials, sharing how-to videos, and maintaining webforum chats with the staff.

"What the machines can do today is not wildly different from what they could do 5 years ago. It's what people can come up with. And I think that is where the complexity of the things,

the daring of our designers, our community, is growing and growing and growing. Sometimes that drives us mad because they come up with things that are so on the edge of what the machines can do . . . but I think, still, a lot of stuff that you can do conceptually with 3D printing is not done yet."

—Peter Weijmarshausen, interviewed for
TheVerge.com's Small Empires show

For independent designers running small businesses, shorter time to market and unlimited iteration to meet customer demand are crucial for business development and survival. Designer Pekka Salokannel designed and launched an iPad case in 4 days, soon after the announcement of the iPad in 2010. An established fashion brand, Kimberly Ovitz, was able to put on sale a new jewelry collection immediately after its première on the runway show.

Designers create several versions of products and iterate on-the-fly along with customer feedback without bearing the risks and costs of mass production. Designer Christina Westbrook sells iPhone cases in her shop on Shapeways. Within 2 years, she released the 25th iteration of her iPhone case based on user feedback that she continuously integrated into the design.

"No longer do we have to wait for a cast to come back and move through thousands or tens of thousands of pieces, only soon to realize that we might want to iterate on that and then have to throw way all of the excess product that we haven't sold. All we've lost is the time that it takes to design a product."

—Charlie Maddock, Director,
Business Development, at
SBS Seoul Digital Forum talk

Lowering Barriers for Independent Small Businesses

Shapeways' 3D printing strategy reduces the barriers to manufacturing for small businesses, in particular for independent designers. According to an internal survey, in 2013 more than half of shop owners were first-time entrepreneurs and a wide majority wished that running their shop was a full-time job. Almost all of surveyed shop owners spent altogether less than $1000 in setting up their shop on Shapeways. Such a low entry cost contrasts with conventional start-up costs for consumer product businesses that rely on traditional mass manufacturing.

> *"It's a design system that's very democratized . . . in 5 or 6 years, when all the designing software is simple enough, anyone will be able to make their own jewelry."*
>
> —Jewelry designer with a shop
> in Shapeways[3]

So far, Shapeways generated a marketplace for 3D printed goods that features more than 14,000 designer shops that display the products and often allow buyers to customize their features. This marketplace built upon the digital manufacturing infrastructure supports the creation of consumer product businesses with low capital investment. Setting up a shop in Shapeways is free of charge. Thus, for the shop owner there are virtually no costs to manufacture, sell, and deliver a product. Before displaying a product for sale, designers get quotes from Shapeways and decide how much to mark it up. In addition, the company offers an end-to-end service that includes customer service on behalf of the shop owner.

> *"If it becomes a hit, that's great. If it becomes popular then we get really busy and you just get your paycheck at the end of the month. If it doesn't sell at all, no worries, you just go on and design something else."*
>
> —Community manager
> Bart Veldhuizen[4]

According to a Shapeways' survey, in 2013, 8000 shop owners earned nearly $500,000 in profit, whereas a few managed to achieve

---

[3]*The New York Times*, "New Technology Opens Horizons at a Lesser Cost," May 15, 2013 (accessed online October 13, 2014).

[4]Interview published on YouTube on June 10, 2013 (accessed online October 13, 2014).

reasonably high amounts. One of the latter is Michiel Cornelissen who created a simple iPad stand that made more than $30,000 in sales revenue.

Wayne Losey, a former employee of toy companies Hasbro and Kenner created his own line of toys, Modibot, posable characters that combine LEGO with action figures. Losey had previously failed to start up his own toy business due to poor retail sales in spite of a growing fan base. Shapeways enabled him to take another chance due to the possibilities of producing on demand and controlling the retail margins. Losey found that the creative process is faster than in toy companies and using mass manufacturing:

> "It's an extremely sustainable business model. There's no over-purchase of inventory and subsequent mad rush to sell that inventory and invest it back into the next batch. Like many software businesses, it's a constant beta mentality, where it's tweaked until it works."[5]

Shapeways tries to augment the generative potential of this creative community. Duann Scott, the company's designer evangelist, searches for shop owners with eye-catching products and exceptional skills in design and communication, and takes them under the spotlight as examples to the whole shop owners' community. Shapeways also supports autodidacts who lack business, marketing, and design skills to make their ideas more appealing and grow the business. The company runs boot camps for shop owners on varied topics such as design concepts, branding, photography, reputation, and sales relationships, including a small business symposium hosted by venture capital firm Union Square Ventures. By boosting the potential of the creative community, Shapeways builds awareness of the market and attracts an increasing number of users.

Furthermore, the company created application programming interfaces (APIs) for developers to build their own creation apps and link them to Shapeways' platform. The idea is to offer a digital to physical experience. An example is Crayon Creatures, an application that transforms children's drawings in 3D models to become figurines that decorate parents' homes. Another is Kinematics, an application

---

[5]Wired, *Print-to-Order Service Helps 3-D Designer Revive Forgotten Figurines*, January 23, 2013 (accessed online October 13, 2014).

developed by design team Nervous System to create custom-made foldable jewelry with complex forms.

Shapeways also supports existing businesses. For instance, it facilitates the replacement of spare parts. An employee of Shapeways made a 3D-printed replacement part for his baby stroller after asking the brand to send him CAD/CAM files of that part's model. Teenage Engineering, a Swedish manufacturer of music workstations and synthesizers, released the digital files of their products' spare parts on Shapeways. People can order it from Shapeways or download and 3D print them in a local hub. Teenage Engineering benefits from this arrangement because it avoids having an inventory of spare parts waiting for customers' need to repair their devices. In addition, Shapeways helps communities of users to hack their products. Fans of GoPro cameras have come up with custom add-ons and accessories that allow them to use the cameras in unusual circumstances which diversified and expanded camera use.

OOMPH: Development and Growth

The 3D printing market grew bottom-up from the community of early adopters. Shapeways has a large community of users in Europe and also in the United States. Yet its customers are based in 120 different countries. Between 2012 and 2014, the number of independent shops increased from 8000 to more than 16,000. While in 2012 the company sold about 100,000 objects a month, mostly jewelry and phone covers, in 2013 that was the average number of models uploaded per month. By summer 2014, Shapeways had sold $2.2 million products.

Production capacity increased to follow a growing customer base. In 2012 Shapeways raised venture capital funding to set up a factory close to the main office so that production, design, and business development teams worked together to learn faster. In mid-2013, 11 large industrial 3D printers made 1000 to 12,000 products on a daily basis. Production facilities in New York hold capacity for 30 to 50 machines that can make 2 to 3 million products annually. This capacity increase was backed by another round of funding for future business development raised in October 2013. According to Chris Dixon of the prestigious venture capital firm Andreesen Horowitz, investors valued Shapeways' creation of a strong community, a strong service model, and a factory footprint.

Challenges

Weijmarshausen thinks that product design education is still focused on a design for mass manufacturing paradigm that has not acknowledged yet the potential and quality of 3D printing, despite the growing base of users witnessed by Shapeways. Shapeways works to make itself relevant to designers and increase awareness of its potential among prospective users and brands. Although much 3D modeling software is free and 3D printing is appealing, according to Weijmarshausen the challenge lies in "making sure more people see the use in our service. We want to make this real for people."[6] The company deals with this challenge by making their service more accessible. The website is full of tutorials to help creative users go through the process of ideation, design, prototyping, and iteration of a product, as well as presenting and sharing a new product launch. Shapeways also tried to build bridges to mainstream retailing. It had a partnership with Neiman Marcus, an upscale U.S. retailer, to display a limited set of 3D-printed items exclusively on the retailer's online shop—a pendant necklace and a stainless steel sculpture.

Outlook: Shapeways as an Alternative to Mass Manufacturing

Shapeways turns production for the masses upside down into production by the masses. The massive number of creative people around the world making unique products is *shaping their way* into the consumer market, thanks to Shapeways. Interviewed by Fortune in early 2014, Weijmarshausen shared a piece of advice from his own father. Work out problems like elephants push over trees in Southeast Asia: Slowly approach them and push until the tree cracks and breaks down. Is Shapeways cracking the solution to making 3D printing a new paradigm for manufacturing?

Shapeways foresees its development as driven toward a local manufacturing model in which products are manufactured as close as possible to where they will be delivered. According to plan, the more Shapeways factories are built globally, the faster iteration and delivery are, even at lower costs and with lower environmental impact.

---

[6]Venture Beat, April 23, 2013 (accessed online October 13, 2014).

Weijmarshausen claims that, while the mass manufacturing model forces concern with the mass appeal of products, 3D printing flips this equation on its head. Additive manufacturing enables products to be made on demand, allows for customization at a very low cost and obviates the need for inventory. In addition, by using Shapeways, designers run product businesses with low costs, offer unique items, iterate their products faster in response to customer feedback, and can be more adaptive to trends and customer needs. Shapeways is not cracking a joke. It is shipping products made in the future as we write.

From the Perspective of Pekka Salokannel, Designer and Entrepreneur

Transcribed verbatim from an interview by Inês Peixoto on December 4, 2014

I found Shapeways in 2009 or 2010 and I've been using their services since then. How it started was that I found Janne Kyttanen's designs online, perhaps in 2005 when I was studying and I was amazed by the shapes 3D printing could create. I got excited about the technology and used it for designing wristwatches at school where we had the possibility to try it out. Then at Aalto University School of Art and Design there was a 3D printer which I used for my graduation project.

When I found Shapeways I started to think again about what 3D-printed designs should be like. What products would 3D printing be good at? First, I thought small personal products and that's why I started by creating jewelry, which is very typical. Jewelry is the biggest hobbyist category of products that people create with 3D printing. Then I also started creating eyewear. I took it as a challenge. I was interested in it. The more I got into it, the more I realized how difficult it is to design good eyewear. It should fit many people, not only one person. However, I believe that in the future, maybe in 2 years, eyewear will evolve into bespoke, personalized products. We scan the face and the head and we get perfect fit. We are quite close to getting there. It's just necessary that digital scanning becomes more reliable, as it is already cheap. 3D scanning is a little bit behind 3D printing. The big players are already investigating the field, for instance Apple which bought the sensor company who made Kinect or Google that has a project for scanning indoor spaces. Eyewear has become a major project for me because it's challenging and because there's not so much competition as in jewelry. There are thousands of people making jewelry. One kind of drowns in that mass, so I don't see much potential there. I have also created lamps as well as wearable products.

I had been working on designing for 3D printing for a few years when I joined Tinkercad. Before, I used Shapeways for the 3D-printed products I designed in my free time and participated in design competitions. At Tinkercad I created tutorials for people using the software. I also did inspirational designs, a few of them ordered from Shapeways.

I have a couple of projects directly with Shapeways. Two years ago I did a business card case for them which they handed out in SXSW. Then I designed a ceramic vase. There had been a few problems with ceramic 3D-printing regarding delivery time. That's why Shapeways started to look for alternative options and eventually created their own method. They create a mold from a nylon-based material and pour real porcelain onto the mold, which makes the product's quality as good as a porcelain object bought in a high street shop. First it was not public and only available for designers applying to test the material with new designs in cooperation with Shapeways. I designed a flower vase, for this cooperation, in ceramics.

Shapeways announces the new materials and technologies in the blog and says that designers can only use them for their own designs. You can't buy it as a consumer, only as a content creator. If you send the application (saying why you want to use it and what product you want to create with that material) then you provide the link to your shop so that Shapeways knows about the kind of designs you're creating and check that you have potential to get into this trial program. They assess whether you have experience in a certain type of product or whether you are skilled enough to be part of the trial. In the beginning they're doing research, for instance on how to set the price level. They assess how long it takes to print, how long it takes to clean an object in post-production . . . and these aspects influence the price point. There are usually a couple of months of trial period to evaluate, through designers and makers' work, whether it's feasible to go commercial, and whether there would be enough requests for certain materials. Ceramics is easy; there are nowadays specifications to use it, but when it comes to different plastics it is a lot more complex to understand what the best solutions are. It's necessary to understand the material, the basic physics, and test whether it works in certain types of products.

About protecting my products, if some product would become a hit that I'd really make money of it—I mean they have been recognized but they haven't sold thousands—then I could think about it. It's the same thing for companies: they don't want to sue anyone if they see that they're not popular and are not making money with it. People tend to make replicas of things of which they're fans. Kids, for instance, usually draw their heroes together with the logos like in Batman. In early days we drew these things on paper and perhaps offered the drawing to our parents or grandparents. No problem. Nowadays we can create a design and sell it right away. That becomes a problem. It's natural that people copy, but in the sense of using combinations of existing things or following trends. Anyway companies typically don't sue unless the product sells a lot. For instance, HBO owns the rights for the design of the King's throne made of blades from Game of Thrones. It was used as an inspiration for an iPhone dock, which became popular as many blogs wrote about it and eventually a lot of people bought it. That was the problem, in a way. If things become popular and start to sell, companies start to be interested in taking legal action by asking the design to be taken down. It's natural that people start copying things; when you're not an artist that's what you do. This will create more legal issues in the future. Although there are the Creative Commons licenses, the truth is that were still living in a Napster time if we compare it with music. It's like the Wild West. There's a lot of free content and people use free tools. It's uncertain how it's going to evolve, but, as digital content, the model might evolve toward subscription types of services, such as iTunes. There is already a streaming option for 3D printing digital content that streams the file in bits which allows people to 3D print remotely but avoids people having the complete file in their computer. The downside of it is that desktop 3D printers are not yet reliable enough.

Back in the early days of the hype about 3D printing, it was all about these incredible and almost impossible forms that could be created, although that is not so much the case nowadays. It is very typical to create complex designs for 3D printing, so there's the possibility of failure, of doing something wrong, and the risk becomes higher. The good thing about 3D printing is that it is relatively affordable to get a prototype so you can test it out. You're not creating concepts at the computer only, but you actually get a finished product and you can try it out.

The media don't talk about those kinds of things anymore. The time has passed and now we are creating real products and real services. I see it has evolved in a similar way as the Internet. First, there was talk about the endless possibilities. In every new technology or new service, people get scared about new things but they get used to it. Slowly 3D printing has become a regular tool for people and companies. It just takes some time. Similarly, the earlier Internet-boom and overheating of the market might come also to 3D printing. I don't see it as a bad thing at all. First, people don't understand it or don't know about it, and then investors see it as a good opportunity so they put money in it—perhaps too much money—and then it crashes down a little bit. Some people lose money, some people win, but it doesn't matter in the end for the wider audience because things are just rolling and evolving further.

These are interesting times because many different companies are trying now new business models, but the whole business is evolving all the time. But that's always the case with new technologies that they come to market too early. There's not the need yet, consumers can't find you yet, so business may be too small and die; but some survive and succeed. Like in the Internet business, in the 3D printing business the winners will be the ones who are just starting now, not the big companies that have a long history.

9

"One Size Does Not Need to Fit All"— Nor1 eStandby Upgrade Solution

by Liis Männamaa

A stay in a hotel room is a complex product.

A product that is answering the consumers' needs to sleep and rest, being a blend of hardware (bed, furniture, bathroom), **services** (F&B, housekeeping, concierge), and many other aspects that help satisfying a guest's requirements during the stay (i.e., location, view, space, entertainment solutions, quietness). For its *consumers* it can be a very emotional product, especially for those who choose to travel for leisure, not for business. For those *selling* the product it is highly perishable: If a room is not sold before the break of dawn, never again will they be able to create a contribution to their need for revenue for that very night. They may try to sell that room again the next night, but for the one that has just passed chances are gone forever if it had been left empty.

Burdened with fixed capacities and costs, operating in a highly competitive market with Online Travel Agencies that are controlling large chunks of consumer demand and are charging high commissions, hotels are struggling to put heads to beds while ensuring their guests have a great experience during their stay. Great enough to come back or to at least talk positively about it in social media channels and trip review sites—a main influencer to other guests' trip preparations. Finding a solution to fill those perishable rooms, adding incremental revenue that goes straight to the bottom line, and increasing guest satisfaction is the mission of Nor1, a global travel merchandizing provider founded in 2004 with institutional investments from Accel Partners, Concur, and Goldman Sachs. Nor1 challenged the way upselling and merchandizing was performed so far by introducing an advanced, analytics-based upsell technology solution that brought a new spin to the actual buying process. Global brands such as Hilton,

CarlsonRezidor, IHG, Accor, Fairmont, and Kempinski, to name a few, are using this unique technology-based standby buying process that created a brand new option of merchandizing hotel products by determining what consumers want and will pay for, thus improving the way those products and services are offered.

Nor1 proves that "one size does not need to fit all" and that customized, relevant upsell offers drive better results in terms of incremental revenue, guest satisfaction, and loyalty.

WOW: Nor1—How Did It All Start?

The original concept of Nor1 is based on the traveling experiences of its founder and co-CEO, Art Norins. He noticed that numerous rooms and suites went unused at hotels night after night, and many travelers wished they had taken advantage of better rooms and services. So he created and patented the process of monetizing that unsold inventory and matching it with travelers who would be willing to pay a reduced price for it upon check-in: Nor1 and its patented eStandby Upgrade® solution were thus born, providing companies with perishable inventories (such as hotel rooms) the ability to add bottom-line value. This *standby* concept can also be found in the air travel industry, struggling with a similar perishable product—the plane seat. Some airlines enable standby upgrades for a first class seat, should one open due to a cancellation, no show, or any other reason. When the flight is boarding, any available seats will be given to those passengers on the standby list. It is a tool to level out overbooking in their base categories and to please their most frequent customers, and we will later have a closer look at similar challenges in the hotel industry.

OOMPH: Don't Leave Money on the Table—Upsell!

As it is more costly to bring in a new customer than to maintain an existing one, it is becoming growingly popular to attract customers to buy up to higher room categories or purchase additional products to the already bought ones in order to increase per-guest revenue with little additional costs. In the airline industry it can be a change from economy to business class, in the hotel business an upgrade from standard to superior room, or to a room providing a sunset view.

There is a high chance that many guests will respond positively to a chance to learn how paying a little extra could let them have a premium room category, and benefit from all those high-class room features, amenities, and add-ons that come along with such an upgrade. If the guest has already committed to the hotel by booking a room, why not use the opportunity and persuade them to spend even more during their stay? Hotel guests increasingly want to make choices about their stay and enhance their experience by making decisions over arrival and departure times, service levels, size of the room, decor, furniture, audio-visual facilities, amenities, and food and beverage options. It is suggested that the more adaptable a product is to consumers, the more valuable it becomes to them because it is no longer just an inanimate object, but an extension of themselves and their personality. In reality large groups of guests are often opting for a hotel's base room categories, either because of their price sensitivity or because they are overwhelmed by the multitude of room-rate combinations and options they got exposed to, during the booking process. Let's be honest: Who outside the hotel industry can clearly tell the difference between "Deluxe," "Comfort," "Superior," or "Executive" categories? With the largest group of guests being interested in inexpensive standard room categories, we often observe hotels applying a strategy we came across already in airlines: They **overbook** their base product, for which they get most demand. It is often a hotel's premium and luxury room inventory that sells last. The more expensive, the less likely such suites will find a guest staying there.

Overbooking standard room types allows capturing more business at lower rates, but it is assumed that each guest is adding to the contribution margin of a hotel, with extra spending expected in F&B outlets or the spa. At the same time, overbooking practice is eliminating revenue potential for a hotel's suite inventory, as guests having reserved an overbooked room category are typically upgraded complimentary to a suite. The more dramatic the overbooking situation and the higher the displacement pressure from base room categories, the less likely it is that hotel front desk staff upsells a guest to a higher category. To avoid conflict and in order to balance the house, way too often guests get upgraded for free. This is where the new standby concept of Nor1's upsell solution can unveil its true beauty, as described later.

Nor1 eStandby Upgrade Technology—the Outstanding Effects of a Standby Buying Process

The Safety Net

Through the Nor1 eStandby Upgrade solution, guests are offered an opportunity to request a room upgrade or an extra service for a discounted price at the time of booking or some days before arrival, which is not confirmed until the time of arrival. Guests are on "standby" for that requested premium room or service, and as a tradeoff to that uncertainty the hotel is willing to give concessions on pricing for such premium rooms and services. However, if such a request is getting awarded, the guest has to pay the agreed discounted price for the upgrade—there is no more chance to opt out.

With this, eStandby provides a solution that gives the hotel a safety net for perishable premium room and suite inventory: Hotels try to sell their expensive suites as long as they can, but shortly before arrival, if their suites are still empty and if it is unlikely that a full paying guest will request such premium room or suite, they can award such suite to a guest who opted in to be awarded such an upsell on a standby basis. Nor1 is creating a pipeline of extra demand for premium inventory, and hotels are left with a simple choice every day: In case suites are still empty, would they rather leave the suites empty or would they give them to someone who is willing to pay a reduced extra amount compared to the regular supplement?

With luxury suites being empty most times of the year it proves to be an interesting opportunity for hotels to drive extra revenue (for a room that otherwise would have remained empty) and enhance the guest experience in a unique way. Often this way guests get exposed to a suite product they may not have been choosing in the first place.

The House Balancer

It also helps hotels during the aforementioned overbooking situation: In case a standard category is overbooked, Nor1 will provide a queue of guests who "volunteered" to be upsold, and that standby list of guests is made available to the hotel way before the guests have even arrived. With eStandby Upgrade from Nor1, hotels are enabled to move guests from an overbooked category to a suite, capturing an upsell amount from a guest who does not know that eventually he could have been upgraded complimentary to that very suite. An elegant way of getting relief during times of high occupancy! Clearly, the application of Nor1's patented buying process that is obliging the guest to pay a discounted price for an upsell before they know if it materializes, allows new ways of selling, thus giving hotels more control on their premium inventory. More importantly, the standby nature of the guest requests gathered before their arrival opens the door to test products and services.

The Market Tester

Imagine a hotel that wants to verify that demand exists for a newly created category, say, a family room. Let's assume the hotel envisions buying a few video game devices for such room, a microwave oven for warming up milk, and a bunk bed for the kids. With eStandby, hotels can suggest to families that booked a room in their hotel, the option to a room with all these new features, without even having them in place already. As the offers are on standby, they can test demand of their target group and based on the results decide whether they want to invest in those new amenities.

The Feature Monetizer

Remember the hotel room being a complex product? The blend of hardware, services, and features? Hotels try their best to create predefined packages of those components, branded as a category. A Comfort Room may be the base category of a hotel. A junior suite consists of additional space and furniture beyond bed, desk, and chair. A suite consists of two or more separate rooms, providing more space and exclusivity. Soft features such as a certain view from your room may get portrayed as a "Deluxe" item. For instance, a deluxe junior suite or deluxe suite can be arranged by adding sea view to the other set of features that make up a regular room category.

What though, if certain isolated features are only rarely spread in a hotel? Imagine a hotel with 350 rooms, and two of them have a daylight bathroom. One of the two rooms is a suite, another one is a Deluxe Room. How to monetize such features without creating another category? How about rooms on floor 1 versus rooms on floor 10? Lots of guests prefer a high floor and are willing to pay extra for that. How about a connecting room? How about a room with a balcony?

Again, the standby nature of Nor1's upsell solution is allowing new selling opportunities. Detached from an actual room category the hotel can sell isolated features at a specific price point. That way, brand new revenue streams are created, allowing monetizing aspects of the hotel that were not considered before.

Strategies—How Does It Work Exactly?

A hotel guest booking a room at a Nor1 eStandby partner hotel could benefit from further standby upgrade options—room upgrades or add-on offers (suites, view, floor, location, F&B, etc.). In exchange to the uncertainty of that offer, the offer is discounted. Via integration to other technology solutions, guests can get exposed to an offer on different touch points: Via the Internet booking engine, on the confirmation e-mail or on a pre-arrival e-mail; guests get invited to learn more about an upsell opportunity. The invite is in form of a small banner, placed on the confirmation page of a booking process, a confirmation e-mail, or a pre-arrival e-mail. Such a banner is linked to Nor1's technology platform, and by clicking on it guests are presented with an offer screen, branded like the respective hotel, stating the name of the guest, the originally booked room, generic booking details as well as more information about the terms and conditions of eStandby.

Guests can choose between different upsell options and select the ones they are interested in and make their requests by clicking on corresponding buttons. The offers are presented with a compelling image, brief bullet-pointed descriptions underlining the added value of the upgradable room categories and services.

Consider a hotel with a multitude of existing room categories, additional services in their restaurant, bar or spa, with room features like views, high floors or a balcony could easily be 15 to 30 different upsell offers. This is a challenge, as consumers are easily overwhelmed, not being able to properly decide when too many options are in hand. The dramatic explosion in choice—from the mundane to the profound challenges of balancing career, family, and individual needs—has already paradoxically been identified to become a problem instead of a solution. Nor1 actually found that conversion dropped significantly as soon as more than six offers were presented to a guest.

This represents an additional complexity for the upsell task: creating a relevant and targeted offer set that is optimized toward the highest potential revenue that is resonating with the guest.

But what offer to choose? At what price? With what combination of offers should they be presented with? And in what order should they get displayed?

OOMPH: Right Offer, for the Right Price, at the Right Time, and for the Right Person

In any business, but especially in the tourism industry as an experience economy, it is important to recognize the customers as the ultimate focus and hence thrive to understand their needs. Consumer markets vary significantly, and one cannot please everyone with the same product as consumers come with different backgrounds and motivations which influence the degree of involvement. If the product does not "speak to the guest," no successful commercial exchange will occur. Moreover, "the customer is the king" and is increasingly accustomed to being offered the right offer at the right time. They are looking for a hotel that caters to them as individuals, having their interests, booking history, and spending behavior in focus.

Whether the price is too low or too high, both can influence the consumer behavior. Customers usually have a range of possible, tolerable prices in their mind and if there is a fluctuation in any direction, the business might be cut. If the price is too low, there is a good chance that some potential revenue would be lost, as the consumer would have been willing to pay more, or/and the product might be perceived as of low quality. On the other hand, if the price is too high, there is a risk of losing customers to competitors because the price went outside of their perceived boundaries.

Price is often used as an attractive call to action and can be such a crucial motivator that people find themselves buying things that they didn't plan to buy—only because the price is "good." As price is often described as a sacrifice one has to do in order to receive some value, a discount counts as a decrease in the sacrifice and therefore is perceived as a bargain and an increase in value. To be successful, the ultimate goal should be to meet the customer in the middle by applying a "good price" where both parties can benefit.

Technology allows hospitality organizations to know more about their customers by collecting and analyzing the information that can be provided, for example, by a hotel reservation. There are millions of bookings made every day. This means a lot of generic aggregated information about the customers such as gender, age, geographical location, interest patterns, and so forth. Nowadays, companies understand that such information is valuable but not every organization knows what to do with it and how to collect and utilize it. As a matter of fact, every booking provides the property important information, which can be used as a basis for targeted offers and could bring higher guest satisfaction. The key to success is the right offer, for the right price, at the right time, and to the right person.

But how could the tourism organization know when is the right time and how much exactly to ask for an offer? How should they realize the needs of the guests?

As technology advances, artificial intelligence and complex algorithms support and facilitate the decision-making process by analyzing and storing experiences, patterns, and information across different organizations, ultimately helping to better merchandize a company's offering to the needs of their customers. To some extent, behavior-related information such as a travel arrangement may already be regarded as "Big Data"—too large of a dataset where regular processing tools fail to detect the right patterns from such information. Leveraging such information becomes key to the success of all companies involved in merchandizing a complex product such as a hotel stay experience.

Developing personalized offers through identifying unique needs is very time and resource consuming. Therefore, it is beneficial to outsource this task to third-parties who have the skills, personnel, and technologies for identifying the unique characteristics of consumers and match them with individually designed products. Nor1 is one of these companies helping the hotels to deepen their relationships with guests by contributing its knowledge, data, and technology, to help solve the problem of composing a right mix of offers, priced with a focus on maximum revenue capture. Not only did Nor1 challenge the way upscale services are presented and positioned (standby buying process), but also it challenges the guesswork in today's hotel merchandizing practice, where experience of hotel marketers is the main driver for offer composition.

PRiME—the Right Offer for the Right Guest at the Right Price

PRiME® is Nor1's real-time, data-driven pricing and merchandising engine that serves as the intelligence engine of Nor1's Merchandising Platform. This patented predictive "decision intelligence" engine is a technology-first for the travel industry and its true purpose is to maximize revenue for hotels while maintaining the rate integrity of their perishable inventories. Anyone would agree that it is fairly simple to find the price when guests are willing to opt in for an upsell: You give it out for $1. The art though is finding the right offer set and the highest price that maximizes incremental revenue—Nor1 answered this need with PRiME, a solution built with the most advanced mathematics and technology in Silicon Valley. Using sophisticated algorithms trained on millions of historical transactions, it can better predict guests' willingness to pay for upgrades over and above the amount they already paid for their confirmed reservations.

Unlike a mere recommendation engine, PRiME accurately identifies in real-time which products and pricing to show to a particular guest and then actually presents an offer set to the guest on behalf of the hotel. It is this "decision intelligence" that increases a property's revenue and strengthens customer loyalty. PRiME also identifies which variables and interactions matter most when applying pricing and merchandising strategies to upsell offers. The data points that matter are typically a combination of booking-specific variables, guest-specific information, and information that's specific to the property.

Each of the variables have a certain weighting, and the weighting itself changes for each reservation based on the unique intersection of the booking, guest, and property—there is no one size fits all.

PRiME enables hoteliers to better predict how offers for similar bookings by similar guests at similar properties performed in the past, enables them to determine, in real time, which offer to make when a new booking comes through the system. Essentially, we can infer the likely product preferences and price sensitivities of the guest even if we have no historical data for the specific property or guest. The result is that PRiME produces excellent results right from the start.

PRiME can optimize offer sets to help channel demand to underutilized inventory, while ensuring it is in-line with consumer preferences. And that's another key element of the intelligence in PRiME—choosing and setting prices that interact with each other to achieve the optimal outcome.

As we have seen before, there is a strong need for limiting upsell offers to a subset of all possible offers in any given point in time. Hence, with the support of PRiME, eStandby focuses on generating the most relevant offer set for any guest. According to research, the mind has a bandwidth in perception. "There is a limit to the ability of the mind to relate to among a large number of alternatives and accurately make a choice even if there is only one criterion" (based on Miller, "The magical number 7"). For instance, if a person has given the task to choose from 20 different options, he will give inaccurate answers because the range exceeds the bandwidth of his channel for perception. In most cases, seven alternatives are the approximate limit of a person's channel capacity.

eStandby Upgrade—Benefits

With all theoretical technicality outlined before, the benefits that Nor1 provides have real-world advantages for both, the guest as well as the hotel using the service. When attempting to influence guests to purchase services additional to the originally booked room, it is essential that they (the guests) are able to see the benefit in it. It can be a monetary or timely gain, or just a matter of convenience, but the customer should always feel that when they purchase several products or services from the same provider, there is something in it for them. In case of eStandby, the guests are clearly benefiting from further possibilities to enhance their stay right after the original booking was confirmed, and they may consider premium features they had not considered before—at a very attractive price point, due to the uncertainty of acquisition.

For the hotels we count incremental revenue, relief in overbooking situations, higher guest satisfaction, marketing effects for the hotel's premium products and services, as well as loyalty effects on the plus side. Also the hotel team is provided with useful information about the guest upsell performance that facilitates the cooperation between the hotel and the Nor1 team. According to this information, changes in the pricing and offer set can be applied which help to continuously improve the performance beyond the effects of machine learning. All of this is provided with a performance-based revenue model, where only successful upsells are commissioned by Nor1, eliminating the risk to invest in a solution that is not bringing a distinct ROI.

Challenges and Conclusion

eStandby Upgrade solution offers the hotel a "safety net" in case of unsold inventory. The guest is exposed to a customized set of non-guaranteed offers determined by an intelligent decision engine. The benefit of this upselling model is that based on behavioral patterns it is possible to personalize the offer set, so as to make it more appealing, relevant, and thus more interesting to the customer.

When customers are confronted with relevant offers evoking their unconscious desires, instead of feeling "being sold to," they feel motivated and attracted enough to buy the product. More than 2 million guests are exposed to eStandby offers every month, thus contributing to a 1 to 5 percent increase in a hotel's average daily rate and resulting in up to a 32 percent average increase in original booking value for upgraded bookings. With the use of predictive data analytics Nor1 makes upselling personal and successful—and you may ask what would prevent any hotel with different room categories and upsell potential to apply Nor1's new approach.

A challenge that Nor1 faces would be the spread of responsibilities and count of departments within the hotel organization that are touched with the eStandby Upgrade solution. *Revenue Management* appreciates the last minute yielding of perishable rooms; *Front Desk Operations* is affected with the house balancing task and the communication to the guests checking in; *Sales* is chartered to sell the hotels capacity best; *Marketing* has a word to say on the way guest communication shall look and feel; *Hotel IT and e-commerce* needs to support the technology integration—and all of them need to get involved! With so many different stakeholders it could take a while until all buy-in is organized and the solution gets launched.

In addition to the obstacles within the hotel organization there is the need to work with a multitude of other hotel technology solution providers to enable a seamless and secure transfer of guest booking data in line with most current data protection and privacy policy requirements. Only that data is fueling PRiME and eStandby Upgrades' true potential. Keeping up to date with these vendors and their own innovations is a task of its own.

But when all is said and done, it is also a venture worthwhile: Hundreds of thousands of satisfied guests and thousands of hotels are supporting the quest for better services and differentiation while agreeing with Nor1—a stay in a hotel room is a complex product. All that counts is the experience the guest has in his/her room at the end of a day.

From the Perspective of Mario Bellinzona, Senior Vice President, EMEA, Nor1

We asked Mario Bellinzona the following questions for his commentary.

1. The purpose on which the company was founded; what is your (his) passion?

Nor1 was founded by serial entrepreneur *Art Norins*, who happened to travel a lot for his prior businesses. Passionate for people that he worked with and for, exposed to many different nations on different continents, he spends months of his life in airplanes, at airports, and in hotels. Value driven and equipped with an intense sense of fairness and good business practices he always wondered why specifically with airlines so many first and business class seats were left unsold shortly before takeoff, with lots of travelers boarding economy class having a distinct willingness to buy such high class, high service, and maximum legroom travel experience—just not at the original fare requested by the airline for such service! Why leaving those seats empty? Especially when cramped in a coach class seat you would immediately sense the value of such a premium seat.

The airline was more than aware of the perishable nature of its product—a fact certainly reflected it in their numbers when too many premium seats remained unsold. Why not offer such seats to travelers at the last minute that at least were willing to contribute, albeit a *lower* amount, to the revenue of the airline? Why not offer those premium seats on a standby basis, so that they are kept open as long as possible, yet guaranteed to be sold even if no one was willing to pay the full price?

This anticipated win-win situation for the airline and the traveler was a key driver in arriving at the option to offer perishable services on a standby basis. This changed the traditional buying process toward one resembling an auction model, creating a value from uncertainty.

The founders were passionate to create a company that would solve that problem, improving the traveler's experience and creating additional marginal revenue and loyalty for travel providers. Originally with an eye on the airline industry, it clearly deployed this powerful idea in the complex world of hospitality.

2. Its difference relative to incumbents; why is it strategically novel in your view?

Until today, there are really no true incumbents to the solution. The eStandby Upgrade product was and is truly unique, and its uniqueness was underlined in a patent granted for the buying process designed for the purpose of helping to sell perishable goods and services to customers at a discounted rate as well as for the merchandizing algorithm PRiME. The invention on the buying process consequently enabled the purchase of perishable objects by ascertaining and attaching a value to the certainty that the perishable object will be available and adjusting the value of the product or service for purchasers willing to pay the discounted value on the condition that the perishable object may not be available at the time of expiration. Rather than paying the certainty value, the prospective purchaser is given the opportunity to enroll in a pool for the perishable object. At a certain time the perishable is released to the pool of purchasers, who are then selected to purchase the item.

Specifically for the hotel industry which offers a complex service bundle (different room categories, dining options, spa options) that in most case combines into a (hopefully enjoyable and memorable) experience, such an approach was ground breaking—to capture revenue for suites and high-class rooms that otherwise would have been left empty. Unlike other solutions which dealt with the question of upselling travelers for higher value services than the one originally booked, the standby nature of Nor1's approach allowed to unfold more power in creating custom built and custom priced options for the guest.

Speaking to the second novelty, PRiME: Nor1 took the guesswork out of guest satisfaction, by allowing data to speak for itself!

Not only was the unique buying process a strategic asset for the company's success. The data gathered from millions of offers made to millions of guests enabled decision-making regarding what to offer at what price to what guest at what point in time. Truly solving the merchandizing puzzle became the clear mission going forward, with the eStandby Upgrade buying process being a means of successfully presenting the offers calculated and prepared by the PRiME platform.

Using *predictive* analytics was truly new for the business section it was applied to.

3. A quick tour of history; how did you and your colleagues in the company get here in terms of doing something differently? (What rules did you break, etc.?)

The team at Nor1 grouped around a simple yet brilliant business idea, and with most people initially not being from the travel or hospitality industry they were disruptive in their approach and perception for the task at hand: optimizing revenue for a complex set of possible additions to a service just booked by a traveler. PhDs in statistics and mathematics brought an unbiased analytical eye on the challenges of an emotional-, marketing-, and branding-driven industry, challenging merchandizing techniques performed by hotel marketers since decades.

With the perception of a start-up, all attention was focused on over-delivering compared to what was expected—not only providing high-tech, but as well a high-touch service. This included onsite training and implementation of the solution at hotel key customers, creating ambassadors for later rollout phases of that brand. It included decisions such as introducing own photographer teams to create better room imagery than those obtained by the marketing teams of the hotels. Not taking what is as granted, paired with the spirit of creating something new was fueling the passion and energy of a global team, working within and for the hospitality industry.

4. Future intent; what is the next opportunity and related challenges?

With all that was learned the next step is allowing the same merchandizing insights to perform while guests are at the property. The next consequential evolution of the service will allow for the customization of a guest's stay and his experience with custom offers based on a blend of predictive analytics, business rules, and the hotel's business needs.

Acknowledging that consumers are best reached using mobile solutions shaped new services that include exact time and location of the consumer into the mix, opening new opportunities for hotel marketers to promote their products and services.

5. Looking back from the future; why did what you have done matter, more broadly speaking (even beyond this particular company surviving or not)?

Sometimes it is hard to truly value what you do in your profession, not being a physician or involved in studies fighting cancer or world famine problems. So many businesses focus on small problems that eventually are part of another niche problem that eventually only affects selected industries. Still—many such businesses contribute to our world advancing to become a better place.

Introducing new ways of positioning and pricing perishable products and services led to more companies picking up the aspect of upselling, each in their own way. Beyond the boundaries of our company's world a new practice was born that helped hotel operators to better merchandize their products and services. Thinking about upselling is a given these days, however now it is supported by data to support.

Having allowed thousands of couples to celebrate their wedding anniversary in a great hotel suite that they would not have dared request, also matters! Many guests have enhanced their stay in thousands of hotels, and what was planned to be a great holiday eventually became an even better holiday for all of them. Asking those travelers today, they would agree that what happened to them after getting exposed to an eStandby Upgrade offer truly mattered to them.

10

Sculpteo: A Factory in the Cloud for the 3D Printing Revolution

In 2007, Eric Carrell and Clément Moreau at Sculpteo acquired the first 3D printers for their start-up. What amazed them was the revolutionary potential of this new way of manufacturing: the possibility for individuals to design and produce whatever objects they wanted and, more broadly, the untapped potential for a democratization of manufacturing. Sculpteo is an online 3D printing service for the additive manufacturing of objects on demand.

The idea behind Sculpteo was to make this technology available to the common consumer, so that many could benefit from it. However, as its 3D printing service set off, the grand majority of the digital design files received had defects that made them un-printable. Soon, Carrell and Moreau realized that making 3D printing available to a wider audience, who clearly was not familiar with the process, required considerable efforts to analyze and repair the files. What came next was a refocus on developing software that would make designing for 3D printing an easy, risk-free task and a burgeoning attention to the professional market in an attempt to make 3D printing an attractive option for mid-scale manufacturing of a few thousand objects at a time.

> *"We think that, taking into account the ease of use, the consumer market will take off quickly, and that we'll go from a world of consumers to a world of co-creators. People are seduced by customization but they're discouraged quickly because results aren't very good if one's not a professional. The consumer market isn't as important as we've expected it to be. We are certain that 3D printing technology will be part of a revolution, but a less exciting revolution: the consumer market*

won't be aware of it. But it will change the life of manufacturers, those who manufacture products for the consumer markets. For us, the true growth is there."

—Eric Carrell, quoted in *La Tribune*
(May 22, 2014), speaking at a venture capital event

Sculpteo was founded in 2009 in France by Eric Carrell and Clément Moreau, from the consumer electronics business, and Jacques Lewiner, a physicist. The founders gathered €2 million in equity from XAnge, a Private Equity and Venture Capital Fund subsidiary of the French Post Bank, and developed Sculpteo with the support of public programs to promote innovation, the beneficial status of a young innovative company, and research tax credits. They invested €700,000 in R&D over the first 2 years to quickly develop 3D printing solutions.

The services provided by Sculpteo are similar to those offered by other 3D printing services, such as Shapeways and i.materialise. The company operates globally, receiving digital 3D files and shipping objects all over the world. In addition, designers and brands can connect their online shops and 3D modeling applications with Sculpteo's manufacturing platform that leaves the necessary manufacturing details and expertise to the company.

Yet, Sculpteo developed a strong focus on professional users and businesses, as it realized that the largest demand came from small and medium enterprises that ordered batches of dozens or hundreds of objects and parts. Gradually, it strengthened its efforts to developing specialized tools for turning 3D printing into an uncomplicated, trouble-free manufacturing option for professionals and businesses, which make up around a half of its whole production.

In 2013, the company opened an office in San Francisco to tap into a pool of potential clients in the start-ups that populate the region. This move helped Sculpteo develop a burgeoning market in the United States which, in 2014, represented half of its entire business. In the same year, Sculpteo built a new factory in France because its facilities were running at full capacity and demand was growing in the professional market. The recently built facilities are located close to large international transportation hubs that will serve international clients, in order to increase operational efficiency and meet higher demand in less time.

Clément Moreau commented, at the Consumer Electronics Show in Las Vegas that took place in 2015, that an increasing number of manufacturing clients were looking toward Sculpteo to produce parts, in particular those parts with complex geometries that otherwise cannot be manufactured. As such, Sculpteo has dedicated more of its attention to the manufacturing of batch series of around 10,000 objects using software developed in-house and third-party 3D printing technology. As a result, its cloud-based digital manufacturing platform is continuously improved by developing software that makes 3D printing a hassle-free manufacturing option and that supports designers and engineers in developing capabilities for designing for 3D printing.

WOW: Cloud-Based Software Platform Underlies the Manufacturing Service

Sculpteo's 3D Printing Cloud Engine launched in 2012 supports e-commerce businesses connected to it to enable remote on-demand product manufacturing directly from a brand's website or web applications. It is also a backbone to manage the consumer functionalities and professional grade services offered by Sculpteo to extend 3D printing's reach and expand its base of users. The functionalities suited to the consumers market include a free web and iOS application for the customization of mobile phone covers (3DPCase), an iOS app that turns human data from one's photograph into design parameters applied to objects, and the integration of Sculpteo manufacturing platform into third-party games and into leading 3D modeling software, for instance from Autodesk and Dassault Systèmes.

Professional clients can easily embed a Sculpteo shop into their websites, in order to access tools for customizing the 3D models available in Sculpteo's interface and to directly connect to the manufacturing service. For instance, the telecommunications company Orange offers an application on their website to customize iPhone covers and order them from Sculpteo. Another example is a digital game to create virtual pottery that can be 3D printed through Sculpteo as real ceramic objects. This "factory in the cloud" can be integrated as well with popular e-commerce platforms, such as Shopify or Magento.

Furthermore, Sculpteo rewards companies that manage libraries of 3D models or that own 3D modeling software for their integration in Sculpteo's Cloud Engine, paying a set percentage of the turnover of each order made through their platforms. Dassault Systèmes 3DVia and Autodesk 123D integrated their 3D modeling software with Sculpteo, allowing designers to order an object directly from the software where it is being modeled. Dassault Systèmes' 3DVia, a professional grade software, enabled users of its open platform for hosting 3D models, to 3D print their digital models through Sculpteo. 3DVia includes the display of models in virtual showrooms. The Cloud Engine is also embedded in Autodesk's 123D Creature App, a web application to create and 3D print original character toys.

Finally, the Cloud Engine also supports the web application 3DPCase created by Sculpteo to make 3D printing available to a wider audience, which was the first mobile application for creating bespoke iPhone cases. 3DPCase was awarded with Best of the Best in Design and Engineering at the Consumer Electronics Show 2013. Users design their own cases by tweaking shapes, changing colors, and adding their own text and images. Alternatively, designers create customizable phone cover templates for users to modify.

While it takes a few minutes to purchase a mass-manufactured phone case on a brick-and-mortar shop, it can take up to 48 hours to ship the 3D-printed phone cases after an order but these can be unique. For instance, a 3DPCase application transforms a photo of someone into a facial profile that is printed in the case. In the advent of 3D printing services and marketplaces, mobile phone cases have been a popular product and a large number of case designs were shared and customized in a myriad of websites. Yet, Sculpteo claims that, comparing with other DIY options, using software such as 3DPCase enables users to design in a shorter time and to get a customized cover at lower cost. 3DPCase's parametric design technology is used by Sculpteo in other applications to design bespoke objects. Another iOS app enables users to embed real human data parameters (e.g., profile of someone's face) into a 3D model feature integrated on various surfaces, for instance ceramic flower pots.

At the very beginning, Sculpteo's founders thought that people would embrace the potential of 3D printing and adopt the technology quickly, in a way that would be transformative for the industry toward personal manufacturing. Since then, the original idea of boosting personal manufacturing evolved to developing capabilities to create software that makes it easy for anyone to create and print a 3D model.

OOMPH: Supporting Designers in Developing Capabilities for 3D Printing

Part of Sculpteo's software development efforts is the creation of tools that allow designers to manipulate manufacturing parameters to their benefit and improve their designs for manufacturability. The software functionalities guide designers into adapting an object's shape and configuration, changing the model to improve the quality of the end product and optimizing the production of higher volumes of a single product to reduce costs.

To help repair the models, Sculpteo offers automated processes that help solve the numerous problems typically associated with 3D printing. Among these are checking the solidity of the object, viewing a cross-section of the model to check structural integrity, and thickening the model in those parts identified as being so thin that they might break. The thickening tool uses a complex algorithm process to find the thin areas, set the area that needs thickening, and reform the 3D model maintaining the original structure.

To increase cost efficiency, Sculpteo offers tools to modify the model and to select among different manufacturing options. One tool hollows out a 3D model for printing, reducing the amount of material needed to manufacture the object and therefore its cost. It suits decorative objects with aesthetic functions because hollowing reduces the resistance of the object. The hollow out tool automatically updates the model when a customer changes the material or the size of the object.

Another tool called Batch Control enables the optimization of the print chamber's volume for mid-sized orders of the same product. It expanded 3D printing from one-off objects to mid-size batches of at least 20 units, decreasing unit costs. Batch Control was created to help clients get the most out of print volume, by optimizing printer capacity, and launched at the International Consumer Electronics Show in the beginning of 2014.

Customers visualize the order inside the printer, including the empty space that can still be filled with objects, and control the items' orientation and positioning to optimize costs and order size, while the tool iterates pricing in real time. In addition, Batch Control allows increasing the layer precision of the printing process for an optimized unit price. Sculpteo reported that the price of an individual unit manufactured with high-layer precision (i.e., smoother surface) could be cut by half by printing a large batch of at least 20 units. Overall, using Batch Control cuts costs in up to 35 percent on average for professional users and businesses ordering series of a few thousand units of the same product. Batch Control is an example of the potential of 3D printing to fulfill mid-size orders and complement mass manufacturing.

Camboutik, a company producing small, specialized cameras for equestrian sports, uses Sculpteo to produce all the plastic parts for this niche business that requires a few thousand parts per month. Small entrepreneurial ventures that seek capital through crowdfunding to launch a product line are also using Sculpteo, at least initially to fulfill the orders made in the crowdfunding campaign. BlueBee and Beast Technologies are two small companies that tried to fund their products on IndieGoGo. Although they did not manage to accomplish their funding goal, both proceeded with developing and producing their products for the early adopters and used Sculpteo to manufacture a Wi-Fi–enabled key chain (BlueBee) and a fitness tracker for monitoring weightlifting (Beast Technologies).

> *Before getting in contact with Sculpteo, we tried to use a FDM 3D printer, but precision was too low and the casings we produced were not matching our high-quality standard. The first prints we received from Sculpteo surprised us in a very good way. We realized that we could use Sculpteo Batch Control feature to produce not only our prototypes but also a first short series. The start-up concept can be summarized in the word "flexibility." We are young and superfast in our deliveries and in developing our products. That's the reason why we need to be able to re-design and re-print in just a few days.*
>
> —Ernst-Vittorio Haendler,
> Beast Technologies, for Sculpteo's blog

Later in October 2014, Sculpteo introduced a Multi-Part Printing tool to improve the printing quality of complex 3D-printed objects that have moving parts or require assembly of multiple parts. It solves the recurrent problem of defective printing of files with multiple volumes. The software in the Cloud Engine counts the number of objects in the 3D files uploaded for printing and transfers them to a multipart uploading page where the customer has the option of printing the parts as a single object or as a multi-piece set to be assembled after printing. The multi-part printing tool also allows Sculpteo to adjust its pricing to the labor involved in handling each piece. Given the labor and time effort involved in post-processing the printed pieces, the company started charging a €6 fee for manual post-processing of multi-piece objects.

In early 2015, Sculpteo launched a Final Proof tool that simulates visually a real 3D-printed object, solving the problematic gap between how the client sees the model on the computer screen and how the object actually looks like in reality. It shows in detail its visual features just like in print and allows users to assess potential defects and loss of detail from the conversion of the file to the print. After an order, it can still take a few hours or days for the client to hold the object in his or her hands, but the simulation tool takes seconds to provide a realistic image of the printed object. Thus, the tool saves re-printing time and reduces frustration with the lack of expertise in 3D printing.

> *"We discovered that a lot of people were deceived by their 3D printing because they over-engineer the file, they put a lot of details and then in the end they were very deceived because the printer destroyed details. If you listen to the comments in the hallway you see that the major problem of 3D printing is that it's not easy enough. In fact it's not easy at all. It doesn't need to be so complex. That's why we work a lot on doing software to make it more simple and to be sure that the customer and the end user will be able to go from his idea to his object very rapidly."*
>
> —Clément Moreau, interviewed for the TCT Show at
> Consumer Electronics Show, Las Vegas, 2015

Sculpteo has sharpened its focus into developing tools that differentiate it from similar services. Some of these tools automate the fixing processes carried out earlier by Sculpteo's internal staff and allow customers to fix their designs while learning how to improve their modeling skills. All the tools enable users to improve the 3D model by changing printing parameters in order to increase printing quality and reduce costs.

Challenges

One challenge that Sculpteo faces is the lack of awareness of the potential of 3D printing and the lack of technical knowledge held by users of its service. These obstacles are shared with other similar 3D printing platform services which have found different ways of tackling them. In recent years, the company tried to be closer to potential customers and to develop software tools that enhance customer experience with modeling and 3D printing. Furthermore, it has turned to professional users and businesses which represent a significant part of its demand.

An additional challenge, pointed out by marketing research firm Gartner as a limitation for growth, is the focus on iOS users in Sculpteo's mobile applications given that the apps are developed for iOS devices only. Nonetheless, it can be deemed a strategic choice of Sculpteo to focus on a growing brand of mobile devices which has been related typically with artists and designers who value the kind of technical expertise the brand conveys.

In their analysis of Cool Vendors in 3D Printing 2013, Gartner also pointed out that Sculpteo would "need clear policies assigning the ownership of any intellectual property for these objects to the maker or Sculpteo." This challenge is pervasive to the emerging 3D printing industry and Sculpteo created a way of dealing with the intellectual property of 3D files.

All the material uploaded to Sculpteo's website by users is property of its authors. Every upload is set as private by default, and kept as confidential in the company's servers, in which case only the designer and people who were sent the link to the file are able to view it within the 3D viewer on the website. Designers can easily change these privacy settings and turn their designs into "Public" mode which allows anyone to view the design and order a 3D print and allows the designer to set a profit margin on the manufacturing of the design. In this case, users authorize Sculpteo to publicly display the 3D model on the website. To generate revenue through the designer's profit margin, designers need to open a virtual shop associated to their Sculpteo account. A shop opened with Sculpteo means granting a non-exclusive license authorizing Sculpteo to sell the object in the name of the designer. Another level of public view is setting the right for other people to customize the design and order the object with modifications to the original design. These rules are suited to small businesses and professional users who wish to display their designs through Sculpteo while ensuring that their intellectual property is protected.

Outlook: Sculpteo and the Digital Factory of the Future

What is the place of 3D printing in the manufacturing landscape? A minuscule detail that sparks the attention of a few or rather a sweeping element that takes control of the scene. One strategy to diffuse the use of additive manufacturing has been to integrate the service with other platforms, such as popular web-based applications and 3D modeling software marketed by industry incumbents. Another strategy has been to improve user experience in order to boost diffusion in the use of the services. Yet, there might be undiscovered terrain out there for additive manufacturing.

Clément Moreau recalled to The Economist the story of a Chinese client, a large manufacturer, who realized in short notice that a few small parts were missing that should have been ordered from an injection molding company. On the verge of a significant delay in shipping the order, it turned to Sculpteo that was able to ship a batch of 5000 parts within days.

While the 3D printing hype is often depicted by desktop 3D printers, do-it-yourself objects with an unfinished look and artistically sophisticated pieces, Sculpteo is catering to professional users and small businesses which make up the largest demand for its services. This is worthy of note, especially combined with the need to develop a tool that supports mid-size production batches. Sculpteo has sought to make 3D printing more mainstream, by developing tools that cater to the needs of its professional grade users, and reduce the user frustration involved in using a largely underexplored means of manufacturing. Will a company such as Sculpteo find room in the manufacturing space to be a valuable complement?

11

BUG: Friendly Wasps for Pest Control in Farming

What if farmers adopted friendly wasps that took care of eating the larvae that fed off their crops? A friendly army of bugs helping out farmers control pests just like human antibodies work through an infectious disease by attacking the menace and leaving us healthy. What if farmers could mimic nature's way of controlling large populations of pests, effectively and without damage to soil, water, and biodiversity? BUG Agentes Biológicos, a Brazilian agroindustrial company, developed an effective scalable method by which to provide biological forms of pest control for farming which are a more sustainable alternative to the commonly used pesticides.

We can think of BUG as a mass producer of armies of countless wasps that are released onto cultivated land and eliminate the moths and caterpillars that threaten arable land crops and vegetable farms. BUG takes advantage of the parasitic behavior of insects and commercializes natural parasites that eliminate pests before they cause large-scale damages. In spite of the nasty warfare just depicted, this kind of biological pest control protects soil, water, and biodiversity from chemical pesticides, protects the surrounding ecosystem and human health in the long term, and defends farmers from uncontrollable pesticide-resistant pests that ruin farming revenues.

Bioagents reduce the need for pesticides, whose use can endanger health and natural ecosystems and eliminate natural pest control dynamics. Whereas in grain crops bioagents can substitute around 40 to 50 percent of chemicals, in sugarcane crops they can substitute 100 percent of chemicals. Contrarily to pesticides, bioagents do not create resistance in pests, pollute water and soil, bioaccumulate in the food chain, or intoxicate farmers and consumers. Contrarily to other macroorganism-based crop protection, parasite wasps cannot easily become invasive because they depend on the parasite-host relationship to survive. BUG's pest control is self-regulating because wasps have a short life span and a limited flying range when there is lack of food (i.e., pests' eggs).

The method for producing and deploying the biological agents was developed by BUG's founders, the biologist Heraldo Negri and the agronomist Diogo Carvalho, who initially saw an opportunity to market the wasps to organic farmers with small-scale tomato crops. BUG started up in 2001 in a technology incubator in the State of São Paulo, Brazil (EsalqTec, part of Agriculture School of University of São Paulo) supported by a seed fund for the initial R&D (around €615,000 today) from FAPESP—São Paulo Research foundation, a public foundation funded through government budgets. Later, in 2007, BUG was funded by Criatec, a venture capital investment program of the Brazilian Development Bank (BNDES) for nascent firms with innovative profile, which works as an acceleration platform advised by SPVentures, a venture capital management firm. Recently BUG has been recognized as one of the world's *most innovative* companies by the World Economic Forum as well as Fast Company magazine.

Going Back and Toward the Future in Biological Pest Control

The *Trichogramma* variety of wasps used by BUG is not a novel discovery. In fact, it has been studied extensively and for a long time as a natural parasite of insects and a beneficial means for pest control. The biological control of insects has been used for centuries. Back in the third century, in China, farmers used ants to protect oranges growing on trees from hungry insects. Farmers' markets sold nests of ants surrounded by twigs and leaves that would be attached to mandarin orange trees to protect them from the insects that would eat the fruits.

After the use of chemical pesticides became widespread, biological methods remained in use in many countries for occasions when pests had resisted the chemical treatment and spread uncontrollably. Between 1950 and 2000, the number of arthropod pest species with resistance to one or more types of pesticides grew in an S-shaped curve from close to zero to more than 500 (Hajek, 2004).

Typically, biological control methods are more specific than chemicals in targeting particular pest species, but the various types of methods differ in their degree of efficacy. The most used methods are *microbial biopesticides*, typically bacteria, viruses, and fungi which eliminate moths, beetles, and flies, and are usually mixed in water and sprayed across the fields. They are relatively host-specific but less so than parasite insects. These organisms "infect" the pests causing their elimination and are easily produced at industrial scale. Another method is the use of *pheromones* that disrupts pest mating or lures pests to be killed.

Finally, *macroorganisms* such as predator and parasitic insects are used also to track down and eliminate insect pests. A paramount issue in using biological methods is making sure they do not cause damage by propagating uncontrollably. For instance, using ladybugs to eliminate plant lice led to the elimination of other important species because ladybugs are massive predators. Cane toads from South and Central America were used successfully to control sugarcane beetles in Hawaii. However, when they were introduced in Australia in 1935 they not only failed to eliminate the beetles but also became an invasive species that today is still hard to control.

On the contrary, parasites like BUG's *Trichogramma* wasps are host-specific, able to search for their host, and able to kill the hosts and reproduce at their expense. In addition, they have a short life cycle, from a few days to a few weeks. Mass production of these parasites is challenging, and requires highly technical skills developed with cumulative experience and knowledge in the continuous production of colonies. This biological method is a first stage preventive measure that avoids the massive use of chemical pesticides that are known to be environmentally harmful and damaging to human health damages all while increasing the resistance of targeted pests.

WOW: How Parasitic Wasps Control Insect Pests Naturally

Moths and caterpillars cause damage to crops early in their larval phase when they feed on the crops. BUG's parasite wasps lay their eggs inside those larvae eggs. As the wasps develop inside the eggs, they feed on the nutrients found inside them, eating these from the inside. Hence, the eggs of pests never get to hatch.

BUG's advantage is to deploy the natural "intelligence" found in the parasitic relationship and to deploy it as a product to protect crops. The wasps have a strong chemical perception and scan the pest's eggs to check whether they have adequate nutritional conditions for the wasp's eggs to be inserted. Moreover, adult wasps segregate a protein that guarantees that their larvae will have enough food to survive and grow inside the pest's eggs, as well as a substance that signals to other female wasps that the egg is already taken, in order to block competition for food inside the egg. A single wasp can lay eggs in more than 50 pests' eggs.

This way the wasps multiply while restraining the proliferation of the pest. As the pest population dies, the wasps run out of food resources, eventually disappearing as well. The natural life span of BUG's parasitic wasps is about 2 weeks. Therefore, the natural biological defense disappears when its mission is accomplished and the farmland returns to an equilibrium that ensures regular crop growth.

OOMPH: BUG Scales Up Natural Processes for Pest Control

First, a team visits the client's crop area, looks for existing populations of parasite wasps, and samples wasps from the field. The collected wasps enable BUG to reproduce the same wasp breed that is the natural parasite of insect pests. This breed has the advantage of being naturally adapted to the climatic conditions of the farmland. Furthermore, the wasps only eliminate their natural targets and no other species that might be favorable to the land.

BUG developed a scalable mass-production method to breed the wasps and an effective method to release them onto the fields supported by extensive testing of the wasps' flying range under particular climatic conditions. After testing the wasps for life span and flying range under laboratory conditions, BUG mass produces them using an automated procedure protected by trade secrets.

Wasps are released onto the crop area either manually by farmers, in patent-protected small cartridges that contain hundreds of wasps in close-to-adult stage, or directly from a drone or an agricultural aircraft. Previously, BUG relied solely on the manual release method, shipping the cartridges to farmers and training them on how to place the cartridges on the plants. Recently, BUG worked out a way to spray the wasps from an aircraft, just as pesticides are crop-dusted over the fields. Upon release, wasps are still developing, inside a cocoon that hatches in the field. To cover about 25 hectares of land, BUG is able to release around 1 million wasps.

Although manual release remains in use for small-scale crops, currently the company uses aircraft release for larger areas. The airborne method was important for BUG to expand its operations to bigger farming areas, attract clients in the large-scale agriculture business, and create a level playing field to compete with chemical pest control.

The application of parasite wasps in an open field environment is more difficult than in greenhouses because conditions cannot be controlled. Parasitic insects are very small and their flying range is influenced by wind conditions which is a problem for the effectiveness of their application. Doing this effectively requires competences in the species ecology and behavior in open environments.

SO WHAT? Radical Cost Reduction in Pest Control

BUG's control method helps farmers to reduce their pest control expenses and to curtail potential losses from damages caused by pests because wasps are extremely effective in eliminating pests as a preventive measure. Higher effectiveness leads to cost reduction in the control of pests and in the limitation of pest-related damage. Yet, BUG needed to develop competences in mass producing and delivering the wasps so that its pest control method is scalable and effective.

First, mass production requires technical capabilities because wasps are living organisms and need to maintain their pest elimination efficacy. Furthermore, wasps cannot be stocked because their life cycle is very short and must be released onto the fields at a specific moment of their development, just before the cocoons hatch, so that adult wasps lay as many eggs as possible inside the pest's eggs. Wasps are sensitive to environmental conditions and need special packaging and transport conditions to the fields in order to prevent them from losing their pest control properties.

Second, the method's effectiveness draws on a naturally occurring parasite-host relationship that was enhanced by research and development carried out by BUG. The biofactory collaborates with academic research groups to transform more parasite species into bioagent products. Relying on host-specificity is crucial because earlier attempts to deploy biological control with macroorganisms have had negative repercussions. Furthermore, chemical control brings about the problem of increasing resistance of pests to pesticides which results in larger use of pesticides and lower effectiveness in pest management.

Third, bioagents that are target-specific and crop-specific make pest control effective and collateral effects minimized. BUG customizes their pest management solutions by sampling the bioagents from the cultivated land, as they naturally occur at that point in time, and bringing them to the laboratory to develop the most effective bioagent breed. In the laboratory, BUG constantly tests which kinds of breeds are more adapted to several different climates. The farmer receives a bioagent product that is tailored to the climate of its land, to the type of crops, and to the natural parasites present there.

Finally, BUG uses two methods for releasing the bioagents, adapted to small-scale (man-handled cartridges) and large-scale areas (drones and agricultural aircraft). The cartridge method was designed to be simple to use and does not require safety equipment because wasps are not dangerous to human health contrary to pesticides. In the airborne release method, wasps are sprayed over the field "in the right dose, at the right speed, and with the right protection so they can be effective" (Francisco Jardim, Member of the Board and Investor).

BUG draws on a combination of various techniques and competences to increase the effectiveness of bioagents, allowing farmers to act early and contain the pest by eliminating their eggs with precision without endangering health and the ecosystem. This represents an immediate cost reduction for farmers in comparison with the release of pesticides. Furthermore, the company markets its bioagents to farmers as a preventive solution that enables them to save in pesticides and in future extraordinary measures that would be required as pests become resistant to chemicals.

How BUG Is Different from Incumbents

The market for biological pest control has grown in recent years, partly due to environmental regulations in agriculture, but remains a niche market. In 2008, the biological crop protection market represented 2.5 percent of the global chemical pesticides market and was valued at €60 million. Biopesticides were the fastest growing segment of the insecticides market, increasing at a rate of more than 20 percent per year. In 2005, the market share of microbial biopesticides corresponded to 65 to 70 percent of the whole biological pest control market, whereas parasite and predator insects for crop protection accounted for only 15 percent.

In the past years, several companies in the biological pest control industry were acquired by leading agrochemicals multinationals. U.S.-based technology leader AgraQuest was acquired by Bayer CropScience in 2012, fulfilling Bayer's intention of building a technology platform for green products that offer farmers solutions for integrated pest management that combine seeds, traits, chemical protection, and biological control. AgraQuest technologies complemented the microbial biopesticide sold by Bayer and leveraged their biotechnology platform. Also in 2012, BASF acquired U.S.-based Becker Underwood which was included in their Functional Crop Care division. With Becker Underwood, BASF strengthened its microbial biopesticides solutions that work in the presence of chemical insecticides and fungicides. Novozymes acquired Natural Industries in 2012 and established a partnership in microbial biopesticides with Monsanto in 2013 (the BioAg Alliance). In 2013, Syngenta launched a microbial biopesticides line based on technology acquired in 2012 from Pasteuria BioScience.

Although agrochemical multinationals have developed and acquired technology for production of biological control agents, such as fungi, bacteria, and viruses, they have dedicated much less effort in developing macro-scale solutions. Agrochemical incumbents have focused also on genetic improvement of seeds, which require significantly less expenditure in R&D. Datamonitor reported that developing a new insecticide costs $40 to $100 million, whereas developing a new plant variety costs under $1 million.

According to technology experts, the potential of predators and parasitoids remains untapped. Recently, a variety of *Trichogramma* was introduced in China to help control an insect that became known in North America as one of the most destructive. *Trichogramma* wasps were used as biological agents in over 30 countries and more than 32 million hectares in 2006, but mostly in South and Central America and in China. However, it remains a niche market solution. Dutch company Koppert is a market leader in commercializing parasite bioagents along with microbial biopesticides, pollinators, and predator insects. In 2012 it acquired the Brazilian Itaforte Bioprodutos which became its subsidiary in Brazil, producing microbial biopesticides, parasitoids, and predator insects. Koppert Brazil competes with BUG in this market, as it also produces and commercializes the *Trichogramma* variety of parasitic wasps.

The use of parasitic wasps is able to compete to a certain extent with chemical pest control methods, which remain the most widely used method in agriculture. One problem with pesticides is that they have a broad spectrum of action and kill both pests and their natural predators. Furthermore, with continued use of pesticides, pests adapt to their chemical environment and develop resistance which makes them less effective, just as bacteria develop resistance to antibiotics in humans. This forces farmers to spend increasing amounts of money to use larger quantities of pesticides, while companies develop additional chemical compounds to tackle pests' resistance.

Notably, a turning point for BUG's business came about in 2012 when Brazilian soy farmers were confronted with the resistance of a *Helicover* caterpillar to pesticides. Before entering Brazil, the pest had devastated crops in other countries. In the first year in Brazil, losses amounted to $2 billion and pesticides failed to control further damage. As farmers looked desperately for solutions, BUG already possessed a fully developed bioagent that had controlled the same pest in Australia. Using the parasite wasps, farmers were able to control *Helicover* and reduce the use of pesticides by 60 percent in soy crops. For every five airborne releases of parasite wasps, only one crop dusting of pesticides was carried out. In 2015, BUG launched a new bioagent for pest control in soy crops (*Telenomus podisi*) with a control efficacy of up to 80 percent.

The soy caterpillar invasion was a window of opportunity for BUG to expand its business given the success of its bioagents. Compared to incumbents in the agroindustry sector, the company had very little resources for marketing and research and development. Multinational companies organize conferences and social events to market their products to farmers. Moreover, they invest substantially in internal and external research and development.

BUG does not have an internal R&D unit and relies heavily on publicly funded research. Therefore, it establishes partnerships with academic research units and other small biological control companies to carry out R&D. Only after getting public seed funding and later private venture capital did BUG conduct research that revealed its business potential was higher than they thought.

In the aftermath of the soy crop devastation, BUG expanded its target market to reach large-scale farmers and, in 2 years, extended its coverage to over half a million hectares of land in Brazil. BUG's bioagents have an effectiveness rate of 90 percent in eliminating pests. In 2011, the biofactories were working at full capacity and expanded in 2012 due to growing demand in order to produce enough to double the acreage covered. The production of bioagents rose from 27 billion wasps in 2011 to 150 billion in 2014. This growth path is remarkable for a company who had planned to focus on niche and organic farming markets, notwithstanding the recent growth of these sectors in Brazil.

Challenges

In spite of its superior environmental profile, BUG's business faces legal restrictions on the release of living macroorganisms in the fields. Strict testing is required for the approval of BUG's products in order to ensure that an introduced species will not become invasive. Yet, BUG is well positioned to benefit from changes in the regulation that controls the use of agrochemicals. In 2013, Brazilian authorities banned one of the most used pesticides for soy crops, *endosulfan*, due to its toxicity and potential for endangering farmers' health. The ban left no choices for many farmers who waited for the regulatory approval of alternative pesticides. BUG took advantage of this opportunity by developing a bioagent that had been identified 10 years earlier during research carried out in collaboration with Embrapa Soja, a Brazilian agriculture research company. The application of this bioagent, which achieves an efficacy of up to 80 percent, can provide solution for the 32 million hectares of soy crops in Brazil, for which uncontrolled pest damage could represent a loss of $10 billion.

Recently, however, agricultural regulation and policies in many countries have promoted integrated pest management programs, which incentivize environmental friendly forms of pest control along with pest forecasting and monitoring in detriment of the use of chemical pesticides. Organic farming and biodynamic farming are market niches that have used biological pest control methods for a long time due to the sustainability values they are based on as well as to the regulations and standards that define organic production conditions.

Nonetheless, variations of these methods are penetrating conventional agriculture practices. BUG sees its biological methods as a fit to the integrated pest management programs that combine biological and chemical control with the use of seeds that are genetically engineered to resist pests. Yet, recently agrochemical incumbents acquired biological control companies in order to integrate these companies' technological capabilities and product portfolios in their crop protection product portfolios. Incumbents' ability to acquire smaller innovative companies can be problematic for BUG's differentiated value proposition given that farmers have shown reluctance in adopting a fully non-chemical pest control method.

Finally, another challenge for BUG is the expansion of their portfolio to increase the number of parasite species. BUG's production method is scalable within the portfolio of biological agents that they commercialize. In Brazil, the company uses four different species of bioagents authorized for commercial production, while globally around 250 species are used. However, expanding the portfolio of biological agents can be determinant for BUG, as farmers might resist using products from different companies. Agrochemical incumbents have been keen to offer complete turn-key solutions for crop management that include seeds, fertilization, and pest control in the same crop protection package.

Outlook: BUG's Biomimicry for Radical Cost Reduction

In its early days, BUG's pest control by bioagents was ridiculed by farmers who did not believe it could work. Admittedly, it was far-fetched to think such fragile small creatures would rise to the challenge. Notably, we read what happened at Orwell's Animal Farm when it was turned over to pigs. Well, BUG's bioagents are friendlier and more productive. It turns out that by choosing bioagents to control pests, farmers are leveraging the power of nature in their favor.

BUG's bioagents favor the natural balance between pest and predator, ensuring the regular growth of crops and limiting damages caused by pests as their proliferation runs out of control. The biological control is adapted to each type of pest and crop, contrarily to pesticides to which pests develop resistance. BUG markets its parasite wasps as an initial, almost preventive, measure so that farmers avoid incurring costs with pesticides and their potential consequences.

Farm produce grown without pesticides can be more valuable for consumers who are both sensitive to sustainability matters and willing to pay more for them. Given the search for farm produce with lower environmental impact and better quality, combined with bioagents' high pest elimination rates, BUG's potential market "is Brazil's entire $7 billion pesticide market" according to board member and investor Francisco Jardim. Crop by crop, acre by acre, these bugs are ready to take over the world.

From the Perspective of Heraldo Negri de Oliveira, Co-Founding Partner and Director of Production, BUG

From the beginning, BUG's goal was the production and commercialization of agents for biological control of agricultural pests. The expertise of the founders in this area made it easy to develop the production technology at an industrial scale and the implementation of a dream, which was the real possibility of contributing to improving crop yields in a safe and sustainable manner. Our great passion is to wake up in the morning every day and do every effort we can to achieve our goals.

In Brazil, the world's second largest agricultural area, chemical control is the most used tactic for controlling pests in farming, which is contrary to the global trend of producing healthier food, while respecting the consumer, the workers, and the environment. In Brazil, a strong culture in farming prefers the use of pesticides for controlling pests. Biological control with parasitoids was limited to small farming areas and greenhouses. Our big project was to overflow large agricultural areas with those biological agents, and compete with pesticides in soy, cotton, corn, sugarcane, tomato, and other crops. To make that dream come true we have persisted in orienting toward and informing about the results and advantages associated with integrating biological control with traditional methods used by farmers. We have been obtaining excellent results with this work.

If we could point out a contribution made by BUG, it would be the fact that never before had biological pest control been so much talked about in Brazil until BUG was created. It has taken us years of persistence, determination, and work until we were able to reach the positive results that we currently have. In a 1-year period, we organized more than 100 talks and technical meetings to spread the results and advantages of adopting biological control technology.

Throughout these years, it is undeniable that BUG has contributed to the advance of biological control in Brazil. We have been always earnest regarding the work with our technology, very technical-oriented in searching for innovations and improvements that would turn into earnings for our company, clients, and the society at large.

Currently, we are working on the development of a new technology that enables the production of an egg parasitoid (*Trissolcus basalis* and *Telenomus podisi*) to control pests that attack soy, a crop that takes up over 32 million hectares of land in Brazil. The first step was to establish partnerships with Brazilian universities and research centers that have been carrying out basic research in this technology. We have started this pilot-project, in collaboration with other groups, to implement the search for improvement steps that will lead to success. In 2014, we released the parasitoid *Telenomus podisi* in crop areas larger than 10,000 hectares. Based on recent assessments, we foresee a success scenario for the coming years.

Our most important step was not giving up in the first 6 years of BUG. Apparently, there was no possibility to get financial return, but work and persistence showed, in time, new windows of opportunity opened and then we started to harvest the fruits of that work and persistence. Currently, we are in a very different situation. After announcing our biological pest control for soy pests, we have been sought out by dozens of farmers who want to use this technology. All of them will be very well served.

12

BioCurious: The Curious Case of the Community Biotech Laboratory

Silicon Valley has seen a number of tech innovations emerge from garages. However, before BioCurious, biotech was largely out of reach for those without access to a university or big biotech company laboratory. In 2010, BioCurious was established to provide shared laboratory space for professional, academic, citizen scientists, as well as anyone else interested in biotech.

Initially BioCurious could have been seen as just another, if exceptionally unconventional, garage-based Silicon Valley idea. However, a successful Kickstarter campaign, led by Eri Gentry, a co-founder, demonstrated that the idea of a shared laboratory space with an emphasis on creativity and openness resonated with an underserved community of amateur enthusiasts and career scientists alike. In addition to the financial support raised through crowdfunding, many volunteered their time and expertise and the laboratory received significant donations of scientific equipment. The world's first hackerspace for biotech was thus born.

After a successful Kickstarter campaign in 2010, BioCurious moved out of the garage and started a non-profit organization with a 2500 square foot laboratory in Silicon Valley. BioCurious provides access to equipment, materials, courses, and a working space to members for experimentation with new entrepreneurial biotech ideas in as well as general creative scientific inquiry. The organization is entirely staffed and run by volunteers, and for a $100 membership fee anyone is welcome to join. Amateurs, inventors, activists, entrepreneurs, students, and anyone else who would like to experiment with DIY Biology is welcome to join and become a citizen scientist. Indeed, nearly 2000 people have joined the MeetUp community and are following BioCurious and its many biotech projects.

SO WHAT Makes BioCurious Special?

BioCurious stands out in the biotech ecosystem as a truly novel organizational model. Biotech laboratories today are generally accessible only to those associated with formal academic institutions, government laboratories, or employees of corporations. BioCurious, however, aims to serve citizen scientists, in the spirit of Benjamin Franklin, and develop a community of experimentation in line with the Royal Society where people showcased their discoveries. To build an open and creative community BioCurious looked for organizational models and found more inspiration from hackerspaces, the BioPunk Manifesto, and organizations such as the Homebrew Computer Club. However, biotech is quite different from computer science and smaller engineering projects which can be executed on an individual scale, with a laptop and some virtual server space. Biotech experimentation requires a physical laboratory and investment in specialized equipment. Thus, BioCurious would be "like TechShop but for Biotech," the first hackerspace for biology, something closer to a Maker Faire community than academic-industrial biotech ventures.

The bioscience conducted at the laboratory is not the only ongoing experiment at BioCurious. The laboratory itself is an experimental and novel space that questions the conventions of formal laboratories and the organization of scientific enquiry. Limited in resources, the laboratory aims to do a lot with a little and thus has been able to develop a very different cost structure and culture than incumbents. The design of the laboratory is innovative in that it rethinks laboratory space workflows and equipment instead of resorting to the conventional sterile looking laboratory where "grey machine sits next to grey machine" (no unnecessary inspiration there!). Indeed, many organizations and companies have visited BioCurious to learn about open innovation and creativity. Delegations of executives and policy makers have visited the laboratory from AkzoNobel, Google, the Atlantic Council, as well as groups of Eisenhower Fellows.

How Is It Different from Incumbents?

The objectives of BioCurious are quite unique in the scientific world. Its priority is to make science accessible to all, not just to the formally qualified top-tier scientists or academics. Unlike in universities or pharma companies, where there is always a focus on the output or efficacy, the BioCurious model does not allow for judgment focus on scrutinizing ideas. The BioCurious movement is more about experimenting and making creative projects come alive. The fact that there are not many hard and fast requirements, deadlines, or specifications to make this evolution possible stimulates a relaxed environment that enhances creativity, a characteristic not associated with formal laboratory structures.

The laboratory space has been used by a diverse group of experimenters. Entrepreneurs have developed ideas for their businesses, talented people without resources have used the laboratory equipment to try out ideas, and science PhDs have come in to share their research and keep their skills fresh. The diversity of the community has also made possible a "grassroots mentorship" program where members share and learn from each other's different approaches to and backgrounds in biotech. In contrast, academic science is largely grant-driven and hinges on Principal Investigators with very similar qualifications, working in very similar laboratories. Members at BioCurious see this homogeneity as a potential limitation to the creativity necessary to solve many problems in biotech.

While there may be a perception that the laboratory caters to hobbyists, as per Fast Company's description of DIY geneticists, ". . . *Tinkering with a vortexer, an ultrasonic bath, and gel electrophoresis to create glow-in-the-dark plants, wormlike creatures that crave butter, and robots that can do your pipetting for you*" (Fastcompany.com), much of the research is very serious. Some of these ideas have evolved to become globally recognized, award-winning projects and many address problems overlooked by the incumbents. Members running projects at BioCurious have also started to apply for research grants—a resource that has largely been the domain of the biotech establishment. In seeking out formal grants the laboratory hopes to demonstrate how serious biotech can be done through innovative methods with a fraction of the resources.

The whole idea behind BioCurious is to be the nexus for this transformation, by making innovations in biology accessible, affordable, and open to a diverse community. To start with, many projects at BioCurious follow a crowdsourcing model. The inclusive nature of the laboratory also leads to a talent pool that can support many different projects. Moreover, it promotes fresher ideas and a greater collaboration between different disciplines. While the community laboratory does not have a policy formal on intellectual property, many of the projects have followed open sharing models allowing people to reproduce, modify, or adapt original creations to further their projects. This commitment to open innovation is something that incumbents may find unsettling. After all, for traditional universities and big biotech companies, a commercially applied solution is the primary measure of output of research.

The Challenges of Novelty

Being one of the frontrunners in the area, BioCurious has had to overcome the challenges faced by first mover innovators. Operating in the biotech space the laboratory has had to think through specific scenarios most start-up companies will never have to consider.

Safety is always a concern in biotech and it is a priority at BioCurious. BioCurious has limited itself to working with equipment and materials at BSL-1, the equivalent of what would be found in a high-school laboratory. The laboratory has a safety committee in place and the open nature of the community that reviews the safety of experiments conducted in the laboratory. BioCurious has put practices in place for training and risk reduction that have been taken up by other community laboratories in the United States and abroad. The laboratory has even led discussions with policy makers, including the Federal Bureau of Investigation, regarding safety, amateur science and community laboratories, as well as thinking about issues ranging from controlled substances to bioterrorism.

Another aspect by which BioCurious stands out of the ecosystem is financial. The laboratory is a non-profit, volunteer-run organization operating in a space populated by universities and companies with impressive budgets. As such, the financial viability of community laboratories has been questioned by, for example, some media outlet. BioCurious, however, aims to punch above its weight by making the most of resources and has pointed to the tremendous resourcefulness of its growing volunteer base and community. Furthermore, BioCurious is regularly approached for guidance and consultation as others look to also start up similar laboratories to serve their communities.

The concept of citizen scientists working in biotech, novel as it is today, poses some challenges too. To start with, some may question the credibility of the research due to the fact that science is being conducted by a group of non-professionals and laypersons possibly without the formal qualifications. However, BioCurious sees this diversity as an asset and source of creativity. The issue of maintaining transparency and open innovation will also drive BioCurious and other community laboratories to standardize their unique approaches to biotech and allow for results and processes to be better communicated and understood across the emerging DIY Bio space.

There are some open questions regarding the next steps of the BioCurious model. The development of standards and common protocols will leverage the open innovation practices and allow community laboratories to be replicated globally adding diversity to the biotech ecosystem that BioCurious seeks. However, the amplification of developing new standards and best practices must be balanced with emergent ideas and creativity. After all it was the experimental nature and eschewing of incumbents' standards that brought about the novelty that is BioCurious. Similarly, the community-based governance model, the development of safety policies, and two-person board may eventually feel stretched thin as the community and interest continue to grow and as new emergent organizations seek guidance.

OOMPH: Curiosity Beyond Bio

BioCurious offers a community platform for discussing and experimenting with anything from health matters and life extension to biofuels by anyone from a casual hobbyist to a formal, establishment scientist. In opening up the scientific laboratory to creativity and people, BioCurious has, at a fraction of the cost of incumbents, enabled its members to experiment with science, instead of merely working with biotech. In doing so they have also experimented with organizational form, challenged assumed industry logics, and contributed to increasing the diversity of the ecosystem—and as any biologist knows the greater the ecological biodiversity, the healthier the system.

From the Perspective of Tito Jankowski, Co-Founder, BioCurious

I'm sitting at BioCurious and I'm not doing any laboratory work. I'm not really a laboratory work person. I'm just sitting reading my e-mail. The whole time, there are people coming into BioCurious, doing experiments, saying hi, talking about experiments, showing me new discoveries and new things, asking me if I've heard about these latest discoveries.

It's still stunning to me. Four years later after we opened the doors at BioCurious, it's still energizing for me to go in and just sit. You don't have to be a biotech expert. You just have to have been frustrated in your life before. You have to have had a job where you were surrounded by people who didn't care. You have to have had a job where your boss didn't care and you didn't care either.

And when you come to BioCurious you realize it's totally different. This is the future of innovation. People are there because they want to be there, on a Wednesday afternoon, or late on a Saturday night. Some members drive all the way to Sunnyvale from San Francisco, it's not a convenient location, and we're pretty far from the train station. People come because they want to try things out at this community biotech laboratory.

And I think of myself 6 years earlier, being in my apartment in Sacramento. I was trying to build a tool called a gel electrophoresis box. I was trying to glue it together myself. It's a mess and I'm frustrated and suddenly the glue spills everywhere, and no one around and I just picked the thing up and I threw it against the wall. And it bounced off, it didn't even break, I was hoping it would shatter into a million pieces. Being alone and working in a field where no one thinks that you should be in is difficult.

Einstein when he first did his research, he was an unknown in physics. His paper was released and no one responded to the idea that $e = mc^2$. I know what that must have felt like. And that's why I'm so amazed to be sitting here at BioCurious.

Last month, we had the head of the U.K. Government Office for Science come to BioCurious and she loved what we were doing. And before that, we had a group of the top executives and engineers from Google come to BioCurious for a 6-hour workshop. A Congressman just e-mailed today. They want to know what are we doing and what it is like. And I just think it's so amazing to see that all these people are able to come to work and be curious.

And what's next is to create this around the world. BioCurious is still kind of one of a kind, though it inspired maybe a dozen or so other laboratories like it around the world. They're all passion projects, and what I want to see is more of these. More people being able to follow their curiosity, experiment with friends, more people being able to learn from others and learn how to make discoveries just like Einstein, who wasn't part of a traditional laboratory, wasn't part of a physics institution.

I think it's really important that we create spaces for people to be curious even if it's not something they've devoted their life to. At the point that I threw that gel box against the wall, I wasn't somebody with a PhD in biology. I had a full-time job doing software consulting for the California State Government, testing software for an automated welfare system. That doesn't have anything to do with biotechnology. But biotech was my passion and it was my interest and that's why I was alone in my apartment, at night, gluing those pieces of plastic together. At BioCurious, we've created a place that all sorts of biotech innovators can be curious, learn, and share with others. Come check it out!

13

TaskRabbit: Hop Online and Pull a Rabbit out of Your Service Network

On a cold night in 2008, when 28-year-old Leah Busque and her husband Kevin ran out of dog food for their Labrador retriever Kobe, an idea was born. Leah and Kevin were on their way to dine out, when they realized Kobe's dinner was not ready. There was no way to contact anybody else to get it for him too. That made Leah thinking, "Wouldn't the world be a better place if there was a platform for contacting people to help you run your errands?" A few months later, Leah quit her engineering job at IBM to focus on creating a viable solution to this problem. Runmyerrand Inc, later known as TaskRabbit,[1] was thus born in September 2008. It was the first location viable, two-way platform for "service networking," a term Leah coined for the activity whereby people and information are brought together online to fulfill a collective business objective.

The company matched people who needed an extra hand to take care of their errands with people who were ready to lend a hand in exchange for money. It was launched in Leah's community of Charlestown. Within 6 months, they had expanded it all the way through Boston and into Cambridge. They participated in fbFund Rev, a seed fund and incubator program by Facebook, Founders Fund, and Accel Partners. They raised $15,000 in funding which Leah used to commence their activities in San Francisco. In May 2008, the company closed a $5 million Series A funding run by Menlo Park, Calif.'s Shasta Ventures. It also raised $1.8 million in seed-round funding. 500 Startups, Lightspeed Venture Partners, and Baseline Ventures are some of the other companies that backed TaskRabbit. In 2011, with a new

---

[1]The name was changed mainly because the word "errand" in Runmyerrand was much too restricting.

funding round, TaskRabbit expanded to New York City, Los Angeles, and Chicago. San Francisco, Orange County, and Boston joined the list later on. By 2014, TaskRabbit had over 1.25 million new users, with over 25,000 taskers working on the platform, and 10 percent of them doing it as a full-time job. The task-posting volume has grown by 50 percent since then. Approximately $4 million of economic activity is requested monthly through the platform. The taskers do a variety of jobs ranging from getting dog food to helping people relocate. This generalist approach is earning the company both fame and criticism at the same time.

Following the "TaskRabbit"—How Does It Work?

By March 2008, there were 100 "runners" ("taskers" as they would be called afterward), the number increasing to more than 2000 within just 3 years. Initially it had an auction house model, where task senders (users) and the taskers negotiate with each other through TaskRabbit's online platform. The senders could declare the maximum amount they are willing to pay for getting a task done. The taskers bid on the task by stating the minimum amount they are willing to accept. The senders then choose from among the bids. Taskers, who are rated highly or available immediately for an urgent job, can insist on substantial premiums. Users could also opt for "TaskRabbit Elites," who are taskers consistently providing best services with proficiency. TaskRabbit takes 12 to 30 percent cut off from each transaction, depending on the value of the jobs. Lower value jobs incur a higher percentage cut off.

At this stage, TaskRabbit had employed game mechanics to keep the taskers from scurrying away. The top taskers were ranked and the level achieved by each tasker was displayed in a leaderboard. The average customer review was also included. The taskers could see their progress bar and know how many additional points they would need to jump to the subsequent level. Points were awarded for accurate bidding, quick bidding, and for recommending TaskRabbit to friends via e-mails.

On July 2014, TaskRabbit changed its model to an "invitation model" also known as "BookerT," by building a computer algorithm that automatically matches customers with available taskers that have the right skills. Each tasker's ratings and hourly rate are displayed and the customer can choose his own rabbit. They also changed their customer model to accommodate businesses. Through TaskRabbit "business portal," companies could outsource work to temporary staffers.

TaskRabbit is guaranteed and has proven to extremely useful for people from homemakers to understaffed companies, from doing grocery shopping to assembling desks for new employees. The taskers are assessed through a four-step process. Initially, upon receiving the application form, an automated phone or video interview is conducted to identify lazy bunnies and reject them. Additionally, a federal criminal background check is done on each prospective tasker by the database company Axiom. Lastly, a social security number tracing is done before making the final selection decision. As Leah Busque says, "it is not an open marketplace where anyone can just sign up." Upon selection, some of the taskers treat the service as a full-time job and earn as much as $5000 per month. A few self-promote themselves via blogs, Google voice accounts, etc., to better their chances.

The taskers hang out together and share their tasker experiences over snacks once a month during "Rabbit Rallies." Majority of the jobs on TaskRabbit involve real work. Improper or "unusual" posts are reviewed and removed by the Operations Manager. An example being the task which requested the tasker to bring an "Attractive/Successful Male, Some Water + Juice," which was taken down 10 minutes later by TaskRabbit.

Apart from connecting the users with the taskers for getting chores done, TaskRabbit is also creating an impact on society by helping people who are looking for jobs but have trouble finding them. People from different backgrounds (ex-military, former medical scientists, and retired handymen) have all benefited from the TaskRabbit project. The taskers praise the company for its positive psychological impact on the job seekers.

WOW: From Hired Hands to Peer Labor?

TaskRabbit is one of the pioneers in the peer-to-peer labor sector. It was brave enough to enter a new space—the peer-to-peer commerce or "do it for me" economy. A lot of companies in our time are more evolutionary than revolutionary. In this scenario, TaskRabbit took the chance to be truly disruptive. The core idea behind this company is motivating many other start-ups, most of them specialist companies, to enter the space. This is proof for the appeal and novelty of TaskRabbit. After all, imitation is the sincerest form of flattery.

With the smart combination of work and gaming in its initial model, TaskRabbit had developed an independent mode of employment and a new kind of entrepreneurship. A particularly remarkable aspect of TaskRabbit made it successful: the competitive dynamics at play. The point system, the review process, etc., created an energetic cadre of taskers who were willing to exchange their services to other people like themselves, for carrots. It also helped in dodging costs associated with inventory, overhead, and hiring full-time employees. The newer fee-based business model was able to maintain these advantages and at the same time, become more straightforward and easier to understand for rabbits and users alike.

The feedback scheme of TaskRabbit has also been quite effective in bringing about constructive adaptations. When Runmyerrand.com was renamed as TaskRabbit in 2010, many new modifications were incorporated as per the suggestions received from members. These involved alterations with respect to the services offered, the networking platform, etc. One such example is "autoposting," by which the service platform could help the user to schedule a task to occur episodically. The user can set it once and would not have to do a manual periodical update.

TaskRabbit introduced its new app in 2011, which made it easier for assigning tasks for people while they are on-the-go. The interface helps to choose the task, indicate the location of the task, estimate the expenses, set the price, and write a description of the task. The user can even include a photo or create a 1-minute voice memo for the task. The app also lets the users browse the profiles of taskers and hire a specific user for the task that needs to be completed. The taskers meanwhile can use the app via the "Browse Tasks" feature. A map of tasks in a particular area is shown and the taskers can choose from various tasks in his locality. The app also has Facebook connectability options. The "Net Promoter Scores" of the company,[2] which were comparable to those of Google and Amazon, is proof enough for its phenomenal success.

---

[2]Campaign which asked users whether they would recommend this service to a friend.

SO WHAT: How Is TaskRabbit Different from Other Job Agencies?

TaskRabbit is quite distinctive from the incumbent companies and the very many adjacent companies that are mushrooming. A temp agency which contracts out temporary workers would be an excellent example of such an incumbent. Unlike such agencies, TaskRabbit helps job seekers to develop their own business model, aggressively pursue suitable jobs afterward, and build their own reputation. It is also relatively cheaper.

TaskRabbit has sound strategic differences when compared to its many adjacent companies as well. For instance, *Angie's List* offers services similar to that of a business directory, *Lyft* provides affordable riders by connecting people to reliable community drivers, *Getaround* lets people rent their cars to strangers, *Yerdle* offers a platform for giving away/lending stuff. Unlike all these companies, TaskRabbit provides a wider network with people from all walks of life, and a wider range of services. Table 13.1 includes some more suitable examples of companies (with even more similar service offerings).

Table 13.1 Adjacent Companies and Strategic Differences in Comparison with TaskRabbit

Company Name	Founded in	Strategic Differences in Comparison with TaskRabbit
Agentanything	2010	Agents are located only in New York and New Jersey. Service providers include only student workforce.
Rockyourblock	2010	Service providers are youngsters only.
Zaask	2012	Offers the services of skilled professionals only.
Ayoudo	2012	Offers the services of skilled professionals only.
Aladom	2007	The platform is devoted to home services alone.
Taskhero	2012	Provides services of fully vetted and verified veterans only.
Yelp	2013	Focuses on storefront type of business.
Fiverr	2012	Services similar to that of TaskRabbit.
Gigwalk	2010	Focuses on fixing retail execution problems and accelerating drive in-store sales. Potential users are brands and retailers.

Challenges

Like any new start-up company in a not-yet-fully-developed arena like peer-to-peer labor, TaskRabbit has also confronted many challenges. In the summer of 2013, the number of tasks posted online started going down drastically. Upon investigating the issues, the auction model of the company was found to be the culprit. Users were not able to decide what starting price to set and had to wait too long for the taskers to start bidding. Rabbits meanwhile had to spend a lot of time scrolling through pages of open tasks, to find one interesting to them. TaskRabbit was able to overcome this challenge by changing its business model to the on-demand "invitation model," automatically matching users with appropriate taskers. This was a replication of what its competitors had done. On the other hand, during this realignment phase, TaskRabbit was forced to lay off employees, which has caused bad publicity.

Likewise, another issue is the fact that the sections of the society whose needs TaskRabbit could cater to is quite small. The upper class has such tasks taken care of for them already and the lower class might not be able to afford it. This leaves only the middle class users. Similarly, the service is now solely focusing on urban areas. For reaching its full potential, it may need to extend outside the urban market. TaskRabbit has also not yet scaled up enough to become a practicable option for a sizable fraction of the workforce.

Identity is another challenge faced by companies like TaskRabbit. The type of jobs TaskRabbit provides (odd jobs) is too broad and fuzzy a category. This "personality fit" is unappealing to many users. As it had been mentioned in the earlier sections of this case study, many new companies with narrower focus are entering the marketspace that once solely belonged to TaskRabbit. These more-focused adjacent companies are in a better shape comparatively too. Ironically, TaskRabbit in a way is the incumbent when compared to these companies. It is possible that TaskRabbit may need to have a look at its (initially disruptive) idea and decide whether it is sustainable in the long run, with more disruptive companies entering its area.

Another challenge TaskRabbit faces is the increasing number of competitors who are entering the market. Many companies are providing similar or better services, when compared to TaskRabbit. TaskRabbit may have lost its first mover advantage because of the same. For instance, Zaarly, *Fiverr*, and *Needto* provide exactly the same services as TaskRabbit. Compared to other similar service providers,

TaskRabbit also lacks control over pricing. Other similar platforms provide more consistent and transparent pricing.

On top of all these, TaskRabbit has not raised any capital in the last 2 years. Regardless of all these challenges, it is quite laudable that TaskRabbit is adaptable and have made changes to support its key business opportunities, namely mobile, geographic expansion, business services, and marketplace operations. Eric Grosse, the new CEO of TaskRabbit, says that the data points are indicating that TaskRabbit is "huge" and still making an impact on the society.

Outlook

TaskRabbit was a pioneer in creating a "neighbor helping neighbor" virtual community. The core idea behind was brilliant, with the current situation of the economy and unemployment. Apart from its business potential, TaskRabbit was also quite successful in connecting people to others in the community, whom they would never have gotten acquainted with otherwise. It has shown remarkable flexibility and has recognized its hitches, rectified them, and are still moving forward in a space which is presently getting crowded. The company has even managed to expand its business to 19 cities (including cities abroad, like London), proving that the fittest can always survive. A feasible way to carry on being "the fittest" would be to decide whether to maintain the generalist identity or constrict the focus to more specific areas of activity. Following the latter path would assist TaskRabbit to sell its services better, make more revenue, streamline the work processes, and most importantly, beat the competition. After all, latecomers can win the race, if and only if the rabbit is asleep.

From the Perspective of Lakshmi B. Nair and Inês Peixoto, Unaffiliated "Taskers"

The following discussion draws on the *Financial Times* article by Sally Davies, February 18, 2015, and other published sources. It was compiled, in a true TaskRabbit fashion, by two unaffiliated Taskers.

1. The purpose on which company was founded; what is TaskRabbit's passion?

The main purpose was to create an on-tap workforce, with the benefits and stability of traditional employment. Also to make our daily lives smarter by spending time focusing on what matters and leaving the errands with people we can trust will take care of them.

TaskRabbit is supposed to make everyone's life easier—just one text message and TaskRabbit takes care of everything that you can't or don't want to take care of. It allows you to focus on what really matters for you. At the same time they created a flexible work model for people seeking for additional income.

2. Its difference relative to incumbents; why is it strategically no?

Compared to incumbents, TaskRabbit offers personalization to its customers. The "taskers" (previously known as "rabbits") can thus build a profile based on the quality of services they provide. In addition, incumbents tend to be specialized by type of service or limited to a geographical area. TaskRabbit provides a web of taskers that offers an urban twist to the good old practice of neighbors helping neighbors.

3. A quick tour of history; how did the founders get here in terms of doing something differently? (What rules did they break, etc.?)

TaskRabbit exists because current hectic daily lives work more smoothly with the help of taskers doing routine or exceptional work. Yet it confronts the barrier of interpreting the practice of contracting errands to taskers as drudgery and exploitative work.

It was actually a Friday night when they ran out of beer and wanted Chinese food. They thought "Why isn't there someone, we can call for that?" So what they did was easy—they set up a number, spread it over the Internet, and waited for people to text. That actually didn't take long. Maybe it was the immediate soft-launch without overthinking, what made them have a good start.

4. Future intent; what is the next opportunity and related challenges?

TaskRabbit plans to expand to Paris, Zurich, Dublin, and Munich. It aims to double its revenue by August 2015. While the next opportunity is expanding to new geographies, the challenge remains in how to reconcile worker protection and fair rewards with taskers bidding against each other in a race to the bottom. In addition, TaskRabbit should be able to respond on demand to an increasing number of same-day services supported by mobile platforms.

As a first step they plan to expand in Germany, afterward Austria and Switzerland. It doesn't make any sense to plan any further before being established in the home markets. It actually doesn't take too much—a solid back office and proper IT landscape is the company's backbone. Since anyone can be a rabbit, they mostly need funding for marketing to hire these people and spread TaskRabbit's mission online.

5. Looking back from the future; why did what you have done matter more broadly?

TaskRabbit created an arena for peer-to-peer marketing, which provided flexible job opportunities to a lot of people. In this arena TaskRabbit offers work opportunities for skilled people who cannot find opportunities for selling their skills in the conventional job market.

I wouldn't go that far and say that the business model really "matters" in the social context. TaskRabbit is simply a platform that brings together two groups of people: (1) the ones, that are willing to pay for more time, and (2) the ones that have some spare time and are eager to make some extra money—that's it. Fairly simple but at the same time economically spoken very efficient.

6. How have you amplified the change, which the company stands for? Or how did you punch above your weight to make impact?

Through the company, the founder tries to revolutionize global workforce by making it more flexible. The change in the labor market that TaskRabbit is enabling is magnified by taskers' talent in promoting their skills and the quality of service they are able to offer. Task-Rabbit taps into the opportunity created by a pool of resources out there in the form of talented and available individuals who possess underutilized, valuable assets such as demanded skills, resources, and free time.

14

Gengo: Winning in Translation Through Crowdsourcing

Who else would understand better the value of enhancing intercultural exchange than Robert Laing and Matthew Romaine, the founders of Gengo? Both of them are multicultural. Robert was born in Australia, and has lived in Britain, Belgium, and Japan. Matthew has American and Japanese lineage and has also lived in both countries. Both of them have experience working in intercultural projects. Matthew had worked with Sony as a member of its international growth strategy team. He was asked to translate a lot during his work there, up until he decided that he wanted to get back to his roots and experience working in a Japanese company. Robert, meanwhile, had previously supervised the creative team of a global branding agency. He wanted to build a company matching his global experience. Both of them got together and created a company (initially a "side project") which offered a human-powered platform for natural, native sounding translations. The company Gengo[1] (meaning "language" in Japanese) was born in June 2009,[2] making the world an even smaller place.

Gengo is a Japan-based company which offers translation services, allowing people to communicate freely across any language. These services span around categories like e-commerce, CMS, Internet media, etc. Gengo employees include about 15,000 translators across 114 countries. It handles both word-based and character-based languages. Currently, there are 37 languages and 63 language pairs that Gengo handles and the list is still growing. It is planning to include

---

[1]Gengo was initially called "Mygengo," as the domain name "Gengo" was not available then. However, when they later managed to get the domain name, they rebranded the company as "Gengo."

[2]The service was launched in December 2008, before the company was established in 2009.

three more pairs to this package—English to Serbian, English to Slovak, and English to Ukrainian.

WOW: Crowd-Based Translation Services

The prices are consistent irrespective of the language pair chosen. However, as the quality goes up, the charges also go up. Some of the clients of Gengo are Alibaba, LinkedIn, Mozilla, Airbnb, Huffington Post, TripAdvisor, and Shiseido. Gengo is also receiving a huge volume of jobs from the travel and e-commerce industries. The company has also grown through collaborations with partners like YouTube and 3Play Media. Gengo is one of the two integrated paid translation services of YouTube.

By 2014, Gengo had received a total of $18.8 million. Investors included Dave McClure (*500 Startups*), Felix Miller (*last.fm*), Joshua Schachter (*Delicious*), Brian Nelson (*ValueCommerce*), Christoph Janz (*Pageflakes*), and Benjamin Joffe (*Plus Eight Star*). Gengo is registered as a company in Delaware, but has its headquarters in Tokyo, with an office in San Mateo, California. San Mateo office has about 10 employees (designers, sales, and marketing staff).

Strategies

How Does Gengo Translate Their Vision into Reality?

Gengo is a pioneer in the translation industry, capitalizing in crowd management and technology. As Robert notices, like in every industry, incumbents in translation industry are engaged in working on high-quality, high-profitable models. Gengo, started with a low-profit model, and then rapidly increased its quality, capacity, and profitability. The quick, scalable, and integrated services Gengo provides have earned it a huge portion of the $33 billion translation market. As on May 2014, it has translated over 200 million words. The translation rate is four words per second (i.e., 240 words per minute). In Maitri Jani's (ex-PR Manager, Gengo) opinion, in a minute Gengo can translate at twice the speed of a live, verbal translator and at six times the speed of an average person.

Gengo noticed that most of the traffic happening in the platform, a.k.a. 75% of the jobs, were for translations under a 500 word count. Most of these contents were also dynamic in nature. This lead to the launch of Gengo's API in April 2010. With the help of API, developers can integrate Gengo's translation platform into websites or other applications. API thus helps manage the large changes, which are required in translating dynamic content (e.g., blog posts). YouTube is one of the main users of Gengo's API.

OOMPH: Gengo as a Recruiter

Gengo receives as many as 8000 applications every day from aspiring translators around the globe. The passing rate to become a translator is approximately 7%. Based on the performance in a two-stage testing process (machine-tested multiple-choice test followed by human-reviewed test), the first level of translators, a.k.a. "Lay Translators," are selected. About 15,000+ Lay Translators are selected from the applicant pool. To climb up successive notches of the ladder (Business and Ultra/Proofreading levels), the translators have to pass additional tests. Higher up in the crowd translation pyramid, the Senior Translators develop and evaluate the pool of translators, oversee testing, and assure quality in their respective language pair. Their other responsibilities include conducting performance reviews to assess translator performance, ensuring timely turnaround of jobs, and creating language-specific translator resources. Professional translators with good experience and track record could apply for this position. About 65 Senior Translators work at Gengo now. Further up, on the apex of the pyramid, the internal "Tops" (Translation Operators) Team consists of four members, who oversee the performance of Senior Translators.

Gengo does not do targeted recruiting. The potential employee pool does not focus on any specialist domains. If the customers require expert knowledge for certain translation tasks, Gengo collaborates with specialist companies to carry them out. The quality of the work is made available individually, to each translator. However, after noticing that some translators are broadcasting their scores publicly, Gengo is planning to publicize the scores of all employees from their end itself.

Gengo as an Open Data Source

Traditionally, translation industry is quite subjective. However, as a people-powered translation platform providing services based on data, Gengo places great importance on transparency, which is currently lacking in the translation industry. The company has an Open

Data Initiative, under which Gengo website gives information about the number of words translated in real time. Gengo's metrics from the measurement of translation quality to the assessment of support performance is available publically (and is updated every week!). Real information on every aspect of the services including support, speed, capacity, and overall performance is available on the platform. This way, the customers can make informed decisions. Gengo feels that providing persistent, complete, and accurate information is a beneficial thing for the company too. They consider this as a way of ensuring them being honest not only with the customers, but with themselves as well.

Gengo as Symbiotic Company

The whole principle behind Gengo is about giving back to the local society. Gengo has connections with local reporters (TechCrunch, Financial Times, etc.), embassy, and local media reporters. This has ensured them some recognition and market visibility. By partnering with and by supporting local entrepreneurs, Gengo advances its symbiotic presence in the local Japanese market. Another way they do this is by collaborating with interested intrapreneurs in enterprises. Gengo also makes sure that it hires local talent more.

Gengo's Quality Policy

Gengo has a unique quality policy with a metric-based assessment mechanism for examining the quality of translation services. The quality is influenced by factors like the understandability of text, clarity of instructions, context, etc. Gengo catalogues the quality differences offered by its different translation levels, a.k.a. *standard*, *business*, and *ultra*. *Standard* translation offers largely accurate output and a 7.0+ Gengo quality score (error tolerance). Usually part-time translators with high proficiency in the language pair take care of the jobs. At *business* level, the translation is for professional usage. It has a quality score of 8.0+ and is taken care by translators with advanced or professional translation skills. Professional use translations can be accompanied by additional proofreading under the *ultra* option. Here, the translators have advanced/professional translation capability with proofreading skills. A quality score of 9.0+ is provided at this level.

SO WHAT Is Gengo Translating Next?

Gengo provides accurate and natural translation services, when compared to a machine translator. Matthew Romaine thinks that machine translators are not competitors, but rather complementary service providers, when compared to Gengo. In his words, language is a living organism. There would always be a need for human translation. Nevertheless, Gengo could offer machine translations as additional, first level services.

Traditional translation agencies typically focus on small jobs, but usually cannot operate on bulk amounts of data. Gengo upgraded the translation industry by introducing a new technology and combining it with crowdsourcing. It provides translation services at a scale. By doing systematic testing, quality checking, and peer reviews, high quality of these services is also assured. All this is done at a much lower cost than a traditional agency, as crowdsourcing reduces overhead and unnecessary transactions. What's more, the online business approach solves the problems related to distribution and geographical barriers.

When compared to translation agencies which have an online presence, Gengo punches above its weight by offering API. Gengo API simplifies human translation by making it efficient and reliable, just like a machine translation. The jobs are ordered, tracked, and managed right from the CMS. Up to 1000 parallel jobs can be handled at the same time through this.

The use of crowdsourcing and API also provides competitive advantages, like more convenience and reliability to customers. This is accomplished by reducing the number of steps and errors involved in the workflow of the company. The average response and delivery times are reduced as the translator pool is spread over all time zones. This results in comparatively shorter lead-time. The flexibility and scalability of Gengo ensure that the customer gets the best deal always. By offering a large pool of translators, regular customers can choose their "preferred translators." This way the end result is consistent and in the required style. To ensure that their daily online postings have a constant tone, industries like media also usually prefer this option.

Low cost is another advantage offered by Gengo. The translators are of the highest quality. Traditional translators who offer high-quality services charge customers a very high rate. By specializing in simple, short texts rather than complex, long ones, Gengo makes the customer pay for just the services he needs. This reduces the cost involved. Gengo services are useful for most applications. By offering customers the option to reject a translation and demand a full refund, Gengo puts its money where its mouth is.

Compared to adjacent companies like *Smartling*, which offers translation project management tools, Gengo is uniquely positioned. Its strength is not just in its technology, but in its crowdsourcing model. The technology is suitable for high-volume transactions. But at the same time, the crowdsourcing component allows for reduced prices.

Challenges

Principally, the translation industry is a very conservative/traditional/ non-technological industry. Apart from the resistance faced due to this, the lack of employee mobility in Japan also caused some sourcing challenges. The lack of flexibility in contracts was also another issue. Another main challenge Gengo faced initially was its low cost. Customers were initially skeptical about using cheap services for jobs which require high quality. However, by looking at Gengo's trajectory, it is safe to conclude that customers have got over this notion.

Another thing that goes against Gengo, when compared to its counterparts, is that it appears to be providing more general services than the specialist services provided by competitors. *OnehourTranslation*, for example, caters to the same customers of traditional agencies, plus developers and digital marketing managers. In this way they are similar to Gengo. The difference lies in the fact that *Onehour-Translation* distinguishes between market segments, and have dedicated departments for each type of customers.

A related challenge for Gengo is the increasing number of competitors entering the market, with some of them providing a wider variety of services than Gengo. *Crowdin*, *Verbalizeit*, *WOVN.io*, etc., are examples. *WOVN.io* is a multilingual localization service offering both machine translation and human translation. *Crowdin* is a localization management platform for translation services. *Transifex* is both a translation and localization platform.

Conyac, a Tokyo-based competitor of Gengo, differentiates itself by having a tiered community review process. The finished work is reviewed several times for accuracy by other translators before being delivered to customers. Gengo responds to this comment by saying that their aim is more to domesticate translation (to provide reasonable, fast, and high-quality translation to people). Possessing API, which Conyac doesn't have, gives them a competitive advantage here. Furthermore, they are rather happy that there are more translation options for people, so translation becomes more convenient for people.

As a final point, the heterogeneity of translation requirements and the associated data security issues raise the criticism that Gengo will never replace traditional translation agencies and Language Service Providers (LSPs). The fact that big LSPs have not yet turned their focus on this segment also arouses suspicion.

Outlook

From the time of founding (when it focused on just one language pairing), till date, Gengo has shown an aptitude to evolve and adapt. Gengo entered an archaic market, contended retention issues, large customer company naïveté, and unwritten employment traditions, and yet managed to be successful on a global scale. Even with an increasing number of competitors entering the market, this is what sets Gengo apart. It is the success story of innovation, crowdsourcing, and human acumen. Referring to Gengo as (better than) the "Mechanical Turk for translations" is not just a play of words (pun intended).

From the Perspective of Nozomi Umenai, Marketing Manager, Gengo

Here are answers (in verbatim) to our questions by the Gengo's Marketing Manager. Even if in a brief format, they provide additional useful background on the company.

1. **The purpose on which Company was founded; what is your passion?**
   - Gengo's website was launched in December 2008, but the company was established in June 2009.
   - Gengo was originally a side project for Rob and Matt, but they received needs soon after they launch Gengo website.
   - Our passion is to create a world without language barrier, "communicate freely."

2. **Future intent; what is the next opportunity and related challenges?**
   - Continue to grow as a global company, help the world communicate.

- We will continue to improve our platform so we can provide the best translation experience for our translators.
- Will start to handle slightly more complex content and higher quality so we can cover more translation orders.
- Will open European office to handle Europe demand.

3. **Company data, stats, etc.**
   - Established in June 2009.
   - About 30 employees in Tokyo, about 45 globally.
   - Office in Tokyo and San Mateo.
   - Rakuten, TripAdvisor, YouTube, Alibaba, Quizup.
   - Sales rep covering Beijing, Shanghai, and Europe.
   - About 15,000 translators around the world.
   - About 307,000,000 words translated.
   - 37 languages.
   - 7 languages pair from Japanese (English, Spanish, Korean, Indonesian, Mandarin, Cantonese, and Thai). Thai is the new edition launched on August 5, 2014.
   - Only 7% of the translators pass the test.
   - Translation done in 8 hours in average.
   - 95% of translation picked up in 60 minutes.
   - About 1000 English to Japanese translators (and vice versa).

15

Microtask: Extreme Approach to Digital Work, Two-Second Tasks at a Time

During his whole life, Ville Miettinen has been an entrepreneur founding software ventures. A programmer since he was a toddler, Ville is a "hacker at heart" who likes to capture the world in photographs while he travels. This passion led him to becoming a semi-professional photographer and surprisingly to the idea underlying Microtask. As told[1] by Ville Miettinen, the first version of Microtask's technology platform was inspired by a problem of photo tagging. Miettinen had returned from a trip to South America and realized he would enjoy having the hundreds of thousands of photographs that he shot classified according to their content. Soon, he understood that it was a task that could not be accomplished with existing computer vision and artificial intelligence and that human intelligence was indispensable. Miettinen then gathered a few experts in the area to develop technology and generate business ideas. Hence, Microtask for distributed work was born of an idea for photo tagging travel memories.

Microtask, a Finnish start-up, is part of an emerging trend in digital services that is changing the nature of work. In 2009, it created a technology service for crowdsourcing and distributed work that combines human labor and computerized work. It breaks down routine work into smaller, short-duration tasks and distributes these to online workers around the world. Therefore, microtasks can be completed anywhere in the world where there is an Internet connection either by freelance or call center workers.

Microtasking is "the crowdsourcing of tiny tasks that can be completed in seconds." It is a core concept of a segment in the nascent

---

[1]Interview published in FoundersLY YouTube Channel.

crowdwork industry that seeks to improve the outsourcing of menial tasks, taking advantage of digital communication technologies. A problem that the company tackles is that not only it is expensive to hire internal staff to carry out routine tasks, but also it is resource-consuming to manage outsourcing. Microtask is not alone in trying to solve this problem. Several companies operate in microwork in different areas and with different business models. Currently, Microtask provides on-demand outsourcing solutions for converting paper documents into digital files, a process requiring large amounts of menial and repetitive tasks, such as text recognition and data entry.

WOW: Human Intelligence in Digitizing Paper-Based Content

The digitization of content from paper documents is a labor-intensive but much needed task. Although nowadays many business processes and communications are conducted digitally, there are still large paper archives in use that are not part of digital workspaces. This places an obstacle for efficient computer-based search and analysis of content. Therefore, the digitization of paper documents has been done using optical character recognition (OCR) technologies that scan a document and figure out the words or numbers from the source, for instance a digital document with handwritten text, using artificial intelligence, computer vision, and machine learning. However, technology is not able to fully replace humans in all kinds of tasks, even in computerized ones.

In the case of the digitization of documents, OCR systems exhibit inaccuracies that can be corrected only using human intelligence. The correction of these errors consists in verifying that the content of the original document matches its digitized version. This is a typically menial, boring, and repetitive task, which does not require highly specialized labor force or a specific work environment. Still, it can be costly and time-consuming to hire human resources to perform these tasks and audit their performance, but it is also costly to possess inaccurate information.

Microtask developed an on-demand solution to bring human intelligence into these digital processes, by transforming large workflows into standardized and uniform tiny tasks that are carried out in a few seconds. By combining artificial and human intelligence, Microtask's service makes the digitization of documents more efficient and effective. The company's core technology can accommodate various kinds of distributed work, such as medical doctors' prescriptions and consumer research questionnaires.

Microtask was founded by four Finnish entrepreneurs—Ville Miettinen, Harri Holopainen, Otto Chrons, and Panu Wilska. Prior to Microtask, members of its founding team had founded companies of real-time 3D graphics (Hybrid Graphics, which later become part of NVidia, a prominent visual computing company) and wireless technologies and applications (Ionific, which later become part of Sasken Communication Technologies, a communications technology and consultancy company). Microtask operates with a technology-oriented team in Finland and a sales and marketing team in the United States. The company received seed funding from Sunstone Capital and from private angel investors, among them executives and entrepreneurs in various fields of digital technology.

SO WHAT: Breaking Down Routine Work into Distributed Microtasks

Technologies have entered various fields of activity to replace humans in order to increase task performance and efficiency. Machines are often able to do things faster and cheaper. For instance, Amazon invested in robots to move goods around warehouses. In addition, its futuristic plan involves delivering orders with autonomous drones that receive GPS coordinates and fly to the destination in the shortest route possible. According to CBS News, on Cyber Monday in 2013, Amazon expected it would receive more than 300 orders per second, so the company welcomes any ways it can reduce costs and delivery time. Notwithstanding the pervasiveness of technology tools to perform tasks that once were carried out by people, some types of work do require human intelligence. Microtask tapped into this need and developed a technology that turns routine work that has to be performed by people into a set of distributed microtasks that increase efficiency in work outsourcing.

"We're bringing human intelligence to the cloud, offering human intelligence as a cloud service. Five years down the road, maybe even quicker, a lot of activities that can only be done by humans, and not by machines, are accessible through API's, 24-7 with near real-time rates. So, if your piece of software

needs access to human intelligence—let's say they need a human to validate something or human face-recognition capabilities or understand speech—you're just able to tap into that at a fairly low cost. Right now we're focusing on challenging the existing outsourcing industry; that part is really what is going to be the big change because it allows building completely new kinds of applications, mind-blowing applications that you cannot even think about right now."

—Ville Miettinen, CEO, interviewed for FounderLY's
YouTube Channel (published on March 13, 2012)

For instance, a client might need to convert into a single digital file the content of a consumer research survey that was conducted by a handful of people interviewing hundreds of random passers-by on the street using paper questionnaires. The paper questionnaires would be converted into digital files using an appropriate scanning and content recognition technology. While the software is able to recognize the handwritten content, there is an accuracy margin that allows for errors in the conversion. For Microtask, a tiny work unit would be verifying that one word converted from handwriting into digital form matches its handwritten original. All these work units, each corresponding to one word, would be sent to thousands of people "microtasking" from anywhere in the world. Another tiny task, for the words that failed the verification test, would be to type the word seen on the screen in handwritten form. Both types of tasks can be performed in a few seconds. This kind of second microtask would correct the errors made by the technology in the conversion. The client would receive only the end result, i.e., the single file with the content of the consumer survey answers in a digital form.

Microtask started when the microwork market was emerging. One of the earliest businesses in microwork platforms is Amazon Web Services' Mechanical Turk. It is a crowdsourcing marketplace for requesting others to perform human intelligence tasks for which computerized processes are unsuitable. Providers of work select a task among the several listed and complete it for a payment amount set by the requester. Another company is CrowdFlower, a market leading crowdsourcing service specialized building optimized workflows for common tasks. CrowdFlower offers microtasking services for collecting, cleaning, and labeling data, with 5 million contributors that work in an assembly line fashion.

Microtask can handle higher volumes of tasks, has a smaller price per independent unit of labor, allows clients to request a certain turn-around time, and does not allow work providers to choose the following set of microtasks assigned to them. Furthermore, Microtask breaks up tasks into pieces and scatters them across several workers in different places, in order to protect the intellectual property and to secure confidentiality over the content of the whole work assignment. In spite of growing competition within the emerging crowd-labor industry, Microtask appears to focus mostly on services that challenge the existing outsourcing industry as that is where they are able to trigger the major changes.

Standardizing Microtasks Enables Quality Assurance and Scalability

At Microtask, the tiny work units are standardized, which facilitates automated quality assurance procedures. In each work set, the company creates "strictly defined inputs and outputs" for each tiny task and "multiple users verify the output" for each unit. Thus, every task is performed three times by different people. Based on this, Microtask calculates reliability by evaluating correlations of task results as part of the quality assurance procedure. This way, Microtask is able to provide automated quality assurance, which allows the company to offer their clients service-level agreements concerning task performance quality and turnaround times. A service-level agreement is a precise guarantee of service quality for clients, a feature that provides advantage relative to the competitors' services.

> *"We have mashed up the document processing industry with crowdsourcing and turned some traditional business processes on their heads. What the Red Herring judges saw in Microtask is a company that is disrupting a $30 billion industry by breaking it apart into 2-second tasks that can be distributed around the world instantly and delivered back to the customer with full service-level agreements and quality controls."*
>
> —Ville Miettinen, CEO, commenting on Microtask winning a prize awarded by *Red Herring*, technology business magazine, in 2011

Moreover, Microtask has long-term relationships with labor service providers, which adds to its capabilities for guaranteeing output quality and delivery time. The company contracts work from call centers all over the world where workers perform microtasks in-between calls. Typically, Microtask uses its own worker pool, keeping 10 to 15 percent of labor cost as its revenue, depending on the number of transactions. In addition to this, in cases where clients wish to use their own employees, Microtask sells "seat licenses" to distribute the tasks exclusively to the clients' workforce.

Standardization and quality assurance address the problem of controlling output quality in outsourced or crowdsourced work, which often requires people to perform additional checks and reviews increasing the amount of resources used. Furthermore, standardization enables a pay-as-you-go pricing structure adapted to each client's needs and resources, which is calculated based on the turnaround time required, on the amount of documents for processing, and on accuracy. As a result of standardization and automated quality assurance, the outcome of work in Microtask can be traded as a commodity because pricing is based on results rather than on an hourly wage.

OOMPH: Microtask's Turn-Key Crowdwork Services for Businesses

Microtask offers two different turn-key services for a business-to-business segment that includes marketing research companies using traditional paper surveys and publishing companies with private archives, as well as insurance companies, banks, libraries, and healthcare services.

Firstly, *Microtask Digest* is a data extraction service for processing large amounts of scanned material that combines machine intelligence with on-demand human intelligence (digital crowd labor). Digest also analyzes the whole set of documents, performing statistical analysis and building custom dictionaries that help to reconstruct broken words and to determine correct characters in poor quality document images. This means that the computerized process can also learn from the integration of human intelligence, which is an advantage over machine-only OCR software that is unable to read low-resolution documents and images.

Secondly, *Microtask Forms* is a service to convert paper forms into digital spreadsheets, which targets businesses that frequently use paper forms, such as insurance, recruitment, or medical companies, primarily in the U.S. market. Clients send the forms by e-mail or fax to Microtask and receive the forms as digitized spreadsheets by the end of the following working day. The service is paid per use, costs $0.36 to $0.60 per form and does not require service subscriptions or long-term contracts.

Nevertheless, Microtask's core technology is a combination of computer vision, machine learning, and artificial intelligence, and has several other potential applications. Ville Miettinen, the CEO, reported[2] that, at the very start of Microtask, the founding team looked into different applications for the technology platform. The first version of the platform, developed during 2000, resulted in 10 different prototypes for different areas of application. What all those prototypes had in common was that they enabled services in which untrained and unsupervised people could perform labor-intensive tasks, for instance as part of business process outsourcing. Microtask's founding team became involved in developing the underlying architecture of tasks that combine artificial and human intelligence, and figuring out "how to route tasks to people all over the world with the Internet, how to reach people, how to compensate for their work, how to ensure the quality of the results, and how to manage the whole process." As reported[3] by Ville Miettinen, the first version of the platform was inspired by a problem of phototagging. Eventually, the company targeted text recognition as the first area of application for their platform. Miettinen stated[4] that, in the future, labor could be outsourced to social games by having people perform tiny repetitive tasks while they play.

DigiTalkoot: An Experiment in the Gamification of Crowd Labor

An illustrative case of crowdsourcing digital labor is DigiTalkoot, a joint project run by Microtask and the National Library of Finland, between 2011 and 2012, to index the Historical Newspapers Library archival content from 1700 to 1900, so that it was searchable on the

---

[2]Interview for FounderLY's YouTube Channel (published on March 13, 2012).
[3]*idem.*
[4]https://gigaom.com/2010/10/08/is-microtask-the-future-of-work/.

Internet. About 2 percent of the National Library's digitized archive, in a total of 4 million digitized pages, had errors in it because the OCR software used was unable to recognize certain characters. While 2 percent was a small percentage, it corresponded to a large amount of pages to be scanned for error search and correction, which required expensive and time-consuming human labor. Furthermore, errors created inaccuracies and prevented information to be found using electronic search.

Microtask created the Mole Chase and the Mole Bridge computer games to easily crowdsource volunteers to help out with the indexing effort. These games consisted of simple captcha solving challenges to be completed in a short period of time. Gamification is present in other crowdsourcing projects. One of the earliest projects was Google Image Labeler, a feature of Google Images in which people helped improve Google's image search results by competing in labeling random images. Other more sophisticated programs for image and pattern recognition include FoldIt, an online puzzle video game that uses human puzzle-solving intuition to predict the structure of proteins which is crucial to understand how diseases work, and GalaxyZoo, a crowdsourced astronomy project in which people help to classify galaxies according to their shapes.

In Mole Chase, players had to choose whether the real word was the same as the computer-recognized word. In Mole Bridge, players had to type erroneous words found in the previous game, as they appeared on the screen, which helped moles cross a bridge over a river. Successful word typing and recognition led them to the next level. The game was designed to that players cross-checked each other, ensuring quality in recognizing the words before final approval. By the end of DigiTalkoot, more than 100,000 volunteers had completed almost 7 million word-fixing tasks.

Challenges

The microwork industry is growing by offering new services and improving labor outsourcing services. Microtask deploys its capabilities in enterprise sales to sell its services to very large organizations with archival needs that involve dealing with massive amounts of handwritten paper forms, including insurance companies, the U.S. military, and organizations in the public sector. One of the challenges that Microtask faces is the improvement of computer vision and artificial intelligence technologies to a point where tasks can be performed solely with computerized systems.

Another challenge is the change in the governance and organization of crowd labor workers. Indeed, a new kind of Internet-based labor marketplace is emerging with the proliferation of the use of crowdsourcing. This raises questions regarding employment relationships, the legal status of workers, and social protection. Some say that the boundaries between empowerment and exploitation are blurry. CrowdFlower was sued by workers who claimed that the company had violated the U.S. Fair Labor Standards Act. The lawsuit included charges of not paying a minimum wage or not paying at all for work done. Following the growth of the digital workers' crowd, these communities began to organize. For instance, researchers at the University of California created an online platform for workers using Mechanical Turk to rate the job posters in order to "report and avoid shady employees."

Others find microwork digital platforms crucial for increasing economic welfare in developing countries. Professors Francesca Gino and Bradley Staats, writing for Harvard Business Review, use the example of Samasource—a non-profit microwork company—to show that economic development in developing communities can be boosted by business process outsourcing supported by digital crowdwork. The authors claim that connecting new workers, who were previously outside of local job markets, to global supply chains and companies can trigger large-scale change for those communities. Clearly, connecting people to jobs online creates many different challenges for the emerging microwork industry, which will have an impact on Microtask's current and future business.

Outlook

Digital office manager Mike Rotask, the mascot of Microtask, invites us to help "save the world from the problem of document processing." Microtask lets us rest assured that the world will not be dominated by robots—not yet. Our brains still beat the machines in some tasks, an advantage that Microtask is daring to explore by making human brains and computer algorithms work together. As MIT-based technology optimists Erik Brynjolfsson and Andrew McAfee (2011) propose, the digital revolution shall impel us to race with the machines instead of against them by leveraging technology and human skills.[5] Microtask goes one step further and allows us to play with moles while doing some work with societal impact.

Microtask created an innovative solution based on artificial and human intelligence which is able to disrupt the business process outsourcing industry. It consists of a software platform that breaks down routine and tedious work into tiny work units that are distributed around the world to a global workforce working remotely on the Internet. These distributed tasks are standardized and can be completed in a few seconds. An automated quality assurance tool that verifies the quality of output, together with standardization of tasks, allows for this kind of crowdwork to be scalable and offered to clients at a fairly low cost per task, which is calculated according to turnaround time, accuracy required, and amount of work. Microtask allows work to be performed from inexpensive Internet-enabled devices or from where workers live, suggesting future changes in the nature of the workplace and in the opportunities for people to perform paid work.

---

[5]Brynjolfsson, Erik and McAfee, Andrew. 2011. *Race Against The Machine: How the Digital Revolution Is Accelerating Innovation, Driving Productivity, and Irreversibly Transforming Employment and the Economy*. Lexington, MA: Digital Frontier Press.

16

Kaggle: Getting Quant Brains to Play Data Games

Context

Four years ago, 28-year-old Australian Anthony Goldbloom won "The Economist" annual essay writing competition. The prize was a 3-month internship, during which Anthony worked on data science and big data. Even more exciting was that he got to interview a lot of people from different companies for his market research. Before long he realized that many of these companies were in dire need of strong and efficient predictive modeling. The responsible taskforce was just not resilient enough to handle this either. This made him think about a business model where the companies would be charged for work based on meritocracy. Drawing upon this idea and his work experience in macroeconomic modeling, Anthony created Kaggle in 2010.

For the ones to whom the name Kaggle[1] doesn't ring a bell, it is a competition-based platform for predictive modeling and analytics. Companies and researchers can publish their data and proposed problems. Top notch statisticians and data scientists (also known as Kagglers) from around the globe will produce models based on the same. This makes sure that an array of solutions is available for the companies to choose from. Right now, Kaggle has around 200,000 scientists from around the globe.

Kaggle received universal acclaim in a very short period. Anthony was named twice in the Forbes' annual "30 Under 30" list of young

---

[1]The name "Kaggle" was selected from a list generated with the help of an algorithm that iterated phonetic domain names.

technology leaders. Fast company presented him in their "Who's Next" series as one of the innovative thinkers who are changing the future of business. He was also a featured speaker at the 2013 Data 2.0 Summit.

WOW: How Does Kaggle Handle the Boggle?

Kaggle started first as a crowdsourcing website for data science competitions. After its move to San Francisco, Kaggle introduced "Kaggle Connect," a new platform which links companies to the growing community of data scientists. Thus it moved from a crowdsourcing website to a marketplace. Competitions are still held prior to the scientists' entry to Kaggle platform. The data scientists are ranked objectively and the best of them are invited to enter the platform. They are matched up with client companies. By measuring the accuracy of the end models or solutions, the performers are rated. The best performers can monetize their expertise.

The Kaggle scientists who use the platform are mainly of three classes: The ones who participate in competitions mainly for fun (and not income), academics who want to get experience in dealing with real-world problems, and finally, people who rely on Kaggle and their Kaggle reputation as a full-time income source. The platform is totally free for data scientists. However, the companies have to make payments to Kaggle for availing their services.

SO WHAT Makes Kaggle a Positive Outlier?

Kaggle offers an exciting, innovative venue for finding solutions to data science problems. When compared to other crowdsourcing solutions in the market, it stands out due to the assortment of key roles it is playing.

Kaggle as a Marketplace

Kaggle offers a platform in the labor market for creating a multitude of solutions from big data, allowing the companies to choose the optimal one from among them. Such choices were earlier complemented by gut feeling and intuition. Kaggle thus offers companies the stage for doing predictive modeling and consequently, making objective decisions.

Kaggle as a Benchmark

Kaggle has also replaced traditional resumes as a more substantial, and valuable indicator of proficiency. The work and value in marketplace have become quantifiable, both in terms of outcomes and process. "Kaggle ranking" has become an essential metric in the data science scenario today. Some companies, like American Express and New York Times, are listing Kaggle rank as an essential qualification in their job advertisements for data scientists.

Kaggle as a Job Market/Recruiting Platform

Kaggle has also solved the problems related to cost of hiring the best people in the field in data science. Through Kaggle, companies can avail of the services of the smartest people in the world. The success of Kaggle has started attracting entrepreneurs from other fields, ranging from designers to doctors, to follow his example. Many new disruptive market places, quite similar to that of Kaggle, are now burgeoning. "99 Designs," a content-based community for designers and "Healthtap," a community of doctors who use their spare time to give health advice, are two examples.

Kaggle Compared to Adjacent Companies

When compared to adjacent companies in its same domain, Kaggle improves upon the open innovation models of "Innocentive" and "Ninesigma" by introducing the element of competition. Competitors can see the results of others in real time, which accelerates motivation levels. Besides, when compared to the latter companies, Kaggle markets crowdsourcing more as a career choice than as a hobby.

Kaggle as a New Corporate Style

The corporate approach of Kaggle is state-of-the-art as well. Statistical modeling has not yet been able to process big data. For the companies who are aware of, and interested in predictive modeling also, deciding on one best option might be difficult. With Kaggle competitions, these companies can match their needs with a variety of solutions, so as to find the best approach. Thus the ultimate quality control of the solutions/research designs proposed in the Kaggle community is by the customer companies. Goldbloom compares this strategy with the architectural design competitions conducted for deciding big property development contracts. Kaggle could be quite useful for companies in a vast range of arenas, from banking to law. Table 16.1 discusses some of the competitions in Kaggle.

OOMPH: Kaggle as a Crowdsourcing Venue

Unlike crowdsourcing companies in more established fields (e.g., creative writing, pharmaceuticals, etc.), Kaggle is creating a disruption in an emerging new field. Kaggle offers a chance for professionals to compete and contribute in the field of data science, irrespective of their location or status. Figure 16.1 shows some examples of customers from different fields and the results achieved via Kaggle. Apart from providing a platform for the resource pool, this also helps participants by offering them opportunities to exchange techniques with others, and thereby advance their own skillset. Besides, unlike in temp agencies, meritocracy (and not bureaucracy or job seniority) is the philosophy behind Kaggle. Kagglers are thus not at the bottom of the job pyramid, rather they are at the apex.

Challenges

One challenge Kaggle faces is the doubt which companies have regarding the Kagglers and their suitability in solving industry-specific or company-specific predicaments. The main question is how someone with no background in their particular industry or domain could solve such problems. Anthony replies to these skeptics by pointing out that Kaggle is a collaboration between the data scientists and the experts. The latter brings in the business content whereas the former joins forces and offers valuable solutions based on this content and data.

However, Kaggle changed its stance regarding this issue in January 2014, when it decided to move from its generalist outlook and focus more on one particular industry, Oil and Gas. "There is a lot to

Table 16.1 A Few Examples of Kaggle Competitions, Compiled from Company Website

Kaggle Project/ Prediction Model	Company	Story
HIV progression	Drexel University in Philadelphia	The scientists had to create a model of the genetic blueprint using records of 1000 patients. The winning crowdsourced model predicts the individual severity of the virus with 77% accuracy, compared with the 70% accuracy previously achieved using conventional methods.
Survival on the Titanic	A "getting started competition"	The scientists had to complete the analysis of what sorts of people were likely to survive, using the tools of machine learning. The main purpose was to introduce people to data science and machine learning. The final model was a data visualization map depicting the survival chances of titanic passengers.
Which patients would go to hospital	Heritage Health Prize	The scientists had to predict who would go to the hospital in the subsequent year. The winning model would predict this with 90% probability. This would help in alerting the provider system about at-risk patients.
Sensor that determines the alertness of drivers	Ford	The company wanted to determine the alertness of drivers through sensor readings. The data included environmental variables (temperature, sun shine, etc.); sensory readings (body temperature, eye movements, heart rate, etc.); and psychological variables (mood of driver). The aim was to equip cars to keep the driver alert. Kaggle scientists built an algorithm that would provide feedback from the sensors.
Mapping dark matter	NASA	Participants were given 100,000 galaxy images, blurred to simulate the effects of dark matter. They had 3 months to create models to find the real shapes of galaxies. The winning team produced a 3× increase in accuracy over the state-of-the-art benchmark that had taken NASA decades to develop. They used the method of Artificial Neural Network.

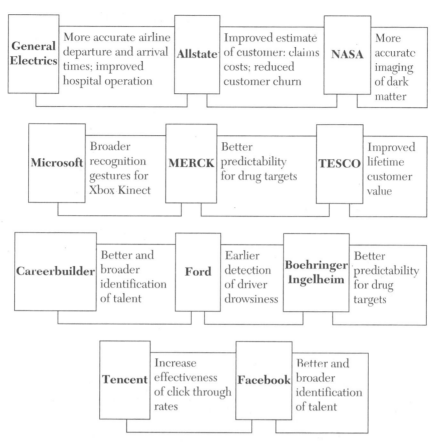

Figure 16.1 Some Kaggle customers and the results delivered, compiled from published sources and company website

learn in each area," says Mr. Goldbloom. "We will still do competitions, they are a great engine for finding talent. But our returns as a business will be higher if we focus." (Excerpt from The New York Times interview.)

Even though it cannot be stated as a challenge per se, another criticism against Kaggle is that it is just another spin on crowdsourcing, which has been around for decades. Quite recently, many other online companies have used crowdsourcing for getting people's jobs done. Kaggle however, easily overrules this criticism through two claims. Firstly, it does not incorporate work from everybody. Only expert professionals who want to compete and win join Kaggle. Furthermore, Kaggle does not create the incidental outcome. Rather it creates a novel, disruptive marketplace for work.

Yet another question thrown at Kaggle is regarding the sufficiency of the data in the competition package. What if there is more suitable data out there elsewhere? This indeed is a limitation of the competition model. Maybe one day, data processing would evolve to a level where data is available to all involved people, in real time. The drawback then would be the issues regarding privacy and data security.

Outlook

From its first day of conception, when Anthony could not afford to purchase a domain name for his website, Kaggle has made quantum leaps in the field of data science crowdsourcing. As Ben Hamner (Chief Scientist, Kaggle) says, with deep learning and single machines, anything and everything from analyzing images to chemoinformatics is possible today. Kaggle's success story vouches this.

From the Perspective of Harikesh Nair, Professor of Marketing, Stanford Graduate School of Business

From an Interview by Dr. Markus Paukku, January 27, 2015

Kaggle is a novel platform currently able to take advantage of two market needs. There is an increasing demand by companies for a type of computational social science and statistical expertise that has primarily been the preserve of academia. Secondly, there is a labor market shortage of these talented data scientists. Indeed, companies rarely have the in-house combination of talent with both the domain knowledge and the requisite statistical know-how by which to leverage big data. Kaggle, together with its competitors, has been successful in filling this gap in the market.

Traditional corporate structures and cultures are not well equipped to experiment with innovative methods. Investing time and resources in novel means to solve problems is a challenge for many companies. Incumbent best practices and processes can even limit the management or bootstrapping of creativity within the organization. Companies have often tried to stoke creativity through skunkworks or through policies of budgeting time earmarked for innovation.

However, many companies have found this approach to be an expensive endeavor yielding uneven results.

Moving a project outside the company's organizational boundary allows external resources, unconstrained by a set of corporate practices and processes, the freedom to solve the problem. Typically this kind of external problem solving has been the domain of hired consultants. However, using a platform such as Kaggle allows for a company to conduct a massive search and leverage the power of the crowd to find a solution. Through Kaggle, multiple project groups can compete for the best solution—a feature rarely seen in the hiring process by which consultants' firms are selected. The openness and transparency of the platform also allow for the external groups to cumulatively build their projects on each other's solutions.

Using an innovative platform such as Kaggle does require some stretch by the client companies. The company must be sold on the value of big data analytics, overcome internal inertia, and be open to the implementation of external, crowdsourced solutions. This requires buy-in from ranking stakeholders on the client corporate ladder and a willingness to experiment with novel practices. However, first and foremost, before a solution can be found the company must have the capacity to identify and frame a problem that can benefit from big data analytics and the answers provided by Kaggle.

Going forward what does the future hold for Kaggle? It will take some time for the market to find equilibrium in terms of training the demanded data scientists and companies to develop in-house big data processes. Thus, Kaggle may see competitors enter the attractive market. Kaggle may address this challenge by splitting the verticals it serves and delivering more value by differentiating its offering by sector. Also, the growth of Kaggle's network may well provide the platform with further network effects raising the switching costs for its current clients and making the company more competitive as an incumbent in a nascent space.

The nature of the analytics' work demanded will also change. Currently data science is largely exploiting methods by which to identify correlation models in which X happens and an impact is measured on Y. However, in the future more nuanced questions will need answering—not just how, but why is something happening? These challenges will require not just today's statistical know-how but specific domain knowledge, knowledge that is challenging for specialized data scientists to gain from outside companies and industries.

From the Perspective of Milena Mend, a Student of Organization and Culture at the University of St. Gallen, on Imaginary Futures

What Will Crowdsourcing Be Like in 2025? And Which Implications Can We Derive for Today?

I proudly present an interview with Anthony Goldbloom who founded Kaggle back in 2010. The interview takes place on the third of March 2025 in San Francisco and the interviewer is M. Mend, a journalist for international press.

Mend: *Mr Goldbloom, thank you for your time, I am very glad to have you here. Now, Kaggle has had an outstanding success compared to other crowdsourcing business models and former competitors like Microtask or Quirky who have vanished by now. As the founder of Kaggle my first question to you is: How do you explain the ongoing success of Kaggle?*

Goldbloom: Well, I think we put all eggs in one basket and it turned out to be the right one. The trend of big data and the need for scientific data analysis started about 20 years ago and has grown ever more since data quantity grew tremendously. On top of that, data quality also improved. As we were the first marketplace to connect data specialists with challenges from the private and public sector we were able to get the most talented workforce for the challenges. Today, we still have Kagglers working for us who started 10 years ago and these people crunch data through our website. They do this for a living. So I think one success factor is that our business model serves a solution to a problem that is widely spread but the knowledge is scarce. We offer the scarce knowledge. And the other success factor is our long-term relationship with our workforce.

The interview is based on the three cases of Kaggle, Quirky, and Microtask.

Mend: *So what did you do different that you have actually a solid and loyal workforce?*

Goldbloom: We work with experts and we value and understand their needs. Being a Kaggler comes along with a lifestyle and an attitude to life. Kagglers are highly independent, very curious, have high intrinsic motivation, and want to solve the big problems of the world. On top of that, they are very competitive and like to win. So first of all, we have always paid attention to the sort of challenges we put out into the cloud. Because what Kagglers value the most is the good and real data bases they get access to and also the challenges from different industries we announce. That was our lesson learned in 2014, when we tried to focus solely on the oil and gas sector. But we realized, our success comes from the variety of industries we collaborate with. So we stayed a generalist after all and this is how we work today still.

But, of course, if a Kaggler wishes to become an expert in one field, we offer enough challenges in each area to become a specialist. But we come to notice that Kagglers hate routine and after a while, if a Kaggler only crunches data from one industry, it becomes routine and he or she wants to switch the industry, which is totally fine for us. That is also the reason why only very little Kagglers ever decide to work for one big company exclusively.

Mend: *In what ways does Kaggler education$^©$ add to your success?*

Goldbloom: Oh, in a great way. We opened Kaggler education$^©$, an online educational system, just when so-called MOOCs (massive open online courses) came to rise. We sensed that Kagglers are individuals that have scarce and unique skills which will rise in demand. So first, we started with educational and learning aspects for our Kagglers only and shared the knowledge of our best Kagglers internally. But in 2017, we decided to expand into education. The reasons were twofold. On the first hand, there are Kagglers out there who find it highly satisfactory to pass on their knowledge to people and we have an interest in keeping them happy so they continue working for us. Secondly, we sensed that school education does not have the necessary focus on big data analysis and predictive modulation in education—but we and the world need these skills.

So today, we can reach schoolchildren from all around the world with our classes through our online seminars. To promote our courses, we collaborate closely with schools. A school can buy our course in their education portfolio and we get great feedback. And of course, it is also a recruiting tool. We ensure that we get to know the best data scientists and if they want, they can join the great Kaggler community.

Mend: *And then how do you explain that Kaggler was not bought by one of the three giants (Google, Facebook, and Amazon) that today almost exclusively dominate the Internet?*

Goldbloom: Well, let me admit that we got offers for mergers and takeovers from all three of them. However, the model of success for us is not merging, but collaboration. We put out challenges from all giants and Kaggle is also dependent on the data basis and the real-world challenges that come from these companies. However, it is of interest from all of us that Kaggle stays an independent corporation. The reason for that is the workforce. Five years ago, in 2020, the official union of crowdworkers was founded. This union fights for the rights of workers and fact is that Kagglers value the heterogenity of challenges and datasets. They do not want to work for one company exclusively. They love their independent life and fight for staying independent.

Mend: *I am sure you have heard from Quirky. Back in 2015 some people predicted a paradigm shift of product innovation and production. Why do you think Quirky does not exist today anymore?*

Goldbloom: Quirky is a very interesting case and the founder Ben Kaufman is a good friend of mine, so I am happy to tell you about what happened in my opinion. I think the crux of the matter was that the basic premise of Quirky did not turn out to be true. Ben's focus has always been on execution, whereas his real unique selling proposition were ideas and the access to a crowd that was motivated enough to submit ideas.

Even though the products that Quirky produced in the beginning were supposed to solve problems, the truth is that these problems were too nitty-gritty in order to hit big. They were personal problems and nice-to-have products, but not real paradigm shifters. Ben realized that he could never reach the economies of scale of the big players in any industry of product production. He realized that and that is why he decided to collaborate with GE. Out of this, WINK was created as a subsidiary. And this was the move to the right direction. So today, Quirky does not exist anymore. BUT the body of thought lives on in the various subsidiaries that serve as idea creators for the big players in the industries. BILAN is one of them, where ideas for the car industry are collected. The subsidiaries serve now as kind of need databanks of engaged customers.

Mend: *And then what about Microtask, why is it not in the crowdsourcing business anymore?*

Goldbloom: Well, Microtask was interesting, but the algorithm they developed in 2018 was so clever that they eliminated themselves in a way. They used to convert audio files and paper documents into digital files by scattering small tasks around the world and combining human intelligence with machine learning. They really pushed machine learning to excess and they finally managed to replace humans in the document processing industry. So today, they don't need the crowd anymore. On top of that they were accused in exploiting their workforce. So it was a good idea of them to only rely on the algorithm which is now their one and only product. But as digitalization of documents is nowadays not a big need anymore, I am curious what they will do next to be honest.

Mend: *Mr Goldbloom, on behalf of international press, I really would like to thank you for your insights and valuable contributions. I wish you all the best for your future and see you another time.*

Goldbloom: Sure, no worries. Have a great time in San Francisco.

Jump in Time

The learnings for today (4th of March, 2015) are:

1. ***For the Outliers:*** Offering a marketplace and distributing problems to be solved is not enough. A marketplace needs to get loaded with products and challenges. Microtask had no incumbents, but abolished itself by technology. Quirky had to realize that it would never really be able to compete with the economies of scale of the incumbents and Kaggler had no incumbents and spotted a real trend.

2. ***For the Incumbents:*** The big stay big and get bigger and the smaller companies have to collaborate with them or get bought by them.

3. ***For the Workforce:*** Crowdworking or not so-called cloud-worker will be the synonym to a lifestyle. One where one has a passion for something and can live it out through the Internet on all of the places of the world. Cloudworkers meet in shared working places and build a large community. They also contribute to a new way of tourism.

All in all what we learn from the outliers now is that if you are an entrepreneur, either make an idea big enough that one of the incumbents buys you (Quirky) or offer a stand-alone solution that really adds value (Kaggle). Don't let technology win over humans, because then we eliminate ourselves (Microtask).

And my question for the future is what humans will do with all that free time, when algorithms and robots (like the robot vacuum cleaner) solve all our problems, work, and duties?

17

MakieLab: Custom-Made, Born-Digital Toys

One afternoon in 2010, at the Digital Kids Conference in New York, Alice Taylor sat at a crowded lunch table full of conference attendants, so close to each other that she could not help but eavesdrop the pitch of an entrepreneur's idea to an executive in the toy industry. She then realized how difficult it was to enter the toy industry. As Digital Kids was co-located with Toy Fair, Alice also came across the huge divide between digital and physical regarding education and entertainment for children. That was when she came up with the idea for MakieLab, inspired by the freedom to create embedded in maker culture and in do-it-yourself communities. What if children could use their fertile imagination to design their own dolls, just like gamers do with avatars? With MakieLab, Alice Taylor wondered whether she could create "an infinite loop of play" by experimenting with blurring the boundaries between the digital and physical world.

"It's incredibly risky to put a product on a toy shelf. To make a doll of this size you would generally spend 4 years in R&D and in production, in secret. You'd mold each piece at a cost of a couple of tens of thousands of dollars per mold, and then you'd run off a minimum order quantity. Usually you then have to get those products into a warehouse in America before they will necessarily be accepted on the shelf. Then, in some cases, with retail you have to pay for the shelf space, in the sense that you have to be able to bid up against Disney or whoever. So, if you want your doll next to those guys you have

to be able to afford it. Again, this is why you don't see start-ups, why you don't see artisanal anymore in those spaces."

—Alice Taylor, speaking at Bay Area
Maker Faire 2014

MakieLab is a U.K.-based toys and games company that created Makies, the first safety-certificated 3D-printed doll for children. Makies are action dolls created and customized by the customer in a web application and turned into real dolls by MakieLab which has them manufactured on demand using 3D printing. At the same time, being born digital, Makies are also avatars that play roles in games. Contrary to traditionally mass-produced toys, Makies are designed according to the preferences of their owners, who modify a doll's facial features, expression, and clothes to their own creative taste. By making unique 3D-printed toys using game technology, MakieLab bridges the digital and the physical worlds in a way that had not been seen yet in mass-manufactured toys.

Founded in London, U.K., MakieLab is the first service in the global mass market to offer full personalization of toys. This is possible, thanks to the additive manufacturing technology but also, to a large extent, to the democratization of access to technology and to the maker culture. MakieLab positions itself in the digital-physical interface of the industries of toys and games. The digital strategy supports the manufacturing platform by providing a source of alternative revenue, as well as other routes to customers, expanding the distribution possibilities of the dolls and being a creative tool to design the physical product.

When the idea for MakieLab started to take shape, Alice Taylor searched in Shapeways for someone who could help her model a sketched doll and have it 3D printed. Producing the dolls at Shapeways was fairly cheap, so they iterated the doll model as necessary, in order to build a prototype to pitch the idea to potential funders. Joining Alice Taylor to set off the company were Jo Roach, also formerly from Channel 4, and Sulka Haro, previously from Sulake, a Finnish company that created Habbo Hotel, a social networking website for teenagers.

WOW: Customized Toys, Manufactured on Demand

MakieLab's on-demand toy manufacturing is hardwired to be driven by the creativity of its customers. "Can we do something where the kids will come along and have a hand in the creation, make a unique thing, stamp their own personality, express themselves their own way?" This was how co-founder Alice Taylor introduced MakieLab's concept at the Bay Area Maker Fair in 2014. Makies were initially targeted to a 14+ age group because they lacked the toy-safety certification. Currently, they target girls and boys over 6 years old, but dolls are safety-certified for children over 3 years old.

Borrowing the idea from games where players create an avatar, the web application enables children to create unique characters from playful imagination. Makies are generated by tweaking pre-set options with a slider to modify sizes, color, and shapes of eyes, ears, noses, and other facial features of dolls. Makie avatars can display multiple variations of each feature. If the child wishes to have a physical doll, it can get one exactly like the computer-generated design provided the child has parental assistance to complete an order using a credit card. After that, dolls are manufactured on demand using industrial grade 3D printing. Doll accessories are also 3D printed and clothes are handmade at MakieLab's headquarters. Finally, Makies are delivered to the customer within 2 weeks after production order.

The first MakieLab product was an online doll building application, launched at demo level in 2012. Alpha versions of software correspond to the testing phase, thus being unstable and prone to crashing or offering limited design options; open means that an unlimited number of people can use the application. MakieLab had decided to use the seed funding to go live early and iterate on the fly using users' feedback as they customized and ordered dolls. Initially, the company received funding from a public innovation agency in the U.K., and privately from friends and family. In the alpha demo version, Makies were offered in the bone-white skin option only and priced at £99, well above the $20 average market price for similar-sized dolls. Although the interface couldn't prove mass-market appeal and could show problems unresolved, going live early gave MakieLab the chance to get an "alpha geek" community of enthusiasts to create avatars and order dolls.

People started to experiment with Makies, alongside the Makies team, for instance using different dying techniques at home to change the skin coloring, adding make-up, and making clothes. Then they posted their accomplishments on the discussion forum. The company followed closely what these early customers made to understand how they used the toy and figure out what they were looking for in such a toy. As the company was prototyping also doll accessories, using a cheap desktop 3D printer, and trying out techniques to obtain different skin tones, it posted on the customers' forum its own development breakthroughs.

> "We said, screw it, we want to put it live anyway, we want to get it out to the alpha geek community; we want to talk to people; we want to see what people want; we want to start figuring out what it is about a customizable doll people love the most. Alpha geeks are the canaries in the coal-mine. They're the ones who will pick something up that most folks maybe wouldn't understand; they'll examine it and say, what is this? How does it work? They'll play with it; iron out the kinks, and in that process the manufacturer or the provider will also learn a lot. And then, when everyone's ready, it will just bleed into the mainstream."
>
> —Alice Taylor in 2013 for *Make*
> magazine (15/03/2013)

The creative exchange between MakieLab and the early owners of dolls became a conversation that fueled user-driven tinkering and engagement of customers, which fed the iteration process. Iterating on-the-fly using early users' experiences and feedback would not have been possible in a traditional model for mass-manufacturing of toys or without additive manufacturing techniques.

Blending Digital and Physical in the Business of Toys and Games

MakieLab extended the universe of Makies from the design tool to games for iOS and Android operating systems that are integrated with the manufacturing platform. It started with Makies Doll Factory, a free app for iPad launched in the Spring of 2013, that is a doll-maker with the same functionalities as the customization software—design, customize, and order 3D-printed Makie dolls. The app was featured by AppStore as number one in the Kids category in the U.K.

> *"We just got an app out, we got skin colors in January, toy safety in February, the CE certification, put an app out in March (2013). The app just sells dolls but the next step is to turn it into a game, which is where this big loop finally closes, where your digital character can be turned into a physical object, but we will be able to create and sell, and maybe people can sell to each other, both digital and physical goods. Using laser printing, for instance, we can have users create patterns for the clothes and then print it on to real cloth and turn it into clothes for your real doll that you've designed in an app."*

> —Alice Taylor speaking at
> NEXT13, April 2013

Makies FabLab was the first actual game developed by MakieLab and launched in 2014 on AppStore for iOS devices. It is a resource management game in which a Makie character grows resources to produce materials that will be turned into clothes and accessories. The game is free, but has purchasable in-app functionalities (priced at €0.89 to €6.99). It features a digital fashion studio and workshop where players design and craft clothes and accessories using a variety of machines, including virtual 3D printers that produce shoes, but also grow the raw materials used in textiles, for instance breeding sheep to produce wool or growing cotton plants. Players can style the dolls, photograph them, and organize lookbooks that can be shared with other players. They can also order a real version of their avatar in the game. MakieLab keeps developing the game and its manufacturing services so that players can order also the clothes that they created in the game.

Finally, the latest game released was Makies Fashion, launched for iOS and Android devices and priced at €2.69. This app allows the player to create fashion for the Makie dolls. It features a fabric customizer, photoshooting of fashion looks and catwalk shows with the virtual Makies. MakieLab's plan is to expand the game's functions to offer more options for creative use.

MakieLab transformed the earlier digital manufacturing platform from an alpha geek app into a series of entertainment games for children. These games are a core part of the digital-physical business strategy, providing a purpose for making real dolls and supporting the interaction between avatars and dolls through stories, characters, and role playing.

SO WHAT: How Are Makies Different from Existing Customized Dolls?

Although MakieLab is unique in its approach to leveraging the digital-physical interface in the toys and games business, it is not the first company to offer customized dolls, which exist both in the mass market and in the collectors market. American Girl is a line of dolls, created in 1986 and owned now by Mattel, whose dolls come in more than 40 different combinations of hair style, hair color, eye color, and skin tone. On its website, children can select among the pre-set combinations as well as from a range of accessories varied enough to meet individual preferences. American Girl dolls are mass-manufactured, more expensive than similar dolls (around €95) and a multi-million dollar business for Mattel in the United States. A doll comes with an access code to a virtual environment with games, quizzes, and challenges called the Innerstar University where children can play online with other doll owners and receive tips for increasing confidence in real-life.

Blythe is a doll, first created in Japan and now owned by Hasbro, which is mass-produced but comes in a large number of variations. When a photographer produced a book in which the dolls posed in different fashion styles, Blythe became a cult doll for collectors. It is priced at around €100, but custom dolls are often sold on eBay for three to four times its original prices. On Etsy there are several shops that sell handmade clothes for Blythe. Doll enthusiasts also created a do-it-yourself community around MakieLab. Moreover, on Etsy there are several shops selling handmade clothes and accessories, such as knitted sweaters, and body painting services, such as make-up and manicure, for Makie dolls.

MakieLab's founder Alice Taylor said that, compared to Makies, "American Girl is the thing that gets the closest, probably, or Lego where you have this combinatorial thing." Yet, she considered American Girl as "bruteforcing customization" while Makies opened up customization possibilities by leveraging the potential of 3D printing and the flexibility of games and digital tools. Furthermore, Makie dolls have hollow backs and heads so that there is enough space to fit batteries or a Lilypad Arduino, a small open-source microcontroller, popular in DIY electronics, which can be programmed to interact with other objects, such as Bluetooth- and wireless-enabled gadgets.

Incumbents in the toy industry are getting their feet wet by experimenting with moving closer to users. In 2012, Disney launched a one-off initiative at its theme parks to make Disney Princess figurines with the facial features of their owners, using 3D modeling from pictures and 3D printing technology. More recently, early in 2014, Hasbro announced a partnership with 3DSystems to "co-develop, co-venture, and deliver new immersive, creative play experiences powered by 3D printing for children and their families." In 2015, Mattel announced it will collaborate with Quirky to create new products that reinvent a few of its brands, including Fisher-Price, Hot Wheels, and Barbie. The mainstream toy industry has not been oblivious to the possibilities brought about by customization, 3D printing, and crowd-collaboration to their business.

How Is MakieLab Different from Incumbents in the Toy Industry?

MakieLab challenges the traditional toy industry in ways that are amplified by 3D printing technology. Firstly, it is a start-up entering the industry space with a lower capital investment than the usually required for new entrants. MakieLab opened up a new space in the toy industry, where it is expensive and difficult to start a business due to high initial investment and risk. Dealing with toy mass manufacturing, an entrepreneur typically needs to bear the high upfront costs of molding, setting up a manufacturing line, keeping inventory, and bargaining for retail space.

Secondly, MakieLab introduced full personalization of action dolls, developing ways for children to create unique toys produced on demand and challenging a conventional divide between designers and users that cuts across many other industries. Finally, it bridged the digital and the physical worlds, which so far have been apart, by integrating gaming technology with creative tools for the design of custom-made action dolls and accessories. Makies are born digital but are also unique objects, which configures a potentially disruptive value proposition. The company foresees its digital-physical strategy to yield a blended margin by balancing the 80 to 90 percent margin in games and applications with around 20 percent margin in physical dolls. The digital strategy supports the growth of MakieLab and the development of the manufacturing strategy.

Challenges

Up until now, MakieLab has had to deal with a low-sales volume, partly due to high prices and poor awareness of its products and services. Founder Jo Roach told Reuters in mid-2013 that the company had sold around 500 custom-made Makies. By then, the doll-building tool had been in open alpha for around 2 years, as the company continued iterating using the feedback of website users that included over 100,000 people. Meanwhile, in 2013, MakieLab was awarded a first prize in the SXSW Accelerator competition, an incubator of cutting-edge technologies and digital creativity, in Entertainment and Gaming category, which offered visibility and credibility. In addition, the company began to sell ready-made dolls at Selfridges and Hamley's in London, drawing attention to the website and its digital doll factory.

Nonetheless, MakieLab continued raising funding to support business development. According to CrunchBase and Angel.Co, it was valued in $3 million in 2012 as it received seed funding of $1.4 million provided by Lifeline Ventures, Sunstone Capital, and game industry veterans. In August 2013, the company was valued at $8 million and raised 2.3 million in seed funding from undisclosed sources.

> "We're a small digital/physical manufacturing start-up, operating in an unproven area. Everyone believes in it, and knows it's going to grow, but there are some really significant questions, like, how long is it going to take for material prices to come down? So we need to stay alive during this alpha geek stage, where the technology stops emerging, and becomes mainstream. And I'm hoping that process takes no longer than 3 or 4 years!"
>
> —Alice Taylor speaking at the
> TCT Show + Personalize, 2013

A pressing issue for MakieLab is costs: 3D printing costs had not decreased as the company expected, which kept the price of the dolls high. It was assumed that the margins on the physical production of toys would increase with scale, and later even more with advances in 3D printing technology and the expiry of patents.

This is the critical point for MakieLab's growth on the manufacturing side because the price of each doll is high in relation to mass manufactured dolls averaging at $20. Although Makies are less expensive than in 2011, a simple doll without accessories around €90, which creates a barrier for adoption at a larger scale. Even though the games for iOS and Android were released in 2014, it is early to know whether they will boost sales of Makie dolls.

Outlook

MakieLab plans to develop a manufacturing platform that integrates the production of custom-made physical toys from multiplayer games and digital toy design platforms. In the future, the ambition is to have a game-toy manufacturing platform that flexibly accommodates any toy brand with customization, complemented with gaming, for any particular target group. To some extent, Makies and their games are a functioning prototype of MakieLab's ambition.

> *"We send dolls as far as Singapore and New Zealand. We didn't need to ask permission for that, we didn't need to ask permission to go on the App store. You go and upload your app and that's how that works, and we also didn't need to ask permission to make physical products. And that's here to stay. When everybody can take part, surely things become more and more amazing."*
>
> —Alice Taylor speaking at the
> TCT Show + Personalize, 2013

Assumed as a "big gamer" and the "nerd in the building," Alice Taylor always wanted to start a games company. Previously, she had created an avatar-builder which became very popular for people on the web to create their virtual character. A serendipitous moment led her to wonder whether one could turn avatars into dolls using 3D printing. Now, MakieLab wonders whether it can be the next LEGO, producing and curating a variety of toy-builders for various age segments. In this quest against dragons plotting "game over" strategies for truly challenging new businesses, MakieLab is the fearless hero making it through every level, gathering props and allies toward creating the next playing field for the toy industry.

Regardless of the challenges that MakieLab faces, Alice Taylor sees a stepchange in the industry, in which innovators will set foot in the market for toys and games. Its ambition is to build upon a basic manufacturing platform that unleashes creativity for design and play. MakieLab aspires to building a distributed manufacturing network that produces customized Makies on demand anywhere in the world where there are professional grade 3D printers. Such a radical change is possible thanks to affordable on-demand manufacturing with 3D printing, and amplified by combining the physical tools with the generativity that a digital platform enables and invites.

From the Perspective of Alice Taylor, Co-Founder and CEO, MakieLab

We asked Alice Taylor the following questions for her commentary.

The purpose on which MakieLab was founded and is being run today: What is your passion?

The purpose of MakieLab is to hold the child's future dear, to celebrate creativity and making, to break stereotypes, and to innovate.

Why is MakieLab strategically novel in your view?

MakieLab makes a difference because it's local, on demand, unique to each owner … that's all novel. Living digitally and physically together is also novel. These are areas of continuous exploration!

How have you and your colleagues at MakieLab get here in terms of doing something differently? What rules did you break?

We treat hardware and consumer products like software: release the demo, and iterate as fast as you can. Don't hold it in secret, and launch with a (marketed) bang 4 years later. We break stereotypes where we can. And we very much rely on word of mouth…!

Both the toy and games industries rely heavily on enormous marketing budgets. This is the toughest hurdle: How to compete with mass-manufactured prices and marketing campaign noise. No one has an answer to this, you can but try.

Future intent: What is the next opportunity and related challenges?

We're developing more products this year; plus we're developing for USA manufacturing, and looking to Japan. We want to find partners and licensing opportunities that help the growth (400% YOY for 2 years in a row, and holding) continue to accelerate.

Looking back from the future: Why did what you have done matter more, broadly speaking?

I think what we have done is a significant technical and manufacturing challenge—done by a company that's 50 percent female in a tech world where that's not the norm! I'd like to think that Makies will influence other doll body image developments, too.

18

ZenRobotics: Riveting Robots to Reduce and Recycle

Q: What happens when two academics and an ex-pop star get together?

A: They do something cool and "trashy" with robots.

When Harri Volpola (PhD, Physics, Mathematics, Neural networks), Tuomas Lukka (PhD, Quantum Chemistry), and Jufo Peltomaa (ex-pop star, serial entrepreneur) got together, that was exactly what they did. After Tuomas and Jufo had sold off their hybrid graphics to Nvidia, they were contemplating what to do next. Their only business plan at that time was that their new venture would involve robots.

To better figure out what it was that they wanted to do with robots, they conducted interviews with potential customers. The interviews helped them understand on what area the customers would like to save money on and need assistance with, simultaneously. The typical interview questions included inquiries about the areas where the companies faced difficulty, areas where they lost money the most, etc. After looking at 200 to 300 companies from a variety of industries, the founders were convinced that recognition and manipulation of odd-form objects in trash was a potential area to focus upon. ZenRobotics estimates that a client would normally pay €100 to dispose of a ton of waste. The metal from the waste however, could earn as much as €250 per ton. Thus they realized that, of the six identified business fields where robotics is most important, the most promising one was recycling. The idea of "robotic recycling" was thus born. Data showed that in European Union alone, 3 billion tons of waste is produced every year, of which construction and demolition waste contributes to 900 million ton. The related recycling and disposal issues could be solved through introducing a new robotic system. With this concept in mind, ZenRobotics was conceived in 2007.

WOW: Robots Sorting Our Trash

ZenRobotics uses artificial intelligence technology to solve the age-old dilemma associated with recycling and waste disposal. It uses a robotic system for identifying the recyclable materials (metal, wood, stone), irrespective of the shape or size, while the trash passes through a conveyor belt. This is quite noteworthy as the differentiation and management of odd-shaped objects were impossible with automation systems before ZenRobotics. In ZenRobotics, the system is equipped with infrared scanners, metal detectors, and load sensors for doing this. The latter detects the surface area and weight of the trash materials. The robot systems weigh the trash while they lift items and calculate the associated price. The adaptive picking motions of the industrial robots are also controlled. The robots used in ZenRobotics are reliable, standard industrial robots ("similar to the ones used in Volkswagen factories"). They are backed up by artificial intelligence software. The systems are monitored so as to check for wear and tear.

In its first funding round ZenRobotics received $17 million from the international equity investor, Invus and the Vigo accelerator, Lifeline ventures. ZenRobotics hired Juho Malmberg (Accenture, Finland), as its CEO and Jorma Eloranta (Metso), as the Board chairman. The initial product launch was in 2012. Within a year, ZenRobotics was able to sell five units, with an approximate per unit price of $1 million.[1]

ZenRobotics contacted 16 waste processing companies in Finland, for its first installation. All the companies were interested in the technology and concept. SITA Finland Ltd., a part of SUEZ Environment, was the keenest one. SITA is Europe's largest environmental company handling waste. Through the collaboration, ZenRobotics launched its product pilot and worked on streamlining the processes. By 2011 February, ZenRobotics had 20 agents in 47 countries, handling the sales. The robotics systems are assembled locally in Finland

---

[1] It could also process a minimum of 12,000 tons of waste in a year (and a maximum of 60,000 tons), making sure that the cost of a unit purchased can be recovered by the buyer company in a year.

and then delivered to customers. Then they are installed through a global reseller network. In May 2014, ZenRobotics opened the world's very first robotic waste processing plant in Finland. They estimate their overall global sales potential to be 8000 units.

Apart from the novelty of the approach, ZenRobotics is also a frontrunner in robotics-based recycling. It is the original robotic waste sorting system in the whole world. Currently, the technology is still a newfangled concept in the Environmental Services Industry. ZenRobotics is working toward making this technology conventional. By adding on to, and creating new applications for existing sensors, ZenRobotics is striving to expand its arena to include more recyclables and a wider array of potential customers.

SO WHAT: Robotics to the Rescue? How Does ZenRobotics Operate?

ZenRobotics systems can handle a maximum of 20 kilograms of recyclable material in one pick (gathering motion). The picking cycle is 3 seconds and a machine can do 1400 picks per hour, 5000 hours per year. By doing the math, quite evidently ZenRobotics can recover more than 10,000 tons of recyclable material per year.

How Is ZenRobotics a Positive Outlier?

Unlike companies that bring a new idea into an existing business, ZenRobotics created a new business with their idea. The idea was born after numerous interviews with potential customers, thus ensuring its relevance and applicability in the contemporary setting. Through robotics recycling, the customer could save on the disposal costs and at the same time, make money on the recyclable material. ZenRobotics identified a market and a business opportunity in the field of Environmental Services and Waste Management. It adapts itself to the present trend toward higher recycling rates. ZenRobotics works along the lines of the model of "Circular economy"—the processes are designed from the start itself to ensure that the waste from one process acts as input to another process. The products are reused and upgraded instead of being discarded.

Compared to manual waste sorting plants, ZenRobotics is a safer option as it prevents exposure of humans to hazardous material (asbestos, mold, toxins, sharp and heavy objects, etc.). The associated labor costs are also reduced as the robots are designed to replace a high number of manual work hours per year. The machines are very durable, capital efficient, and require very less maintenance cost. They also come in different models. For instance, ZenRobotics Recycler comes in three models (with one, two, or three arms). The installation options include retrofit (to be integrated into existing processes), and stand-alone (all in one compact semi-mobile package).

As it is unnecessary to transport the waste material to centralized plants, the transportation cost is much lesser than in conventional models. By eliminating the need to source-separate the customer can increase the profits by single stream collection of waste materials. To top it all, being the company with a "robot waste sorter" attracts media attention and the interest of clients, thereby boosting up business.

ZenRobotics' innovative idea, systematic implementation, and product enhancement attempts have won it many awards and accolades (see Table 18.1).

Challenges

In any field, one of the challenges that frontrunners face is from incumbents and competitors. The incumbents in this context are the

Table 18.1 Awards and Nominations Received by ZenRobotics, Compiled from Published Sources and Company Website

Awards/Nominations	Category	Year	Results
Global Cleantech 100	Top 100 private companies in clean technology	2014	Won
2013 Later-Stage Top 10 Award, Global Cleantech Cluster Association	Waste Management	2013	Won
Gold EEP Award, Pollutec Paris	European companies that improve the environment with innovative technologies	2011	Won
Nordic Cleantech Open	Top 25 early-stage Cleantech companies in the Nordic region	2010	Finalist

manual waste sorting plants. Other recycling facilities designing recycling sorting systems like Machinex are also potential competitors to ZenRobotics. However, Machinex is yet to develop a robotic recycling system that could become a potential contender to ZenRobotics Recycler.

Another significant challenge is the fact that the field of environmental services is a conservative one. The technologies used are conventional and mechanical. Introducing and successfully integrating Robotic systems into this field would require some preparation. Customers might need time and information about the technology to make the transition. On the other hand, ZenRobotics counts on the concept of Best Available Technology (BAT), promoted by the European Union and the United States as an element which would encourage this transition. Juho Malberg (CEO) envisions that in an immediate future, when manual sorting becomes obsolete and illegal, the BAT principle would drive both local and international regulation to the usage of the most efficient technology available, i.e., the one of ZenRobotics (Source: cleantech.com). What is more, he believes that the good results of the technology would be enough to convince even the most conservative people to make the switch.

Outlook

ZenRobotics entered a market which is booming, socially sensitive, and yet facing a lag in efficiency and effectiveness. Waste disposal and recycling is an area which is too complicated and disorganized for standard robot control systems. It is in this field that ZenRobotics entered and created a disruption. By combining sensory fusion, data-mining, machine learning, and real-time robotics, ZenRobotics made the outmoded recycling industry automatic, modern, scalable, and effective. The change which the founders envision through this is quite similar to the one which happened in auto industry, with the advent of robots.

Besides, ZenRobotics is still evolving. It aspires to be able to process new waste streams like Municipal Solid Waste (MSW), End of Life Vehicles (ELV), Waste Electrical & Electronic Equipment (WEEE), hazardous materials, and radioactive waste, among others, in the near future. MSW includes everyday waste items that are discarded by the public, usually disposed of by landfilling. ELV, or motor vehicles which have reached the end of their productive lives, usually constitute about 8 to 9 million tons in the European Union only. Managing them the correct way would involve dismantling and recycling them. ZenRobotics could prove to be extremely prolific in both of these areas. Another line

of work ZenRobotics could involve itself is in the promotion and implementation of facilities for the reuse, recycling, and recovery of electrical and electronic equipment waste (WEEE). Disposal of radioactive
waste in a safe and suitable way is another grave matter of concern.
Spent nuclear fuel from nuclear reactors, high-level radioactive waste
from the reprocessing of spent nuclear fuel, transuranic radioactive
waste from nuclear weapon manufacturing, uranium mill tailings from
the mining, and milling of uranium ore, low-level radioactive waste
(contaminated industrial or research waste), and naturally occurring
radioactive material constitute different kinds of nuclear waste. The
final category on the check list is hazardous waste. It is a big category
and includes subcategories such as household hazardous waste, some
agricultural wastes, drilling wastes, or cement kiln wastes. ZenRobotics
plans to expand to this domain too.

It looks like ZenRobotics has set its aims high. In a distant future,
ZenRobotics might even be able to move robots from factory settings
to the real-life environment. In short, as the founders rightly say,
"what you buy is just the beginning." It looks like the ultimate aim of
ZenRobotics is indeed, world (of trash) domination.

From the Perspective of Tomi Laamanen, Professor of Strategic Management, University of St. Gallen

ZenRobotics is an innovative start-up that was established by three
founders through a careful thought process where the founders were
systematically analyzing alternative industries in which they could enter.
The founding of ZenRobotics resembles the thought processes that Jeff
Bezos, the founder of Amazon, and Austin Ligon, the founder of Car-
max, went through before choosing the product areas they wanted to
focus on. Similarly to Jeff Bezos that was convinced of the opportunities
offered by the Internet and Austin Ligon that wanted to benefit from
the trend toward specialized superstores, the founders of ZenRobotics
were convinced of the opportunities offered by robotics.

The waste recycling business is an interesting, in many respects
attractive business since one has the in-bound and out-bound customers that both provide cash flows for the waste recycling firm. On
the one hand, one is serving the in-bound customers in helping them
dispose their waste and, on the other hand, one is using the valuable
materials or energy retrieved from the waste recycling process and

selling them onward to the out-bound customers that can use them as raw materials in their own processes. Furthermore, as the amount of waste is continuously increasing and the pressures for recycling and environmental consciousness are getting higher, there are without a doubt major global growth opportunities in waste recycling.

ZenRobotics is tapping onto this global trend in helping the waste recycling companies to optimize their processes through robotized waste handling systems. The use of advanced sensor technology combined with artificial intelligence and robots capable of handling odd-shaped objects represents a major innovation for waste recycling that enables the waste recycling firms to further automate and optimize their processes. The major potential associated with the firm was also recognized by investors and, as a consequence, ZenRobotics was able to raise 17 MUSD from a syndicate of reputed early-stage venture capital investors.

While the investment provides ZenRobotics a great opportunity to start expanding its business with the help of its newly recruited CEO, Mr. Juho Malmberg (former CEO of Accenture Finland and former management team member of Kone Corporation), it also puts major pressure on it to be able to sell major customer projects internationally due to its relatively narrow sectoral focus. Moreover, starting to sell internationally an innovative concept that requires major capital expenditures from its customers is not easy, because, in addition to developing a relationship with the potential customers, one has to be able to convince them that the new automated concept works and provides a solid pay-back time for the investment. Moreover, developing an international sales force often tends to take more time than one would have originally anticipated and cost more than initially expected.

This difficulty is clearly visible in the financials of ZenRobotics (see Figure 18.1) where the investments into the international expansion and the further development of the product concept have not yet paid off in terms of higher sales revenue. With the help of the relatively generous initial venture capital funding, the balance sheet of ZenRobotics continues to be strong, but the present burn-rate cannot continue for many more years without an additional funding round if the sales do not dramatically increase. This struggle can also be seen in resignation of the CEO of ZenRobotics at the end of 2014.

One of the further reasons for the challenges of ZenRobotics has been that even though already the initial system worked well, the robotic arms were too slow for industrial scale automated waste recycling. Thus, the ZenRobotics team had to go back to the drawing board in 2014, halt the sales efforts, and redesign the system

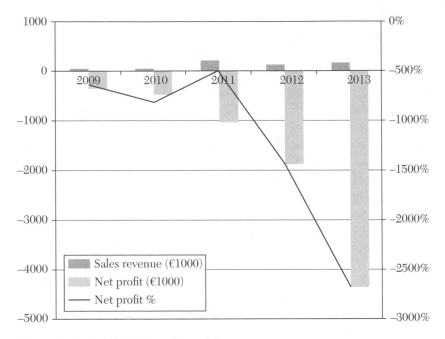

Figure 18.1 ZenRobotics: Financials

to make it faster. A pilot version of the new robot is now already in operation in Finland in SITA's waste plant and the sales efforts of the new product concept were restarted in the RoboBusiness Exhibition in Boston in the Fall 2014. The future will show how the 10 meters long and 4 meters wide system costing roughly €500,000 will sell and how long it will take for ZenRobotics to return back to profitability.

Going beyond the early lessons learned regarding customer requirements, ZenRobotics continues to be well-positioned with an innovative product in a growing industry. A further important consideration for the company will be the business model of the future. A central question for ZenRobotics in this respect will be whether to become a vendor of automated systems or whether to retain the ownership of the systems and rather start selling waste handling as a service with a monthly or yearly service fee.

19

Spire: Launching Crowdfunding Beyond Earth

Peter Platzer was always attracted toward Science and education. He received training at CERN and Max Planck Institute, and dreamt of a day when everyone would be able to have access to space. Attending Singularity University's inaugural Executive Program in 2009 was the final cue. The high-energy physicist-turned-finance guy finally propelled himself to pursue his true passion of commercial space exploration. With this idea in mind, he graduated from the International Space University's master's program, and received internship experience at NASA Ames' Space Portal. In 2012, along with Joel Spark and Jeroen Cappaert (space engineers), Peter found Nanosatisfi, the first remote-sensing platform intended to deliver distinctive data multiple times per hour from anywhere on earth. They deployed *Ardusat*,[1] the world's first crowdfunded satellite the same year. The purpose of the launch was to serve a platform for meeting the crucial need for applied STEM education, and to make space exploration available to everyone.

After fulfilling its initial purpose, i.e., covering the shared mission of Ardusat, Nanosatisfi expanded its satellite network. The business branched into two distinct and dynamic areas. Nanosatisfi went ahead and hired a professional in educational technology sector to become a stand-alone company. It developed its own customer base and industry connections. The close collaboration with the Ardusat team however, is still ongoing.

---

[1] The name "Ardusat" is a portmanteau of the words "Arduino" (an electronic platform on which Ardusat is based) and "Satellite."

WOW: Satellites for Mr. and Mrs. Brown

Soon, Nanosatisfi realized the importance of a name that would be more illustrative of its vision and customer base. "Spire" has expanded fast since then and is aspiring to be the most powerful remote-sensing platform in the world. It has received investments from companies like Emerge, Mitsui & Co. Global Investment, Qihoo 360 Technology, Moose Capital, and RRE Ventures. Currently it has offices in San Francisco and Singapore.

WOW: How Did Spire Launch Itself into the Space?

Spire moves in par with the current market trend where big, costly, single-use traditional technologies are substituted with smaller, cheaper, multi-use standardized technologies. Within 2 years of its launch, Spire has put four satellites in their orbits. However, Spire would not call itself a satellite company, but rather a satellite-powered data company. The satellites are not considered the main focus, but rather as enablers for procurement of space-based data for solving problems. The approach is similar to that of *Skybox Imaging*, which uses satellites to procure imagery.

The company focuses on designing hardware and software simultaneously, in an integrated way. This approach facilitates the fast pace of Spire's development by accelerating the building of additional sensors and satellites. These multi-sensor satellites, which range from 1U to 3U, are built with Commercial Off-The-Shelf (COTS) components for reducing costs. Multiple sensors collect various types of information for customers in 12 verticals across North America, Europe, and Asia. It has ties with a number of launch providers and has purchased numerous launch slots for achieving its several missions. Spire plans to launch 20 nanosatellites ("small enough to fit into one's palms and weighing less than a bottle of wine") by the end of 2015.

SO WHAT Makes Spire a Positive Outlier?

Is smaller better? The Spire satellites come with a range of technologies like sensors, antennas, and infrared cameras. As Spire satellites are much smaller than conventional ones, they require smaller rockets only. A normal size rocket can pack more satellites too. This makes the cost of each launch hundred times lesser. Numerous satellites also give constant coverage by providing better "temporal resolution." As a single spacecraft has a limited time window to capture information for an area before it moves out of range, the constellation of small satellites provides better data than a single, big one. Big satellites also have a big development time and life cycle (5 to 15 years). As nanosatellites are less costly, the life cycle can be reduced (2 years), after which the old satellites burn up in the atmosphere. Then new ones with better hardware can be launched. This iteration cycle is similar to that seen in the software industry.

Spire as a Data Company

Spire aspires to provide better data on areas like maritime insurance, fishing, global trade, weather, piracy, among others, using its satellite technology. For example, the data type—automatic identification system (AIS) assists in tracking ships, measuring weather, etc. Using similar relevant data, Spire could provide data solutions to several problems which require space-based data (see Table 19.1). Spire monitors three-fourths of the earth's circumference, previously neglected by

Table 19.1   Some Areas Where Spire Offers Its Services and the Respective Issues Addressed in Each Area, Compiled from Company Website

A Few Types of Information Provided by Spire	Issues Addressed
Navigational data	• Missing ships
	• Illegal fishing
	• Maneuvered data (usually from international partners)
	• Global piracy
	• Waste in insurance claims
Weather data	• Gap in forecasting due to end of life of traditional weather satellites
	• Forecasting issues due to inconsistent availability of relevant data
Surveillance data and international security	• Geopolitical conflicts
	• International attacks
	• Airline tracking

traditional remote sensing, with the help of these satellites. The monitoring of oceans by the nanosatellites, for instance, checks piracy and illegal overfishing. It also provides more rapid revisit times than other satellite-based data systems.

Spire as a Business

Spire team takes pride in having a global outlook. The team competence and the relationship with customers are well developed for a new company. The company has expanded to Singapore. The economic potential, engineering-inclined education, the political attitude toward space race, and the support from Economic Development Board of Singapore were factors which drove Spire to choose Singapore. This expansion opens up possibilities for Spire's future success in Asia, a zone that is not currently the focus of most space companies.

Spire as an Employer

In Spire, the employees are encouraged to innovate, rather than invent. They are motivated to find smart ways to make use of proven technologies, so as to create new results. The employees do not receive any performance review and neither is there a hierarchical organizational chart. The whole organization functions around the notion of spending time in activities they enjoy. Peter assures that this will bring career success. To supplement this employee-centric corporate culture, Spire offers year-around career coaching, career tests on long-term career goals and aspirations (to ensure job-employee match), and quarterly career progression discussions. These strategies are based on the trends noticed in larger, successful companies in various industries.

Spire When Compared to Similar Companies

When compared to traditional satellite companies, Spire satellites provide a myriad of space-related data, more frequently. Traditional satellites update the AIS roughly four times a day. Spire, meanwhile, tracks AIS data every minute and updates it several times a day. This makes activities like route management and traffic management more effective. By monitoring areas which do not have traditional satellite coverage, Spire increases the coverage and consistency of data services provided. It collects weather information at 100 times more frequent and accurate rate than traditional companies. Even when compared to land-based radar systems, Spire has a competitive advantage because it does not face data loss due to the curvature of earth. It thus has the potential to disrupt legacy platforms set by traditional companies.

Space industry as a whole has been dominated by government for a long time. Spire is one of the pioneers in changing this trend. With the increasing number of niche satellite networks, the customers would soon outspend and move beyond government in the near future itself. Another area in which Spire differs from traditional, governmental companies is in its business model. Traditional companies have their businesses structured around unique needs of government and universities. Companies like Spire are more flexible in the kind of services they provide. The expenses involved (hardware, software, and operation) are quite low as well. Where traditional aerospace project spend hundreds of millions of dollars, Spire spends mere thousands.

The Space industry is an oligopoly with a few companies controlling most of the global market share. Economies of scale and scope act as natural barriers to new companies trying to enter this market. Being disruptively innovative like Spire is one of the very few ways a new company could enter the market. The brilliance of the Spire business model is that its strategies cannot be adopted effortlessly by the incumbents. Doing so would impair the latter's existing business and damage existing strategies. On the other hand, they cannot choose to ignore Spire model either. Not adapting to the current market trend would cause loss of market share.

When compared to adjacent companies like *DigitalGlobe*, the difference of Spire lies in its crowdsourcing model. Also, the focus of the former is mainly on the coverage of the United States and Western Europe. Spire covers Asia also, making its services more wide-reaching. When compared to satellite-imagery companies, Spire stands out by providing data services, instead of imagery. Many other firms are also working toward making the access to space more conceivable to common men. Some examples are *Virgin Galactic, Generation Orbit, Interorbital Systems, Rocket Lab, Garvey Spacecraft Corp.*, and *XCOR Aerospace*. However, most of this activity is seen in the area of rocket launchers, not satellites.

Challenges

The main challenge that Spire faces is, like other outlier companies, its competitors. For instance, big player *DigitalGlobe* provides services similar to Spire, along with images. It also has the most sophisticated and swift high-resolution earth imaging satellites that are capable of collecting over 1 billion km^2 of imagery per year. It even provides intraday revisits around the globe, like Spire. What is more, *DigitalGlobe* analyzes the information available in the form of images and provide meaning to them. For example, WorldView-3, the fifth satellite from *DigitalGlobe*, could analyze the composition of clouds and gases and determine whether there is drought in a particular area. Furthermore, it can map food shortages that could be caused due to this drought. Spire is yet to start providing analytics for the data it delivers. *DigitalGlobe* also offers its best, most secure and fastest "Direct Access Program" for its defense, intelligence, and commercial customers around the world.

Likewise, *PlanetLabs* also provides comprehensive global coverage similar to that of Spire. It even has launched five satellites already (compared to four by Spire). It also provides services for businesses as well as developers. The options for collaboration range from being full-fledged *PlanetLabs* customers or partners, to integrating *PlanetLabs* datasets into products. *Dauriageo*, on the other hand, provides not only its own constellation of satellites, but also a platform for other satellite operators to guarantee data (satellite imagery and derived data layers) with a higher resolution, coverage, and novelty. *Skybox imaging*, recently acquired by Google, combines scalable computing and analytics to find answers to the world's most important geospatial problems.

Another apprehension is regarding Spire products (satellites). Apart from the differences in technology base, development timelines, and launch flexibility Spire satellites also have major physical differences when compared to conventional, big satellites. Most of the nanosatellites cannot be maneuvered further after they are launched. This creates problems at the regulatory level as most of the laws in the area were made with traditional satellites in mind. The areas where this is a concern include state responsibility, liability caused by damage, space debris mitigation, and remediation and so on. Of course, with the gaining popularity and demand for nanosatellites, it is not impossible to amend the laws so as to include the newcomers or even create new laws specifically for them.

Outlook

The vision behind Spire allows people to aim at stars. The developments in technology helped Spire maintain a lean profile. Most importantly, Spire brought space to the people. Commercial customers and venture capitalists already appreciate the magnitude of Spire. With market analyses (by SpaceWorks Enterprises Inc.) showing that commercial customers are likely to dominate the business from 2014 onward, Spire's business is sure to skyrocket.

From the Perspective of Eric Nowak, Professor of Financial Management and Accounting, Università della Svizzera italiana, and Swiss Finance Institute

SPIRE—Crowdfunding as a Success Factor to Shake Up a Sleeping Market

Spire is a high-tech start-up company combining Big Data (software) with nanotechnology satellites (hardware). Start-ups combining innovative data-driven solutions with a hardware component are currently belonging to the hottest sought-after "unicorns" (potentially billion dollar market value companies) in Silicon Valley. Spire is intruding a market—satellites to remote-sensing data about weather and other areas—which in the past, due to its huge initial investment costs to transport satellites with rockets into the stratosphere, used to be dominated by Governments and state-owned companies. Only recently private companies have begun to actively compete in the business of space missiles and rocket launches (e.g., Space-X, Virgin Galactic). Spire is promising to provide these satellite data services more frequently, with more variants, with higher coverage, but albeit with less potential for data loss, and more cost-efficient.

Another intriguing novelty is that beyond regular venture capital financing rounds, Spire has "crowdfunded" a satellite to launch into space. This is a very clever strategy, because we know that crowdfunding works particularly well for high-risk projects, which can mobilize potential investors also emotionally and not just for financial considerations. For satellites or anything connected to space aviation this is certainly the case as there is a gap to be filled by the current lack of ambitious NASA programs, so the crowdfunding of satellite rocket launches can be expected to be successful in the future.

Spire belongs to the "small is better" movement where nanotechnology and the power of connected crowds together challenge established industry players. The company is located in two of the most innovative technology and finance clusters on Earth, the San Francisco Bay area and the Asian market and technology hub Singapore. Furthermore, it is a small high-tech start-up company breaking into the domain of previously Government-owned and very large companies which have more financial resources but are also much less flexible to adapt their business models to rapidly changing environments.

Another domain where Spire has definitely broken industry rules is with respect to its human capital management. The company needs talented people in the most-demanded sectors of the Silicon Valley economy. This is a challenging task for every high-tech start-up. Spire manages this in an innovative fashion by having an extremely selective hiring process where they accept less than 3 percent of applicants but then on the other hand offering the few selected employees a unique challenging and creative working environment. The CEO and founder of the company, Peter Platzer, a physicist who turned into a classical business entrepreneur, offers every employee personal coaching until he or she is fully satisfied with his or her job task. Furthermore, Platzer promises that no employee hired will ever be fired for economic reasons, so everyone has an implicit job guarantee.

Of course, this particular human capital approach to compete in the War for talent is also sort of a future challenge. First, it is very unlikely that Spire will be able to continue this policy with respect to its employees into the future for good. At some point in the future, financial necessities and economic reality might impose to restructure the workforce. Second, while growing in size and number of employees the CEO will not be able to coach every single employee. Access to top talent in data sciences and engineering is key to the future success of Spire so the company will have to stay innovative in order not to face a lack in this area.

Another potential risk in the future is the dependence on crowdfunding. While this works very well with highly innovative projects with a limited financing need, once the company and its services are more established, it will face a higher need for investment capital to be financed while at the same time potential technology enthusiastic investors might prefer to crowdfinance the next big idea and not yet another satellite for weather forecasts. So at some vintage point the company will have to rethink and redesign its financing model. Of course, should the company stay on a successful growth path, it will be easy to convince venture capital funds, strategic investors from the same industry, or shareholders in an Initial Public Offering to finance the growth of Spire. So that is a risk and an opportunity at the same time.

Nevertheless, the strategy of crowdfunding "small is beautiful" high-tech start-ups combining data-technology and hardware will continue to be successful in the future. The investment sizes are manageable and therefore so are the risks. The emotional component for investors in these areas will make it easy for innovative entrepreneurs to generate enough attention in order to attract funds.

The change brought upon by Spire and similar companies is already on the way driving established businesses out of business thereby exercising creative destruction in markets, which have been rigid for years because of government regulation and artificial barriers to entry. In this way Spire reminds me a lot of Uber, another recent unicorn company which is shaking up a formerly sleeping and rigid hence highly regulated market. Similar to Spire, while operating in completely different area, Uber is combining software data (remote location information transmitted through smartphones) with a hardware component (cars to transport people) and is extremely successful in a market which was characterized by state-regulated barriers of entry (licensed taxi transportation). So while this analogy is maybe not intuitive at first sight, Spire could become the "Uber of Space" and given the recent financing round valuations of Uber (around 40 billion USD) Spire could be doomed for a similar level of success.

20

Organovo: Leaving 3D Bioprints for Others to Follow

It all began in 2003, when Dr. Thomas Boland patented ink-jet printing of viable cells at Clemson University. Drawing inspiration from this, Prof. Gabor Forgacs and his multi-institution team began work on organ (bio) printing technology at the University of Missouri the very next year. The subsequent year, the founders of Organovo had discussions regarding the formation of a bioprinting company around the Forgacs organ printing technology. Through bioprinting, printing equipments could be devised to deposit biological material and create tissues that mirror key traits of the native tissues. With this vision in mind, Organovo, Inc. was formally incorporated in Delaware, in 2007.

Under the leadership of Keith Murphy, CEO, Organovo, Inc. began raising start-up funds and receiving $3 million in angel financing in 2008. In 2009, Organovo opened its laboratory in San Diego and completed work on the delivery of NovoGen MMX Bioprinter. It created bioprinted blood vessels and received its first National Institutes of Health (NIH) grant. Organovo, Inc. has had exponential progress since then.

The main focus of Organovo Inc. was on launching 3D bioprinting. Using this technology, the company designs and creates functional human tissues, which are built to function just like native tissues. After it demonstrated the ability to create novel tissues in 3D using primary human cells, it began corporate partnerships (see Table 20.1).

In February 2012, the company went public through a $15.2 million financing round. The same year, Organovo received its company patent and key founder patent. It closed $46.6 million in secondary public offering and stock listed on NYSE MKT in 2013. The same

Table 20.1   Organovo and Its Collaborators, Compiled from Company Website

Year	Collaboration with	Purpose
2012	Autodesk Research	Developing 3D bioprinting software
2013	OHSU Knight Cancer Institute	Cancer research
2013	ZenBio	Constructing 3D tissue models
2013	Methuselah Foundation	Funding of bioprinting research
2014	National Institutes of Health	Technology access collaboration

year, it developed its own 3D human liver model and in 2014, it delivered the first 3D liver tissue to Key Opinion Leader. Not surprisingly, Organovo featured in MIT Technology Review's 2012 list of the world's 50 most innovative technology companies and will be honored as the 2015 Technology Pioneer by the World Economic Forum (WEF).

WOW: Digitally Printed Organs on Demand, or Bioprinting Tissues in Their Own Image

Organovo is a pioneer in 3D bioprinting. Basically, the 3D printing process involves taking particular cells and putting them into a 3D matrix. The cells are internally programmed (by nature) to help create the final tissue. The final tissues are then layered architecturally in the right positions. The tissues formed thus represent the true human biology better than its polymer-based counterparts.

Organovo partners with biopharmaceutical companies (e.g., Pfizer, Janssen Research & Development, L.L.C.), and university medical centers to fashion "preclinical discovery," i.e., to create and authenticate predictive tissues for disease modeling, toxicology, metabolism, and transport studies. This ensures that the preclinical models are safe and efficient, when compared to the 2D animal and cellular (cells in petri dish) models. Sometimes, clinical tests which might work in the 2D models might not work in real human tissues. The failure rate is 20 to 50 percent. This causes a loss of close to 500 million USD yearly. With bioprinting, Organovo solves this problem and ensures the testing and production of more, quicker, safer, and effective drugs. This bridges the gap between preclinical testing and clinical trials by allowing for the testing of drugs in functional human tissues, even before administering them to a human being (see Figure 20.1). The 3D printed liver tissues made commercially available by Organovo in November 2014 is a step in this direction.

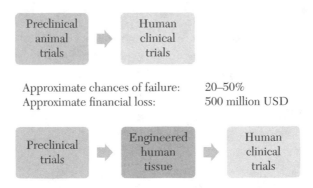

Figure 20.1 Traditional model and Organovo model (created by authors)

SO WHAT Makes Organovo the Fittest?

Organovo When Compared to Human Donors

Another area where Organovo tissues can be useful is in surgery. Organovo aspires to produce small, purely cellular, functional replacement tissues that go through clinical trial pathways like heart muscle patches, nerve graphs, blood vessels, etc. These 3D tissues in turn would repair or replace the diseased or damaged tissues. This not only enhances the chances of availability of tissues for recipients, but also ensures the quality of donors. With human donors, it is difficult to determine the quality of donated tissues or to ascertain whether they carry any traces of chronic diseases. Organovo would be able to ensure that the recipient gets high-quality tissues harnessed from his own cells, thus guaranteeing its safety and suitability. By using the recipient's own cells, organ rejection during transplantation could also be checked. Furthermore, this would solve the problem of the mismatch between the numbers of willing, healthy organ donors and worthy recipients. Likewise, recipients usually have to be in long transplant waiting lists till a suitable donor is identified. With Organovo bioprinting technology, transplant waiting lists would soon be things of past. After all, it would take only less than 30 minutes to create a 5-centimeter section of artery.

Organovo When Compared to Traditional Models

Organovo moves 3D printing beyond building plastic prototypes and metal end products (e.g., work done by companies like *Stratasys, 3D Systems*) and into cardiovascular medicine, medical research, and transplant medicine. It revolutionizes Pharma drug discovery and toxicology testing by enhancing the effectiveness and longevity of testing models. When compared to animal tissues, Organovo tissues are human, as well as have a longer life (more than 40 days).

Organovo as the Future

Organovo's ultimate aim is to harness new organs from the patients' own cells. Even though Gabour Forgacs is uncertain about 3D printing being able to create body parts identical to the ones provided by nature, he is quite sure that creating body parts functionally equivalent to the natural ones would be possible in the future. Science today cannot fix an upper limit on longevity. If Organovo does indeed succeed in this attempt, we could look forward to a future where tissue-on-demand and organs-on-demand would be technologically possible. Shedding defective organs and replacing them with new, functional ones would be a reality (see Table 20.2).

Table 20.2   Potential Future Applications of Organovo's Bioprinting Technology, Compiled from Published Sources and Company Website

Organovo—Potential Future Applications
• Grafting blood vessels for heart bypass surgery
• Building regenerative scaffolds for dental and bone repairs
• In situ bioprinting of skin cells directly onto the human body for healing wounds
• Keyhole bioprinting for repairing internal organs

Challenges

Not many 3D printing companies work with live tissues. Nevertheless, Organovo does have one strong competitor at this point. *Envisiontec*, the 3D rapid manufacturing solutions company, launched its 3D-Bioplotter in April 2014. According to *Envisiontec*, this Bioplotter is a "rapid prototyping tool for processing a great variety of biomaterials within the process of Computer-Aided Tissue Engineering from 3D CAD models and patient CT data to the physical 3D scaffold with a designed and defined outer form and an open inner structure." It comes in two series—the Developer Series (for educational institutions) and the Manufacturer Series (for advanced tissue engineering research and production). Apart from printing bio-ink "tissue spheroids" and supportive scaffold materials (like Organovo), Envisiontec also prints a variety of biomaterials like biodegradable polymers and ceramics for supporting and actuating the formation of artificial organs, and bone substitutes. However, Envisiontec Bioplotter is not capable of bioprinting with high concentrations of living cells. It can work only with biomaterials of very dilute cell mixtures in hydrogels. This process would not be able to yield a "tissue" with the cellular density that approaches native human tissue, the way Organovo does.

Apart from industry adjacents like *Envisiontec*, academic institutions like Columbia, Cornell, and Wake Forest also have researchers working on bioprinting. Wake Forest research team members, under the directorship of Surgeon Anthony Athala, have already lab-grown their first organ (a bladder) which could be implanted into a human being. They are also working on experimental fabrication technology that can print human tissue on demand, just like Organovo envisions.w

Apart from the competition in the field, another challenge Organovo faces is its stock fluctuations. In 2013, the company's stock rose 345 percent based on the potential of its tissue engineering technology. Yet, in 2014, its stock crashed by 40 percent. This can be attributed to the wearing off of the awe-factor and the ambiguity regarding the company breaking even and making profits. The company's full-year profitability is at least 3 to 5 years off. Likewise, another factor contributing to this challenge is the cash burn out rate of the company. According to investment experts, the company might have 3 years of cash viability unless it turns to open market and sells some of its shares. However, selling shares this way would dilute the existing investors. Another way out would be for Organovo to enter into a licensing deal with a larger company.

Outlook

Bioprinting might one day prove to be a potent tool for people pursuing life extension and longevity. Doctors and scientists would be able to manipulate a living tissue at its cellular level itself. As a result, we could anticipate developments in medical fields and pharmacology, which might even lead to bioprinters becoming mandatory in every hospital emergency units. Bioprinting could also cause ripples in fields like nanotechnology, genetic engineering, and plastic surgery. Who knows, in a future not far away, people might be able to use bioprinting to achieve their desired looks and perpetual youth. Maybe the elixir of life is not just a legend after all.

From the Perspective of Michael Renard, Executive Vice President of Commercial Operations, Organovo

The following answers were provided to the questions presented in an e-mail exchange:

1. The purpose on which the company was founded; what is your passion?

The company is driven by the potential for "Changing the shape of medical research and practice"—our brand essence and purpose.

2. Its difference relative to incumbents; why is it strategically novel in your view?

We are the only company able to produce human tissues with the density, composition, and architecture that closely resemble native tissue, and consequently achieve behavior that is representative of native biology. This gives our tissues unique and differentiate performance for a variety of uses.

3. A quick tour of history; how did you and your colleagues in the company get here in terms of doing something differently? (What rules did you break?)

I am not a founder, but the founders saw the opportunity to combine the disciplines of biology and engineering in a way that had never been done before.

4. Future intent; what is the next opportunity and related challenges?

To prove the utility of this new technology with value-added products and services that fulfill our purpose.

5. Looking back from the future; why did what you have done matter more broadly speaking (even beyond this particular company surviving or not)?

We are a leader in this area, and the promise of this is in the creation of a new industry, an industry based on where biology can be engineered—and built by design.

6. How have you amplified the change, which the company stands for? Or how did you punch above your weight to make impact?

We work to leverage our technology with capable and reputable partners, and we remain the first mover, market leader in innovation, allowing us to set the rules for this new and burgeoning industry.

21

Power to the People: Participant-Driven Health Research at Genomera

Technology entrepreneur Greg Biggers is a problem-seeker. In 2008, he came across personal genetics when he listened to Hugh Reinhoff, a medical geneticist and founder of MyDaughtersDNA .org, spell out his lifetime challenge and took participant-driven health research using personal genomics as his own challenge. Reinhoff had set up a laboratory in his attic equipped with second-hand DNA analysis equipment in order to figure out the genetic basis of his daughter's undiagnosed syndrome. Deeply touched by Reinhoff's painstaking and inspiring effort, Biggers realized that analysis of DNA and health data was no longer the exclusive realm of scientists. He also realized that health-related issues were incredibly personal, that deeply touched people's lives. So, he left his job in a software company, raised seed funding, and started Genomera with a small group of software developers and an expert advisory board. By founding Genomera, Biggers embarked on an ambitious journey to change health research.

Genomera is a company doing participant-driven health science research that combines personal health experiments, scientific evidence, and social networking. Described as "health meets Internet and social software" to "heal the world," Genomera explores the intersection of health literacy and citizen science. Does daily meditation or relaxation practices reduce average blood pressure? How does the vitamin D intake affect sleep? These are research questions that initiated scientific protocols at Genomera. Many people are concerned with health issues that might not be interesting for a research laboratory, from scientific and economic point of views, because they are either too mundane or too rare.

In order to address these concerns and interests, Genomera developed a platform for research that is intuitive but rigorous enough to support sophisticated research and rigorous and scalable health science studies. In its online platform for health science, supported by cloud-based software, participants can design and implement scientific studies themselves. The service reaches out to two emerging areas in health research. On the one hand, the company provides a platform for citizen science research that caters to the quantified self and personalized medicine communities that design and carry out experiments by and on themselves. These are trying to answer questions such as, how does magnesium affect my sleep and how does my genomic profile moderate this relationship? On the other hand, the service draws on a trend of crowdsourced clinical trials, providing a way of recruiting trial participants with available personal genomic data who are willing to contribute to research.

This health research platform is participant-driven, bears no hierarchical structures and is enhanced by a social networking component that supports research protocols and discussion of findings. Many members of Genomera have profiled their personal genome and shared it in the platform for research purposes. Therefore, the pool of members with genomic data is a considerably valuable asset for Genomera, which can use it to market its platform as a service to larger pharmaceutical companies.

Joining Biggers at the very early stage of Genomera were other two experimenters in personal health research; Raymond MacCauley, formerly at biotech firm Illumina, and Melanie Swan, founder of DIYgenomics, had been developing Quantified Self experiments and knew Biggers from health-hacking meetups, whom they told they were eager to create a platform to support data collection in those studies. Biggers had begun developing Genomera and they joined the company. In 2011, the seed funding accelerator Rock-Health, specialized in health start-ups, funded Genomera with $20,000. The company proposes an innovative business model for clinical trials and health research, based on personal health collaboration, which is radically different from the current paradigm in pharmaceuticals.

How Does Genomera's Research Platform Work?

Genomera is functioning in private beta mode, which means that the platform is under development and interested people are required to ask for an invitation to become member. Any member interested in a particular health-related problem can propose an experiment. Initially, most study proponents were people who actually suffered from a health condition, or people who related to these problems through a personal relationship. Then, other members will help to formulate testable hypotheses and to design a research protocol in order to create a scientific experiment that will be carried out by the members of the community.

People who participate in the study as *data participants* perform the protocol on themselves and share their data with the group for joint analysis. A myriad of online tools and low-cost genomic tests, accessible today, enable participants to collect a large amount of data about how their body is behaving during the experimental period. After data collection, people enrolled as *discussion participants* collaborate online to produce results and discuss findings.

By facilitating health research carried out by "lay scientists," Genomera is part of an emerging movement for citizen science. In July 2014, there were around 18 public studies in progress and 15 in the design stage. Using Genomera's platform for health studies, as an organizer or as a participant, is free of charge. Revenues are expected to come from sponsorship and from services provided to other companies or organizations, such as test referrals and advanced analytic services.

WOW: Participant-Driven Health Research

Say people start with an interest in, for instance, how nutrition affects sleep or how their diet is appropriate for their genomic profile. By working together with easy access to data collection tools, reaching findings and gaining insights is faster and cheaper than in research laboratories. MacCauley believes that this kind of citizen science is fueled by a personal appeal motivated by a self-interest in one's own health and the possibility of generating immediately actionable information. Eventually, participants running the study can obtain results that are important for science and health practice.

> *"We want to give any individual a voice in health sciences and let them influence or actually set the agenda, so they can use evidence-based science to find answers to the questions that matter most to them."*
>
> —Greg Biggers interviewed for digital
> agency Possible in 2013

One study, Butter Mind, intended to analyze the effect of butter consumption on cognitive skills. It was inspired by a university professor who was intrigued by an intuitive perception that eating butter everyday improved his reasoning. Genomera ran a study lasting for 21 days and engaging 45 people who ate a daily dose of either butter, coconut oil, or none of these, and performed also daily math quizzes. Thus far, there were two different studies following up on the results of Butter Mind.

> *"Since the first study we helped orchestrate [on vitamin B metabolism], we have proven two important items. That participant-driven research is credible and productive, and that Internet study operations bring efficiency and scale to the world of health research."*
>
> —Greg Biggers interviewed
> for *Nature* in 2012

Early studies, such as Butter Mind, contributed to developing Genomera's platform by providing data to improve collaboration process, data collection, participant engagement, and results. Despite acknowledging that these earlier studies have worked as a proof of concept, the company has not disclosed details regarding how the platform introduces scalability in health research or how it is a credible alternative to current clinical trial methods.

For Biggers, a novel health research model, that is more participative and democratic, requires that people are able to develop new roles in science making structures. Science projects at Genomera do not follow hierarchical structures. Everyone involved is a collaborator, either as an organizer or as a participant. Participants can take part in data collection as well as in the discussion of results. Moreover, almost everything in participant-driven studies is openly accessible, including design, participants, results, and unidentified data.

This way of doing science is utterly different from the *modus operandi* of public and private research laboratories, bearing more resemblance with garage laboratories and hackerspaces. Daring to propose a radically different model for doing health research is risky for the research process. Genomera needs to address concerns regarding results bias, random assignment, and experiment control, which are brought about by a model in which scientists who formulate research questions and design study protocols are also participants in those studies. These are challenges that Genomera faces when positioning its health research model as an alternative to conventional health research beyond genome-centered studies and opening up space for participant-driven science.

In addition to this, Genomera seeks to take advantage of how people behave socially regarding health issues and to boost that in favor of health discovery. The company's insight is that participant-driven health research can be enhanced by the fact that people in their daily lives gossip and exchange information about how they deal with health issues, and what works for them and what does not. For instance, many people are self-medicated, others advise their acquaintances or their online readers about health and nutrition matters. A more productive and systematic approach to information exchange for health studies was put in place by PatientsLikeMe, a research network for patients with chronic diseases to share experiences and learn from others with the goal of improving well-being in the face of enduring medical treatment. Meanwhile, at PatientsLikeMe, patients generate data about their condition in everyday life settings, which can be used by researchers, organizations, and regulators to improve products and services.

Users of Genomera are not necessarily suffering from a disease; they can be interested merely in how their body reacts to different physiological and environmental conditions. They create individual profiles, upload personal data, including genomic and phenotypic data, follow research protocols, and track data over time. They also comment on their personal experience throughout the studies and discuss various issues related to the condition or effect being researched. By integrating a social networking component, the company provides a space of communication and interaction, which attracts people into becoming members of the community, in addition to a structure for systematic research.

SO WHAT: Cost Compression in Health Research

Research conducted through Genomera is largely facilitated by the plunging marginal costs of DNA sequencing (see Figure 21.1). Nowadays it is cheaper and faster to gather more data on human genomic profiles, largely due to the plummeting costs of human genome sequencing, the culmination of a decade long, large-scale public and private effort to reduce the cost of DNA sequencing which was previously around $1 billion.

Thanks to personal genomic services, the cost of ordering a DNA test and receiving personal genomic data in digital form has decreased dramatically in recent years. For instance, 23andMe offers personal DNA tests for about $99. Despite the radical cost reduction, in clinical trials and health research, the combination of genomic data with health records is scarce, even though it would help understand the incidence of diseases and the effectiveness of therapeutics at the individual level. An individual-oriented medical research would allow physicians

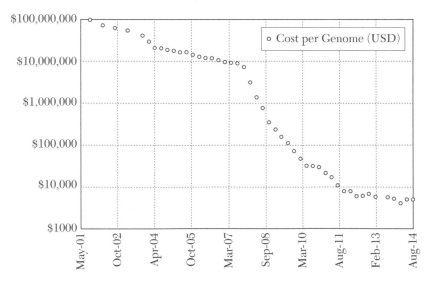

Figure 21.1 Falling DNA sequencing costs[1]

---

[1]Wetterstrand KA. DNA Sequencing Costs: Data from the NHGRI Genome Sequencing Program (GSP). Available at: www.genome.gov/sequencingcosts. Accessed April 16, 2015.

to make personal recommendations and design individual therapeutics instead of prescribing drugs that are effective for the average population but often fail to provide effective results in specific cases.

Researchers affiliated with public and private institutions can launch studies and recruit participants from Genomera's pool of members for academic and commercial studies. A recent study under development, initiated by DIYgenomics and the Center of Cognitive Neurorehabilitation of Geneva University Hospital in Switzerland, examined dopamine genes and rapid reality adaptation in thinking. It is based on ongoing research carried out the University, which aims to determine whether "genetic variants related to dopamine processing in the brain impact the processing of memories according to their relation with ongoing reality—in healthy volunteers." The study involves 85 data participants and 17 discussion participants. The protocol required that participants confirm absence of neurologic disorders, submit personal genetic data, provide background demographic data, and complete memory filtering tasks throughout the study period. Since it will be used by Genomera to learn about collaborating with a university and a hospital, some of the data is also made available to academic research.

By integrating the personal genomic data of participants in its data collection protocols, Genomera designed a research platform that enables clustering the findings according to particular genetic profiles and drawing conclusions that support personalized medicine. This facilitates collaboration with research laboratories and companies, which is advantageous in the recruitment of research participants. Besides having an automated genotype-phenotype recruiting tool, Genomera developed capabilities to mobilize community members around a study, orchestrate protocol tasks, and collect data in digital format in a cost-efficient way.

How Genomera Is Different from Incumbents

Traditional clinical studies are expensive and time-consuming, which results in slow-paced drug development and medical breakthrough. Genomera proposed to break open the bottleneck of clinical trials that constricts the flow of research. In addition, its premise is that it only takes an enough number of people willing to follow a study protocol that can address a problem of their interest. The company is trying to prove that rigorous research can be carried out by a distributed pool of members forming an online community, outside laboratories, yielding useful results.

"In some ways, we want to be to health studies what something like WordPress or Tumblr is to a blog. We're the infrastructure that makes it possible, but the actual work is because the people are doing it."

—Greg Biggers interviewed for digital
agency Possible in 2013

An alternative model of crowdsourced clinical trials is the platform created by Transparency Life Sciences (TLS), launched in 2012, which intends to cut clinical trial costs in half by opening the protocol design process to patients, physicians, researchers, and other stakeholders. The company created a Protocol Builder, which is patient-centered, is comprised of an extensive list of questions targeted at particular drug development programs which focus on drugs for chronic diseases. According to TLS, the goal is to rescue pharma compounds, which were shelved because moving them along the pipeline was too costly, and develop those using ideas from the crowd of patients, patient advocacy groups, physicians associations, and professional groups.

Crowdsourcing methods have called the attention of big pharmaceutical companies that also seek to lower the costs and increase the speed of clinical trials. In 2012, Pfizer terminated a pilot social media recruitment process for a clinical trial of an overactive bladder drug that took place in 10 states in the United States for 1 year. Pfizer's "clinical-trial-in-a-box" expected that participants recruited through social media platforms would carry out the research protocol at home and report results using personal computers and mobile devices.

Eventually, recruitment was deemed very challenging and did not meet the expectations that Pfizer held. The online recruitment carried out in digital patient communities and typical web advertising channels failed to draw a sufficient number of participants. Moreover, the company explained that it was trying to do many different new things at the same time, since the trial included online recruitment, at-home study drug delivery, mobile- and web-based data reporting, online identity verification, and centralized investigator site. The organizers concluded that the recruitment strategy should be improved toward being more tailored to virtual trials and that the support and engagement of trusted healthcare providers could be important.

Contrary to Genomera's research platform, Pfizer's crowdsourced version of clinical trial focused on lowering costs by using online recruitment and allowing participants to perform tasks locally and report remotely. Genomera hosts health studies that are participant-driven, which encompasses a deeper level of engagement from participants, increasing the chances of success.

The company developed an intuitive and friendly system that makes people enthusiastic about what scientist do—formulating questions and looking for answers—and makes them feel comfortable with conducting research on themselves. On the one hand, people armed with their own genetic data are able to carry out simple research protocols, generate data in their real-world setting, and analyze results by comparing them against different genomic profiles. This creates knowledge about each person's responses to physiological and environmental conditions, and to medical substances, enabling the creation of individual therapeutic profiles.

On the other hand, allowing people to organize studies and ask for specialized support to pursue a research question increases the pipeline of new ideas and questions. This could unleash new flows of discovery with a much lower cost compared to research carried out in research laboratories and companies. At this point, Genomera comes closer to a citizen science platform for massive health research. Unlimited study capacity could be generated as people become organizers and investigators in health science studies instead of subjects or participants of trials. Furthermore, a participative model for health research, combined with opportunities emerging from lower technology costs and wider access to testing services, reduces greatly the costs of research.

Genomera claims that, in a participative model, clinical studies will move toward people becoming shareholders of the benefits of research. Yet, the possibility of participants reaping the rewards of research triggers interesting questions concerning the contrast of Genomera's model with the conventional pharma research model. Would participants be co-authors of published scientific outputs? Would they be owners of the intellectual property generated in the research project? The way Genomera evolves in the future may show whether participant-driven health research has the potential for radically redistributing the benefits of research to participant stakeholders, including intellectual property, authorship and patents, and blurring the boundaries between subject and object in research.

Finally, a participant-driven model generates engagement and attracts resources for health problems that are important for a minority of the population with rare diseases or for people in regions of the globe with very little resources. As it is designed, Genomera's research platform may fill the gap of research on therapeutics and health conditions that are not economically attractive to big pharmaceutical companies, or simply are not a priority for organizations with scarce resources.

Challenges

One of the most salient challenges for Genomera is building trust within the group of potential research participants and within the scientific community. Firstly, getting more people involved, as organizers of studies and as participants, is critical in growing a community of "lay scientists" that is one of the most important assets of Genomera's business model. Secondly, the company tries to build legitimacy and credibility among scientists, not only to validate their operations but also to generate business opportunities. In 2012, Biggers reported that the "goal of a prospective, longitudinal study that can yield scientifically valid results has almost been achieved" but no further details were released. In addition, Biggers spoke on behalf of Genomera at the U.S. Presidential Commission for the Study of Bioethical Issues about the company's business model and platform, and how lay people designed and carried out research protocols, but also conducted analyses and collaborated with academics. Ultimately, Genomera aims to generate useful, rigorous clinical studies that may be published in scientific journals.

Outlook

It all started with a group of health hackers wondering how butter increases the brain's ability to focus, and evolved to founder Greg Biggers addressing a U.S. Presidential Commission with a speech on personal genomics and citizen science. Biggers himself acknowledged that, at first at Genomera, they thought the scientific community would think they were insane for being serious about citizen-driven health research, even feel threatened. When Nature Medicine got captivated by their story, Biggers tried to persuade them from not reporting it, as he expected hostility, but when the story came out he came across a rather empathetic reaction from many scientists.

Genomera was trying to make a difference in people's lives and it was just what they had dreamt about when they became scientists. Genomera offers to heal the world by laying out the playground for curious, engaged minds to do health research together, from the mundane to the outstanding kind. It wants to make health research as a no-brainer as finding out how a spoon of butter in the morning can improve our math skills in the afternoon.

Genomera's participatory research model is poised to flourish at the intersection of various mounting trends: citizen science, quantified self, personalized medicine, crowdsourcing in health research, and open innovation in drug development. Its platform for participant-driven health research has pushed down the barriers for doing sophisticated health research by lowering costs and by making it accessible to an increasing number of people.

From the Perspective of Dr. Markus Paukku, a Study Participant

The Genomera website only hinted at what exactly was happening on the social platform. The website modestly stated, "We're crowdsourcing health discovery by helping anyone create group health studies." A quote from a futurist stated that this was the "Facebook of science." The site also had a picture of the CEO of Genomera testifying to the U.S. Presidential Commission on Bioethics. I joined the fray and signed up for the private beta.

Genomera had received some media coverage in Wired, Fast Company and similar outlets heavily slanted to all things technologically novel, start-ups, and Silicon Valley. Genomera is seeking to overcome the bottleneck restricting health science discovery providing consumers demand evidence-based answers, speed and engagement while offering researchers the needed efficiency and scale, as well as cohorts and data. Billed as a platform where anyone can organize scientific trials "working together, sharing data, supporting one another, comparing with one another, achieving insight faster together"—I was curious what exactly this looked like.

The community of trials organizers and participants are engaged in various types of studies investigating everything from the effects of caffeine on sleep to do common variations in the MTHFR gene keep vitamin B-9 from working? The platform offers a wide range of studies—in design, in progress, in analysis, and an archive of instruments utilized in trials.

The high involvement of the participants had been reported in the media but was still surprising. While some studies only required minor changes in diet and behavior, such as eating butter while doing math exercises, many trials on Genomera had a higher threshold for participating. Genomera clearly had a community of dedicated citizen scientists with access to, and interest in sharing, personal medical data. The website made it very easy to upload personal genome raw data from commercial companies such as 23andMe, deCODEme, FTDNA, or Navigenics. At the time of writing the aforementioned vitamin B-9 study had 49 data participants each volunteering their genomic data and committing to blood tests measuring homocysteine levels. I found a relatively less involved study entitled, "Sleep: Magnesium's effect on sleep quality" which only required daily supplements and the monitoring of sleep via survey.

Genomera offered a window into the world of consumers, citizen scientists, amateur geneticists, and those comfortable identifying with personal biological experimentation. The data-driven hacker mentality aimed to rapidly gain results and leverage the social platform to ask new questions, propose new research, and access scientific trials. The falling price of genome sequencing suggests that emerging community will continue to grow potentially renegotiating the traditional divide between the medical community and patient, scientist, and consumer.

As for the results of my magnesium study, I personally did not notice any effect. However, the idea behind the Genomera platform is to build a community that collects and aggregates data from all participants with the aim of teasing out hidden patterns. This data is available to all participating in the study. As for the overall results, at the time of this writing the study was still ongoing, over 2 years after the trial was initiated. While, from this single user's perspective, albeit one without a reference point, the platform had not delivered medical insights "faster" it had created a place where one could ask and seek to answer questions "together."

22

Robin Hood: The Merry Adventures of an Asset Management Cooperative

Once upon a time, researcher Sakari Virkki found that the investment algorithm that he had developed after years of hard work would yield annual rate of return higher (approximately 130 percent) than that of the S&P500.[1] Unlike what most people would have done, he partnered with economist Akseli Virtanen to establish an asset management cooperative. Robin Hood Minor Asset Management Cooperative was thus born in June 2012 in the midst of the European financial crisis. Drawing on the legacy of Robin Hood, the cooperative intended to challenge the conventions and practices of the dominant system. Describing itself as a fund, business, art, bold philosophical and economic experiment Robin Hood aspires to share and democratize the power of finance or as Virtanen says, to "bend the financialization of economy" for the common good. Not only does it allow minor asset investors to benefit from the same systems that cater to Wall Street, it also allows members to direct a percentage of the returns toward philanthropic, artistic, or other fund-sponsored projects.

WOW: Robin Hood and the Parasite Algorithm

The Robin Hood's investment portfolio is guided by the "parasite algorithm," which identifies the most profitable investors and patterns across prominent U.S. stock exchanges such as NYSE, NASDAQ, and

---

[1]The prominent U.S. stock market performance estimate.

AMEX. Virtanen explains that the process is "pretty straightforward." First SEC filing data is collected, combined, organized, adjusted, and corrected. The algorithm calculates the performance of every actor by every instrument resulting in a competence map over the market. The distribution of this competence is used to invest in those stocks where the risk exposure of the most competent actors is very high. The fund follows the swarming behavior and imitates the emerging consensus action of the financial establishment. Thus far the fund has been very successful as the value of the Robin Hood portfolio rose 30.75 percent in the first year. And after the second year now, it is up 40.15 percent. It means that Robin Hood beats almost all of the funds operating on the U.S. stock market in the world.

Robin Hood and the Profit Allocation Structure

The profit allocation structure of Robin Hood is exceptional. When a member buys shares, he has the option to choose (six options) how the net profit should be divided between himself and Robin Hood Fund. When the shares start growing in value, the profits are split between the cooperative and the person, according to different options like 50/50, 80/20, etc. The amount which is remaining after the members partake of the profits is put toward a community pool called Robin Hood Fund. The members can vote and decide how to allocate the money in this pool (e.g, as no-interest loans or grants). Every member receives only one vote, irrespective of the number of shares they own. This makes sure that the decision-making process is collective, democratic, and not unduly influenced by any one person(s). Virtanen compares this to a "social experiment on the cooperation to come."

A board of (maximum) six members, selected according to the rules of Robin Hood, includes Akseli Virtanen (chairman), Tiziana Terranova, Tere Vadén, and Liisa Välikangas. Currently, it has more than 550 members from different walks of life, from more than 15 countries. The shares can be bought by anyone, anytime and are in turn invested in a suitable stock portfolio. The membership fee and the fee of each share are both €30 each. Each member is required to buy at least one, "obligatory" share.

An investor in Robin Hood can always see how much profit his share has generated (for himself and for Robin Hood Projects) and what amount is allocated for the Robin Hood Fund, both via the robinhoodcoop website. The results of investments are also available and are updated every day. The website also gives information about currency fluctuations and their relative effects on the investments.

SO WHAT Makes Robin Hood a Positive Outlier?

In the whole world, approximately 10 big investment banks control 90 percent of the whole derivative market. This is close to $1400 million billion and 20 times the GNP of the entire world—a figure reflecting the leveraging of debt for profit. These profits from these interest-driven financial instruments, however, are out of reach of the average individual who only carries the debts and the associated risks. There is also an asymmetry between people whose income is not tied to the necessity to work and those whose income is. This is where Robin Hood differs from conventional asset management firms.

Unlike conventional financial firms, the focus of Robin Hood is on common men. It speaks to the portion of the population who, even after working persistently, are unable to invest. Robin Hood Cooperative's philosophy is to be able to service these "precarious workers" with a rate of return that matches the world's top investment without the costs. Robin Hood is the very first "cheap bank" of asset management. It has extremely small operating costs when compared to normal asset management firms like ordinary and private banks. After all, Virtanen argues banks typically spend money on 20 to 30 salespeople for every analyst they employ.

Challenges

Many in the financial community do not know what to make of Robin Hood. The financial regulators and civil servants have been neutral on the fund and its activities. The media was initially skeptical but has been reassured having seen the books and formal audits. The financial professionals, however, have been the most suspicious of all. Virtanen suggests "they are unable to think finance in any other terms than those established in their education."

Ironically, the unconventional strategy of Robin Hood, the very element that differentiates it from the traditional firms, may result in

Robin Hood being misconstrued as a fraudulent practice. Potential investors, being asked to allocate some of their profits to the fund may mistake Robin Hood to be a fake, Ponzi scheme. As Robin Hood is not a bank offering financial services, it does not have a Finnish Financial Supervisory Authority (Finanssivalvonta) bank permit, per se. These heavy regulations enable big banks in blocking new entrants such as Robin Hood from entering their field. By breaking the industry norm, what it does is something so new that it could come across as confusing and untrustworthy. Robin Hood sees that the only way to overcome suspiciousness is to keep educating, explaining the paradigm, providing audited information and documents, and doing everything by the book. This may become easier as the 2014 EU Directive on alternative investment fund (AIF), a category that Robin Hood may potentially fall under, aims to substantially simplify reporting duties and capital requirements.

Outlook

Robin Hood Cooperative is an ingenious new initiative for making finance available to a wider public. In addition, through Robin Hood, people think of money not just as a means of payment and exchange, but also as a means of independence and escape from the archaic financial market fiends. Virtanen reflects that Robin Hood is an experiment in creating a new social form. In doing so Robin Hood certainly aims to provoke the system and feels comfortable experimenting on the "wild side of finance."

From the Perspective of Dr. Liisa Välikangas, Board Member, Robin Hood Minor Asset Management (with Comments from Dr. Akseli Virtanen)

Becoming Robin Hood and Its Minor Implications

The origins of Robin Hood date back to 2012 in Finland. Dr. Akseli Virtanen, one of the founders, explains in an interview (Lovink, 2015): "So, minor asset management is a very special way of managing assets—a way that makes something new possible when it looks like nothing new is possible. A becoming. This is our invention. . . ." Such an invention matured during the founder's stay at Aalto University's Future Art

Base from which the organization was expelled due to its radical or perhaps hard-to-imagine approach, called by some a freak in the world of finance, others suspected a pyramid scheme. But rather than an analytical scheme looking for an economic rational, Robin Hood was rather an aesthetic, the future art of finance, or its "wild side."

Minor plays an important part, already in the name of the organization. "But it is also management of the assets of minorities . . . who will and can never become major, but will always remain like spit in the salad. And it is the management of minor assets, small assets, this is our other particularity: a lot of small assets working together. We don't mind the connotation of being underage—not legally responsible, a minor, in a process of still becoming—neither as an attribute to our way of managing assets or to the assets managed, there is something true there."

After being expelled from Future Art Base, Robin Hood had to reimagine itself as a fully autonomous entity. It lost the project funding that Future Art Base provided for some of its founders and some of its affiliates. Robin Hood had staged various artistic exhibitions around the world, including Finland, Germany, and Brazil; now was the time to reimagine the economic side, to radically expand capital under management to survive as an organization. Robin Hood had reimagined itself as a global financier.

Robin Hood expanded to the United States in 2014 together with its founder who moved to University of California, Santa Cruz. The new U.S.-based Benefit Corporation started exploring the possibility of launching its own cryptocurrency for its members to trade. The members could use the "Hoodies" to invest in each other's artistic enterprises. This would also create a secondary market for Robin Hood ownership, which would become more liquid as a result, and giving the members use of an alternative form of capital. (Currently selling one's shares is cumbersome.) The cryptocurrency invites interest from many Silicon Valley investors, and it opens up yet another strategy to "make something possible when it looks like nothing is possible" by refining the arenas for action. The "Hoodies" (the preliminary name) are likely backed by the Robin Hood investment portfolio, to begin with, and they allow for entirely new way of transacting using an emergent technology called the Blockchain. Such synthetic finance is the next Robin Hood frontier.

Amplification of impact is baked in to the concept of Robin Hood: " . . . it is always something collectively produced. It changes power relations by changing the conditions of situation. It allows for 'a people to come' by opening new routes and processes of becoming." Robin Hood has gained new members—the member base exceeding

500 at the time of this writing—and appears to be riding a trend that suggests further amplification. "[W]hat is really important is the approach behind it, i.e., the understanding of the changed nature of creation of value. That is why we are now capable of coming up with new products too." Its political dimension has potential transformative consequences. "[It] is an attempt to think about political means, means of change. . . . [The concept of] minor is something that always brings together personal and political. It is . . . about making our existential territories more habitable."

Whether Robin Hood becomes something more than a fading footnote in the collective story of the precariat, capitalism, and democracy, remains to be seen. Yet it has implications to understanding how imagination, or learning from things that have not happened yet, can be used to creating novel strategy. Robin Hood is a play in the future, and as a play, it requires the engagement of its audience, or its members, for making it real. To assess it with rational financial logic is to undervalue its true meaning and potential strategic impact: It is an aesthetic (Strati, 1992) rather than a calculation, and a minor (Deleuze and Guattari, 1975) rather than a major enticement to novel thinking and to the creation of new opportunities, even when they are precarious.

23

Bang & Olufsen: Modulating Strategic Renewal Through Innovation and Organizational Design

by Giacomo Cattaneo, Lars Frederiksen, and Andrea Carugati

The history of Bang & Olufsen (B&O) started in Struer, a small village in the North of Denmark. In 1925 the two young engineers, Peter Bang and Svend Olufsen, pursued the dream of developing the perfect radio. Struggling in the first years to make a real profit, they did not falter in their determination—not even when saboteurs burnt down one of their early factories during World War II as they refused to collaborate with the Nazis. The persistence of the two young and undeterred engineers eventually paid off, and they built a company that evolved into an enterprise unanimously accepted as one of the hallmarks of Danish quality. B&O's uncompromising attention to quality and design earned the company worldwide recognition and a spot in the permanent collection of New York's Museum of Modern Art in 1972.

If success is hard to achieve, it is even harder to maintain; B&O faced several challenges on many fronts over decades, first from the low-price and high-volume Japanese products in the '70s, then by the economic downturn and loss of direction in the '80s, which brought the company to the brink of collapse.[1] However, at the beginning of the '90s, B&O's brand and profits began to shine again under the leadership of CEO Anders Knutsen and his vision "The best of

---

[1]For more details on the '70s, '80s, and '90s, see also Ravasi and Schultz (2006). For an encompassing history of B&O since the early days, see Bang (2005).

both worlds: Bang & Olufsen, the unique combination of technological excellence and emotional appeal." The re-establishment of B&O's great design and technological innovation was championed new icons like the Beosound 9000, a music system that rapidly became one of the company's most recognized products.[2] The section below describes the recent history of B&O, together with the challenges and strategic choices that accompanied it.

Strategies

WOW: How to Continually Renew for Success in a Fast-Moving Industry?

For organizations like B&O, continuous strategic renewal is a key capability, in which the link between environmental change and corporate strategy is continuously modified over time. Closing the gap between the current core capabilities and the evolving base of competitive advantage, however, is a challenging process that clashes against the core norms and institutionalized practices of any organization. Renewal is only achieved through promoting, accommodating, and utilizing new knowledge and innovative behavior to refresh or replace the company's tangible and intangible resources, to substantially affect its long-term prospects. A look into the history of B&O illustrates how they took up this challenge.

The Enduring History of B&O

The most recent chapter of B&O started in the early 2000 and challenged the now 90-year old company like never before. The rise of digital technology as the new paradigm affected all of B&O's product lines. The market was stormed by companies like Apple or Google that still today are both competitors and partners and present throughout all levels of the value chain. Furthermore, the generational shift of B&O's target customers from the "Baby boomers" to "Generation X" implied a completely new way of listening to music.

To meet up with the changing market, in 2001 new CEO Torben Ballegaard enhanced the product development process, leading to an

---

[2]For more details on the end of the '90's and the first years of 2000s, see Austin and Beyersdorfer (2007).

increased production output and a reinforced position of recognized design *and* technological excellence. The production of Beolab 5 in 2003, employing the "acoustical lens technology," achieved a new standard in technological excellence and triggered a partnership with Audi, which paved the road for the introduction of their new car stereo system. The brand kept on increasing its value, reaching a total turnover of DKK 4.38 billion in the financial year 2006 to 2007, and a peak in its operating profits of DKK 530 million.

However, the tide was about to turn. Following the outbreak of the financial crisis in 2008, the sales of luxury goods in the European market, 83 percent of B&O's total turnover, were hit drastically. CEO Ballegaard was dismissed after a sharp 30 percent decline in turnover, and a 350 percent decline in profit[3] in the financial year 2008–2009. Unprofitable explorative projects like the Serene mobile phone or ill-timed high-end products like the 103-inch plasma TV were indications of a troubled product pipeline. The underlying vulnerability was embodied by slow new product development process and problematic strategic direction, which largely failed to keep up with the convergence of digital technologies. B&O's successful competences—crafting sculptural hardware while finely developing each product's core from scratch—became a source of inertia and rigidity in developing the necessary capabilities for the new paradigm and in expanding the strategic horizon to effectively include and exploit them.

In 2008, new CEO Karl "Kalle" Hvidt Nielsen improved the speed of product development by radically changing the technology strategy and developing technology platforms. This ensured shared development across products, thus decreasing complexities and development time.[4] In 2009 Beosound 5, a music system that aims at creating one's own digital library, was released as the first consistent attempt at digital technology—considerably later than the introduction of iPod and iTunes by Apple in 2001. Yet, despite stabilizing the company the company did not achieve growth under his guidance.

In 2011, the new CEO Tue Mantoni stepped in to shift the overly product-centric B&O toward becoming an international lifestyle brand, a move structured into a 6-year long strategy called *Leaner, Faster, Stronger*. Its key drivers have been a stronger customer-focused orientation and a clear re-focus on the core capabilities that

---

[3]Data from B&O annual reports.
[4]Wheelwright and Clark (1992).

have made the B&O brand strong: sound, design, and craftsmanship. "B&O Play," the new product line for attracting younger customers was a first step in this direction, together with an increased focus on the profitable automotive business, the consolidation of the retail network by trimming off the least profitable shops, and an increased presence of B&O in BRIC countries.

As of the beginning of 2015, the new areas of business—Automotive and B&O Play—are growing strong and providing positive brand exposure through continuous awards of excellence. Sales per store increased, achieving overall profitability, supported by a complete product portfolio turnaround. The new generation of B&O's products is championed by the wireless speaker series like Beolab 18 and the 4K TV Avant, followed by Beosound Moment, launched in January 2015. Despite the new launches however, the core product categories—Audio and Video—are still lacking the expected growth that was forecasted in the strategy.

How Is B&O a Positive Outlier?

A Look from Within

As Marie Schmidt (Vice president, Brand, Design & Marketing) noted, "If there is a place around the world where everyone is often convinced this product is his or her chance to create a masterpiece, that place has got to be B&O. Everybody knows about it, and everyone is proud about it."[5] The core essence of B&O can be defined as a delicate balance between meaning-driven[6] (i.e., design and user experience) and technology-driven innovation, which needs to be synergistically integrated. Still, *how* B&O creates its products has changed over time. It has largely been affected by, and has itself affected the strategic direction of the company, as is summarized in Figure 23.1. Each phase is championed by a different CEO, and is characterized by the modification of the existing organizational design and the unit in charge of the innovation process.

In the so-called "IdeaLAND," B&O's concept developers linked a pool of highly skilled engineers to some of the world's best designers,

---

[5]Interview on December 9, 2014.

[6]For meaning-driven innovation, see Norman and Verganti (2013); Verganti (2006).

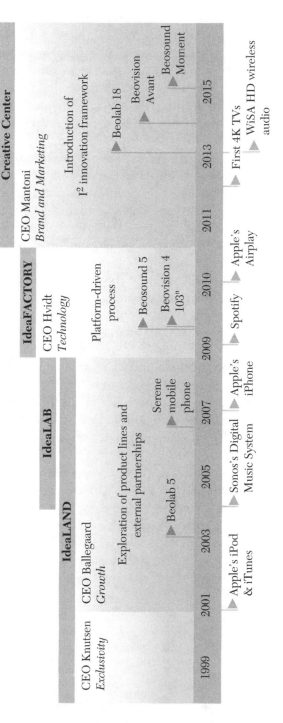

Figure 23.1 Innovation evolution at B&O

who are still today employed from outside the company so that they are not restrained by its dynamics and limitations. By relying on their understanding of the world, B&O delivered iconic products that would have been difficult to develop being bound to a standard technology-push approach. Designers were given total freedom of maneuvering when creating concepts and limited technological constraint, leading engineers to be constantly challenged by their often unique and extravagant ideas. In a predictable and fairly stable market, such approach allowed B&O to create a recipe for success—however, since the advent of the digital technology and players like Apple, Sonos, and Spotify, B&O has been challenged by a faster developing, more complex, and more design-conscious technology paradigm. In 2004, "IdeaLAB" was created to explore opportunities provided by the new landscape. The new unit was kept separate to avoid its immature projects being overruled. At the same time, they were put in situations of explicit conflict to emphasize B&O's distinct process of continuous clashes between conflicting ideas by designers and engineers to reach an optimal synthesis.[7] However, this worked only partially—on one hand, IdeaLAB took longer than expected to produce tangible results and thus justify its existence, on the other the product development process was clearly still dominated by the figures heading IdeaLAND. This led to a tendency to allocate more resources to IdeaLAND projects than to combined ideas and resulted in a series of either frozen or aborted projects. To tackle the problem, in 2008 CEO Hvidt Nielsen merged IdeaLAND with IdeaLAB to create the new "Idea Factory." Initially reporting directly to the CEO, over the years the leadership of Idea Factory passed through a few top executives and a few restructuring processes before becoming the "Creative Centre,"[8] reporting directly to the CEO again today.

In 2014, the "Technology Centre" underwent restructuring as well. Tensions in the product development domain, which accompanied the partial relocation of production from Struer to the Czech Republic in 2006, and the subsequent undesired delays and quality

---

[7]Austin and Beyersdorfer (2007) present this concept revamping the classic philosophical idea that a clash between competing ideas can lead to a superior idea as their synthesis.

[8]In February 2014, the Creative Centre (at the time brand, design, and concepting) absorbed the department of marketing to ensure a continuity in the value chain and was rebranded in today's "Brand, Design, and Marketing."

issues,[9] required a new COO—Stefan Persson—to take over and integrate R&D, Product Management, and Operations under his guidance.

With regard to the process of new product development, it was left to an informal sequence of interactions between designers, concept developers, and engineers until 2012. This process, while never formalized, became institutionalized, a norm the organization would fight to preserve. Realizing that such a process design left too many uncertainties and inefficiencies unsolved, the new top management launched a new framework to professionalize the process from idea creation to implementation, scrapping old ways. Despite some resistance, the unanimous recognition of the need for a faster and more efficient development process brought most of the people to formally align. The new innovation process, called "I^2," consisted of two blocks: one for the development of ideas and opportunities, and the other for execution and production.[10] In 2014, an increased focus on ideation was signaled with two new processes: the first one connecting the most innovative people in the company through a series of workshops, to develop a set of creative ideas to be evaluated by top management. This led to the definition of many new opportunities, some of which are already positioned on the roadmap for development. The second process involved an internal idea management system supporting the opportunity process with an ongoing source of creativity—a larger base of skilled B&O employees—both in terms of product and process innovation. Besides the process of pure ideation, concepts at B&O are also created through the management of roadmaps, which could lead to either the improvement of an old product or the filling of a void in terms of features or revenues. However, the front-end of the new opportunity phase and the back-end of the execution phase are often felt to be distant from each other, leaving a gap of uncertainty for the implementation of the more explorative ideas. To fill such a gap, elements of new ideas are sometimes trimmed to land onto safer concepts, similar to how exploitation is often favored over exploration for its better-articulated propositions.[11] Two activities increasingly

---

[9]Press release No. 14.23, 22.12.2014.

[10]Despite its focus on execution, the second block also includes a framing track for projects benefitting a larger product base, as well as an exploration track for concepts needing additional resources to be investigated.

[11]Crossan and Berdrow (2003).

support the innovation process by ensuring an assessment of feasibility and consistency of B&O's competences. The first one advances members' interaction from the "tough triangle" (creative, technology and business centers) to an earlier point in the conceptualization phase. The second involves a newly developed "maturity matrix" to assess each concept element of proposed briefs.

What Next?

With regard to product development, the concept of success is still open for discussion. Projects of incremental nature, like the new wireless speaker series, are articulated by firm employees as the result of a successful process, respecting time and budget plans. On the other hand, projects involving unbalanced concepts and inefficient processes, like Beosound Moment, are praised for being radically innovative when hitting the market. For which product should B&O strive, and which process should support it? The current stage-gate system of I^2 has worked fine for incremental innovation, but has proven inadequate for more radical projects. Radical innovation, despite its potential, requires more process flexibility, and should be measured differently than based on straight execution. Balancing the concept development in terms of early participation of the "tough triangle's" members, as mentioned earlier, is increasingly being considered a potential solution that would not require the redefinition of the whole framework.[12] Without renouncing the characteristic "initial spark of genius" from concept developers,[13] a more comprehensive technology-market linkage process before entering the execution phase could anticipate and find solutions to uncertainties that today are discovered too late in the process. This could more effectively lead to a successful product development. Moreover, doing so would serve the purpose of consistently integrating the opportunities provided by in-house research and pioneering technologies like the current sound zones systems early in the process.[14]

---

[12]Also suggested by Dougherty (1992).

[13]Perhaps this is the spark from outliers the authors are referring to here.

[14]See Baykaner et al. (2015); Francombe, Mason, Dewhirst, and Bech (2015).

SO WHAT: Comparison with Other Companies (Incumbents and Adjacents)

When compared to the incumbent companies in the field (and many adjacents), what makes B&O stand out is its resilience and willingness to continuously challenge itself through a process of strategic renewal. There are three main lessons B&O can teach: the first involves strategic renewal and organizational design, in which the company adopts a new explicit strategy to be embraced by a newly established innovation unit. Today's fast pace of industry developments emphasizes the act of balancing the exploitation of current business on one hand, and the creation of a competence base supporting exploration of new opportunities on the other. This cross-pressure is often embodied in such a new innovation unit, and can serve as a signal for change, especially for companies with mind-sets and culture strongly anchored in their previous successes. Failing to move on by resisting the renewal of the strategic direction, independent of its outcomes, is likely to result in a situation of complacency, which has led too many companies to fail.[15]

Secondly, B&O illustrates how organizational design affects the shifts in power and relationships among different groups involved in the innovation process, in this case, design and technology. Creative tension can be achieved across groups by acknowledging the other side's expertise in a dynamic friendly fighting, or by overlapping knowledge domains with boundary spanning activities. The overpowering of one side (or individual) over the other might lead to a strong reliance on the former's ability to synthesize them, leading to iconic products in lucky cases and to risky and unbalanced concepts in others.

The third lesson is to take strategy renewal to the innovation process, namely the process of translating a new vision into market-technology opportunities and subsequently crafting the resulting concepts into products. Despite the use of comprehensive frameworks defining roles and stages, the struggles in linking the various bits of the process and concretizing abstract visions into feasible projects make bridging activities by the individuals connected to the innovation process extremely valuable.

---

[15] See, e.g., the case of Polaroid by Tripsas (2013).

Challenges

As seen in the previous sections, B&O has faced several challenges over its 90-year history in the form of sabotage, competition, economic crisis, volatile market, quality issues, and many more. During these stages, B&O learned that many of these external contingencies could and should be overcome by adopting an encompassing process of strategic renewal, i.e., hitting the core product development process from the angles of strategy, organizational design, and innovation. Such processes however, often led to internal tensions related to the orchestrating and harmonizing strategy, organization design, and innovation processes, and to separate attempts to propose changes (design), to resist them (inertia), and, if any, to support them (entropy).[16] Now, the critical challenge for B&O is to clearly frame the future direction of the company and move on from the past paradigms, both in terms of business model and operations. Moreover, while the balance of the creative and technology centers can be considered as the golden rule to B&O's success, it is also the major source of inertia, together with tensions across managerial levels that often turn persistence into resistance from all sides.

The current competitive landscape of B&O puts an even stronger pressure for B&O to become *Leaner, Faster, and Stronger*. Bose and Harman are tough competitors in terms of sound quality and product selection, while Sonos is pushing B&O to include a comparable system of multi-channel and multi-room speakers in its portfolio. The hurdle for B&O is, with comparable resources, to compete on similar technical features and assortment while at the same time ensuring the integration of TVs and products from the Play line into the B&O system.

Such external and internal obstacles have seen the company struggling to deliver the expected growth. In June 2014, B&O issued additional shares worth 10 percent of the existing shared capital, aimed at raising resources for improving and strengthening sales and distribution channels, as well as maintaining the current level of investment in the continuous renewal of the product portfolio.[17] Additionally, the second quarter of the financial year 2014–2015 saw B&O's shares fall to the lowest level since 2009. In response to this

---

[16]Oliver (1992).

[17]B&O Press release No. 14.02, 19.06.2014, Harman Press release 31.03.2015.

challenge, Chairman Ole Andersen has announced that B&O would consider bid approaches by larger incumbents and adjacents, while CEO Mantoni announced the acquisition of B&O's automotive division by Harman.[18]

Outlook

B&O illustrates how the renewal of an organization needs to be considered through the relentless engagement of the triangle of strategy, organizational design, and innovation process. The current developments of market and technology make a continuous adaptation of the company's capabilities necessary, yet increasingly complex. Companies' strategies need to find their unique answer to the question of exploration and exploitation, and infuse clear direction even in daily activities. At the same time, companies should recognize that these activities could already embody partial answers to such questions, and hence should be embraced as part of the company's future direction. Moving forward, like B&O is trying to do, is the only option. The open question is: Will the company be fast enough to generate the potential growth and re-establish themselves with a new wave of customers?

From the Perspective of Nicolai J. Foss, Professor of Strategy and Organization, Copenhagen Business School

Changing the Business Model of Bang & Olufsen

Cattaneo, Frederiksen, and Carugati (2015) provide a nice account of the strategic challenges of a company that while small in comparison to its huge competitors in the consumer electronics markets stands out on account of a long history of design-driven innovation that spans at least most of the nine decades of existence of the company. They make the reasonable point that choices related to overall strategic direction, innovation, and organizational design are strongly intertwined (or, "complementary"), which surely is a general

---

[18]Thomson Reuters, "Denmark's Bang & Olufsen would listen to bid approaches." http://www.reuters.com/article/2015/01/05/bang-olufsen-ma-idUSL6N0UK21X201 50105 (accessed online January 15, 2015).

proposition, but applies with perhaps particular force to B&O. The reason is that B&O is forced to find a new business model for its traditional video and audio products because of the increasingly strong competition from Internet-based services, and the likely decline of the traditional TV set.

Cattaneo et al. also seek to foster a discussion "about the existing models of strategic renewal," based on how these fit with the case description. Specifically, they point to the importance of the organization of the innovation process in a company such as B&O that is entirely based on design-driven innovation, i.e., the notion that design is not about adding aesthetics to a product but at the very core of the product development process. This is an interesting point because discussion of internal organization tends to be sidelined in discussions of business model change (Foss and Saebi, 2015).

Bang & Olufsen: Icarus in Jutland?

Cattaneo et al.'s account is mainly focused on the B&O of the last decade. B&O suffered a major setback under the financial crisis of 2008–2009 (e.g., revenues dropped by 30+ percent), from which it has not yet recovered. Indeed, many commentators have argued, and Cattaneo et al. echo this, that B&O was, and still is, in the danger of falling victim to what Miller (1990) called the "Icarus Paradox," i.e., the situation where a company fails massively and rather suddenly, after a long period of success—*and* the failure is brought about by the self-same reasons that drove success. The underlying drivers of the paradox are self-sufficiency, overconfidence, and complacency, an illusion of being (wholly) in control (e.g., neglecting technological change and competitor action), anchoring on too optimistic assumptions (about costs, sales, etc.) or misrepresenting these (to get projects accepted internally), and excessive specialization that introduce cognitive blinders that reduce flexibility.

Many such factors can be discerned in Cattaneo et al.'s account. For example, we learn of a "problematic strategic direction" which fails to keep up with digital developments in audio and video technologies and excessive focus on B&O's core competence, the crafting of "sculptural hardware" in the context of a rock-bottom product development approach that emphasizes developing everything from scratch rather than relying on economies of scope across products and systems (p. 3). We similarly learn of overly targeting small, stagnant, and highly exclusive customer segments, and neglecting the markets that lie closer to consumer goods mass markets. In the light of such challenges, the new strategy (Bang & Olufsen, 2011) with its emphasis on lower-end markets, speedier and somewhat more formalized product development and improved customer focus, would seem to make much sense.

The Innovation Process in a Small Company

Of course, retrospective accounts easily falls prey to confirmation biases (e.g., Rosenzweig, 2007), i.e., the information looked for, presented, and discussed is driven by one hypothesis alone, to the neglect of rival hypotheses. Basic rival hypotheses are the financial crisis, changing consumer preferences (not everyone would agree that all B&O products are top-notch in the aesthetics/design dimension), difficulties of controlling internal costs and/or the distributor network, and internal conflicts and tensions (e.g., see Krause-Jensen's [2010] account of the rise and fall of value-based management in B&O). Here is a brief attempt at a very simple alternative account of the troubles of B&O in recent years that centers on diseconomies in the innovation process.

Fundamentally, B&O is a tiny player in most of its markets, in particular, B2C markets, like consumer electronics, high-end consumer electronics, high-end audio systems, home luxury products, e.g., high-end furniture, etc. The exception is its position in the B2B market, where it was the dominant producer of exclusive sound systems for high-end cars (until the automotive division was divested in March 2015). In any case, the brand name value of B&O is arguably out of proportion compared to the size of the company (e.g., in terms of employees or sales; 2013 revenues of around 500 million USD is not a lot). Although a significant fraction of B&O employees are rather directly involved in the innovation process, the relatively small size of B&O places inherent limits on the number of trials in terms of new ideas, development efforts, and product launches that the company can perform.

To be sure, small size is not just a handicap from the point of view of innovation. In particular, it is easier to incentivize and motivate key innovation people in a small company and smallness also facilitates knowledge sharing and trust. Smallness may also mean close physical proximity between product development and production (as is the case in B&O). However, smallness may also impede innovation. One reason is that if the innovation process is mainly internal, access to external weak ties that can bring new insights and ideas is hampered, and the innovation process involves a relatively small number of internal ties. In fact, B&O has tried to handle this problem in a number of ways. Most importantly, many design services have been externally sourced. Thus, some of the fundamental design-breakthroughs have been supplied external designers, such as Jacob Jensen and David Lewis. Also, when B&O began to explore flat-screen TV technology, they did so by, among other things, arranging an ideas competition among nine designers from different parts of the world.

The deeper problem is arguably the small size of the company in combination with a rather sluggish product development process. In non-perfect capital markets, small size means fewer funds for explorative efforts. Companies seek to engage in innovation for a variety of reasons, but one has to do with the creation of real options that can produce flexibility when consumer/customer preferences and technologies change, often in ways that are far from predictable. However, creating such real options is costly, and small size therefore translates into creating few real options. Moreover, it seems likely that there are economies of scale in the process of creating real options, as larger firms typically control more technologies, and therefore can produce more combinations and recombinations of these technologies.

As a small, specialized company B&O is clearly disadvantaged in these respects. Moreover, B&O may be additionally disadvantaged because of what is often seen as a product development process that is both extremely ambitious and quite sluggish—and therefore costly. A number of B&O products (e.g., Beosound 9000) were initially "unmanufacturable" and took many years from concept to actual production. Betting on relatively few, very ambitious concepts that may take several years to commercialize is a risky strategy indeed in a market that moves fast and unpredictably, including those markets where B&O is present. Sometimes you win, sometimes you lose, and with only few bets, losses can have a heavy impact.

The current B&O Strategy (Bang & Olufsen, 2011) may be interpreted as trying to grapple with the issue of an innovation process that is not only ambitious, costly, and sluggish, but also forms a very large part of the cost base of the company. Thus, the ambition is to double, perhaps even triple, the current revenues within a few years to spread cost of innovation across more units. The means to do this is investing more in the core business, targeting new segments with higher potential sales (as represented in the B&O Play business unit), and strengthening sales channels (idem.). Part of the cost of these

investments comes from the recent divestment of the highly successful B&O automotive business unit.

Coda

It is surely safest to pass judgment on the soundness of corporate strategy in a retrospective mode. However, the danger here is
that one falls victim to the confirmation bias and present facts in a
way that lend credence to only one interpretation. The claim here
is not that this is what Cattaneo et al. are doing. Rather, the claim is
that their case description and general information about B&O lend
support to another interpretation, namely that B&O has faced difficulties because the small size of the company and the peculiar characteristics of its innovation process mean that it engages in "too little"
exploration in the context of fast-moving markets and technologies
and because its ambitious innovation process has also been associated
with high costs.

Seen in this perspective, the emphasis of the current management
on providing more structure around the B&O product development
process, engaging the company more in external collaboration (Bang
& Olufsen, 2011), and spreading costs of innovation across more units
as volume is increased through more efficient sales channels make
much sense. The potential danger is providing too much structure
around the process, stifling development efforts.

24

Outlook for the Strategist

Toward Strategic Resilience: Learning from Strategic Novelty (or What Is About to Leap at You)

"Everybody always wants to know what's next. I always say that what I can imagine is rather dull. What I can't imagine is what excites me."

—Arthur Schawlow, Stanford physicist and Nobel Laureate[1]

Strategists beware. In 2 years, this book and the world will look different. Some of the outliers here may have fallen by the wayside. Some might turn into incumbents (i.e., the major firms in their industry or form entirely new sectors). Take this book as a guide by which to sample strategic novelty—novelty that will keep on reinventing itself whilst causing disruption. As we've shown over in the preceding pages, the most successful outliers revitalize our world not only by experimenting with strategic novelty but also by amplifying its effects. Thus, the kinds of disruptions that are most powerful are the ones we do not expect. Not only do they surprise us, they take us by force. They leap on us.

---

[1]A History of the OTL. Stanford University. http://otl.stanford.edu/about/about_history.html.

Where does such a force come from? One of the researchers involved in this project, Lakshmi Nair, described the companies as follows.

> "I think these are companies with a permeable flow of information and resources between themselves and the customers. They are creative in uncovering unmet customer needs and are open to feedback from the users/customers. They continuously revise their ideas in response to such feedback. They envision growing beyond their current base, into something bigger and more impactful in the market."

Another researcher, Inês Peixoto, described her learnings as follows:

> "These companies are not afraid of making themselves vulnerable: like launching in alpha stage and iterating on the fly, as MakieLab did, putting the novelty out there and see what people make of it. It can seem a little foolish to by-the-book advice. Yet, I find it interesting beyond the "fail early" or "fail fast" mantras. While exposing vulnerability bears risks in two extremes: from being ridiculed to being imitated very easily by more powerful incumbents, it can be used to reduce the risk of growing/evolving the business, by learning. These companies don't ask for permission either. Beyond boldness, I relate this to harnessing resources—e.g., digital platforms for social interaction, either pre-existing or custom-made—in order to create value. As discussed in the Introduction, the Internet makes this possible."

Emergent Outlier-Incumbent Arenas

Which areas (even 2 years from now) do we think will be most affected by the dynamics we illustrated in this book? Let's look at the arena of outlier-incumbent interaction to situate the forces we outlined industry-wise. Our case studies point to three arenas in which outliers' and incumbents' knowledge processes, organizational structures, technology, business models, etc., interact with significant potential for transformative impact that can cascade beyond any single industry. These arenas are *open manufacturing, participant architectures,* and *inclusive financing*.

Innovation in manufacturing currently encompasses the digitization of manufacturing and technologies such as 3D printing, an increasingly inexpensive technology enabling small-scale, localized production activity. Open manufacturing is thus a term that indicates the transformation ongoing in production and logistics activities that take many of these activities out of a dedicated factory and cause them to eventually become much more distributed and diffused, under no central planning or decision authority. Thus, these new open manufacturing models bring in new participants, from individuals to organizations. In the process it also changes the production and creation of knowledge as well as the processes by which it is transferred. This is an arena ripe for incumbent-outlier collaboration.

Architecting such participant contribution is a theme that cuts across all emergent outliers yet deserves to be distinguished in its own right. From companies such as Kaggle where data scientists compete to solve difficult tasks, to BioCurious where laboratory members work with biotech, to Genomera where anyone can seek to improve their physical well-being by collaborating online; participating in organizational activity is radically changing. The participants—amateurs—are sometimes people with (occasionally double) PhD degrees or impassioned autodidacts both with fantastic community connections in part due to their shared activities. They build new ways of working which are better suited for people who have a passion for doing something, irrespective of the pay. Such an amateur, or a "lover of" something, influences management professionals by insinuating the need to develop new attitudes toward organizing. It may not be fruitful to think about how to capture value and tie the resources to the organizations contractually, but rather about how to make the organization—the architecture of contribution—as attractive as possible and thus no longer requiring conventional ties. The resulting participant contributions may be fleeting, yet important. Kaggle organizes competitions through which the best scientists are recognized. BioCurious maintains a laboratory that members can use for doing whatever they are interested in. Strategically this means that emergent technologies are less noteworthy for what they enable in terms of new content of offering, but more so for how they make the offering possible, and how the people producing the new possibilities participate in their making and consumption. It is the organization of technology that enables people that matters. Resources are becoming increasingly mutable. Managers of incumbent companies need new organizing tools and managerial attitudes[2] to collaborate with these outliers.

A third arena in which outlier knowledge models appear to be having industry-crossing repercussions is the theme of inclusiveness, particularly in financing. New models are extending financing to wider numbers of participants and organizations and, in doing so, are "democratizing finance" and shifting the channels for entrepreneurial competence flows, for example. This change will benefit from inclusive finance in the sense that capital, not just financial but also sweat equity and knowledge, will become much more available, transferable, and be governed by different rules and conditions compared to the previously dominant funding logics. Such shifts will not only result in a relative change of power positions in different industries (lessening the role of traditional banks, for instance) and societal arenas (with many new non-profits becoming players) but also alter underlying knowledge flows. Many established financial veteran companies are already vested in the opportunity frontiers that outlier finance firms are opening up in, for example, crowdfunding. Other firms will also benefit in broader funding for innovation, most importantly in expanding the range of innovation that attracts funding. Grow VC Group is an example of a firm funding innovation beyond the relatively few start-ups of interest to venture capitalists. Such new funding models are radically enlarging opportunities for financing innovation across the world beyond the small fraction that venture capitalists are interested in.

Strategic Resilience, or Learning from Things That Have Not Yet Happened

This book has important leadership implications in leveraging novelty. We call for strategic resilience. Being able to anticipate and adapt to change before a crisis forces a company into a painful reckoning is the hallmark of strategic resilience (Hamel and Välikangas, 2003; Välikangas, 2010). Such proactivity requires that a company and its leadership are able to learn from things that have not yet happened,

---

[2]G. Sevon and Liisa Välikangas: Strategies of Detachment—Of Mutable Resources and Late Modernity, Paper presented at EGOS Colloquium, July 5–7, 2012, Helsinki, Finland.

in other words, from the peeks behind the curtain of the future that is embodied by outliers. These opportunity horizons that outliers point to may take a year or 10 to materialize but eventually many of these ideas will, through some outlet, become the mainstream. By then, those strategically resilient have made full use of the potential while the rest of the incumbents are still trying to make sense of the disruption at hand (see Figure 24.1).

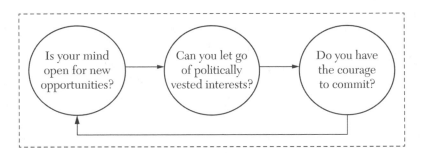

Figure 24.1 Key leadership issues in strategic resilience

Strategic resilience is the ability to undergo such ongoing change without having to resort to the production of great urgency—how many times a year can you evoke a "burning platform" or a must-win battle—or call for a crisis before people will burn out? A true crisis will bring its own change, and hence leaders who resort to such crisis tactics have abandoned leadership to the force of inevitability. Crises are also, by definition, not very manageable and may result in outcomes that may not be strategically desirable. Creative destruction then makes outliers into incumbents, until the next crisis arises.

The first key to strategic resilience is the ability to have the cognitive flexibility to constantly assess the strategic novelty horizon such as described here and accept the challenge and uncertainty it proposes. The acceptance may mean incrementally experimenting with the implications of the new and adopt new ways of business while there is still time to learn from the outliers. Most importantly, such acceptance calls for the abandonment of unnecessary nostalgia for the tired past while mustering the courage to take up the new. The company mission may remain but the form by which the mission is implemented and executed that must be renewed.

The second key to strategic resilience is political. The pursuit of novelty requires the vesting of power from those that for reasons of self-preservation may resist renewal. It is very important to distinguish between resistance to novelty that is caused by a lack of courage to move on and the kind of resistance that may be justifiable—it may indeed be too early to make the big leap. A good test is this willingness to de-risk the effort and embark on related discovery and experimentation. An upfront dismissal often indicates that a person's own interests are put ahead of those of the organization's. Occasionally such resistance may simply be a matter of not caring or laziness—it is easy to keep doing what has been done in the past. Then it is even more important to infuse the organization with positive energy and commitment to the future.

The third key to strategic resilience is moving beyond the experimentation phase that does not yet require commitment to a transformation. If such a commitment continues to be postponed due to "not enough" evidence or information, or the opportunity horizon is always too far out to make the leap, these are signs of a lack of strategic resilience. The inevitable crisis will then eventually force the situation. To maintain strategic resilience capability, the organization ought to rehearse changing regularly, change even when it is not absolutely necessary, just to stay in shape. Organizations are a lot like people that inhabit them in that if the change is not exercised, the capability is lost. The change muscles decay and lose their mass. Strategic resilience means that change by crisis will never be necessary. However, if this capability has never been created, rehearsed, nor tested, as one executive puts it: "When the tiger is on your tail, it is too late to learn to run." By then those who are strategically resilient have already spurted away, having long since leveraged the lessons from "things that have not yet happened."

Reference Summary on Outliers

Outlier Case	What's Novel: Wow!	Why Potentially Strategic: So What?	How to Amplify Impact: Oomph!!!
Fondia	New type of firm that brings transparency to pricing legal services. Fondia lowers costs and adds predictability to legal services. All employees, not just partners, are shareholders challenging the dominant industry's partnership model.	The new business model unbundles professional services by standardizing, routinizing, and repricing legal services. A new kind of partnership with a client with access to broad base of expertise. The VirtualLawyer empowers start-up clients to use specialized legal services at a lower cost.	The unbundled business model can be scaled across other types of professional service firms driving down costs. The shareholder model has the potential to restructure companies and career paths across professional service industries such as consulting. Innovative use of digital technology in services to expand capacity.

Outlier Case	What's Novel: Wow!	Why Potentially Strategic: So What?	How to Amplify Impact: Oomph!!!
Quirky	Quirky brings together, manufacturing know-how, partnerships with major corporations, and, yes, over 1 million collaborators/ co-innovators. Quirky considers thousands of product ideas, and is able to launch three new consumer products, per week. A pioneer in collective innovation.	The open business model is able to efficiently leverage the ideas of 1 million co-innovators in a community-grounded product development process.	Through its product development process Quirky launches products to a community of already interested, involved consumers. The company has teamed up with major established companies (e.g., GE, Mattel) looking to better leverage creativity.
Grow VC Group	Grow VC Group is redefining who can be a global investor. By experimenting with peer-to-peer and crowdfunding platforms the group's companies are building new markets expanding the demand and supply of investment opportunities.	Grow VC Group's companies are exposed to many opportunities and sources of intelligence throughout their ecosystems giving them a competitive advantage relative to closed-model incumbents such as investment banks.	Creating new markets through technology and new business models financially connects increasing numbers of people and opportunities globally and democratizes access to finance. Partnering with established players for new business models.

Outlier Case	What's Novel: Wow!	Why Potentially Strategic: So What?	How to Amplify Impact: Oomph!!!
Scoopshot	Over 600,000 users have registered with Scoopshot to provide on-demand, verified, genuine photographs. Scoopshot uses crowdsourcing (sourcing photographs snapped with cell phone cameras) to meet commercial and other photography needs.	Scoopshot has built a market that monetizes the activity that many users are already doing, i.e., taking pictures using their smartphone camera.	Scoopshot's platform provides verification to the wild west of the Internet content without losing the flexibility of crowdsourcing. Traditional news outlets can quickly leverage online communities to gain localized, personalized content.
Shapeways	Shapeways prints products "on demand," "self-publishing" business model for physical goods. The spin-off from Philips created a platform for the creativity and emerging business of 3D printing.	Shapeways' "Made in the Future" stands for zero inventory, customization and design flexibility, redefining the scale of efficient manufacturing from large volumes to single units.	The platform business model creates an efficient, accessible market for emerging 3D content generators (designers, artists) as well as consumers of 3D printing. Builds a pioneering manufacturing model that rewards uniqueness, design complexity, and customization.
Sculpteo	Sculpteo provides a supported 3D printing platform lowering the threshold to engage in additive design/production.	Sculpteo bridges cutting-edge technology and consumer markets by providing automated design support.	3D printing's potential is made available to greater numbers through a supported platform. Sculpteo is partnering with brands to offer personalized products to consumers.

Outlier Case	What's Novel: Wow!	Why Potentially Strategic: So What?	How to Amplify Impact: Oomph!!!
BUG	BUG uses insects instead of pesticide to control pests helping farmers and saving the environment.	Breakthrough methods in deploying biological pest controls allow for a natural solution for a problem generally addressed through harmful, inorganic means.	BUG is an example of biomimicry being used to address current problems. With the forecast of further environmental tumult all, including natural, approaches are expected to be in demand. Leveraging natural processes BUG provides alternatives to chemical industrial solutions and brings down short- and long-term costs for farmers.
BioCurious	BioCurious opens up an accessible and affordable biotech laboratory to any citizen scientist in the community. Its motto "Experiment with Friends" suggests the citizen scientists are taking charge of their well-being and performance.	Established industry companies have visited the community laboratory to learn about creativity and open innovation. Policy makers and government are also looking to learn from BioCurious.	BioCurious blends organizational models from tech and the maker movement and introduced diversity to the biotech. Numerous community laboratories from around the world are looking to learn from BioCurious.

Outlier Case	What's Novel: Wow!	Why Potentially Strategic: So What?	How to Amplify Impact: Oomph!!!
TaskRabbit	Distributed workforce for distributed tasks on demand, built on the foundations of networking and flexibility of work. Some of the taskers make as much as 70,000 per year![1] Exploits the competitive dynamics of play.	This market is an example of the re-organization of the supply and demand of work and contracting, e.g., the gig economy.	The open and distributed organizational model has already emerged in different industries from consulting to technology testing and development.
Gengo	Crowdsourcing and crowd-managing translation expertise globally, on demand using technology. Gengo has processed over 300 million pieces of translation to date (and raised a funding of $23 million).[2]	Gengo provides a human powered, natural voiced Internet service.	Accurate and natural translation will allow for further market penetration and personalization of the Internet-driven services across emerging markets.

---

[1]http://fox4kc.com/2015/05/06/on-demand-economy-taskrabbit-is-the-new -way-to-get-things-done/.

[2]http://techcrunch.com/2015/04/22/gengo-series-c/.

Outlier Case	What's Novel: Wow!	Why Potentially Strategic: So What?	How to Amplify Impact: Oomph!!!
Microtask	Unbundles complex tasks combining high-powered digital processing and human cognition into a seamless microtask platform. Promises anonymity, reliability, and speed.	Redefining the location and time of work, "micro gigs" can be completed anywhere, anytime there is an Internet connection and a computer.	The efficiency of Microtask's model brings computer power, with human support, into a wide range of analog transactions.
Kaggle	Efficient modeling algorithms through competition. Uses crowdsourced and resource pooled domain knowledge and big data expertise, for solving (companies') data-related problems. The platform hosts the $3 million Heritage Health Prize.[3]	Kaggle's business model reinterprets outsourcing by having highly skilled and much-in-demand experts compete for solutions, globally.	The reorganization of external consultative work brings openness and transparency to the evidence-based solutions provided by consultants and advisors. Taps the kind of expertise in predictive analytics that may not otherwise be available for hire. Peer-based competition.
MakieLab	Creating personalized physical toys based on consumers' own digital designs and choices.	MakieLab blurs boundaries creating "an infinite loop of play" between the digital and physical world.	MakieLab is making artisanal, locally produced products possible in an industry dominated by large corporate players.

---

[3]http://www.economist.com/blogs/babbage/2011/04/incentive_prizes.

Outlier Case	What's Novel: Wow!	Why Potentially Strategic: So What?	How to Amplify Impact: Oomph!!!
ZenRobotics	Created the world's first robotic waste sorting system: ZenRobotics Recycler. Bringing automation and robotics into scalable and effective waste disposal and recycling.	Waste is a growth industry, and solving environmental problems is also a potential business opportunity.	A reduced impact growth-based economy requires increased recycling. Automation and intelligent software will allow for sustainability at scale.
Spire	Made public the plans to launch and maneuver 20 commercial weather "'SmallSats" before 2016.[4] Spire has launched four satellites but still considers itself a "data company."	Commercial off-the-shelf components make low cost, private nanosatellites, and the data streams they generate, possible.	With space-based data there will be few dark spots left on earth, ensuring safety for ships, tracking weather, etc.
Organovo	Organovo launched exVive3D: the very first commercially available 3D-printed human tissue in the world.[5] 3D prints live "bioprints," high-quality human tissues from one's own cells.	Bioprinting has tremendous implications for drug testing and medicine development. Radical cost reduction. Potentially more humane.	The technology ensures safe and sustainable replacement of damaged tissues with healthy, compatible ones and thus redefines life. Organovo has also partnered with L'Oreal to 3D print skin.

---

[4]http://www.satellitetoday.com/technology/2015/01/29/spire-to-launch-20-satellite-weather-constellation-this-year/.

[5]http://3dprint.com/60245/organovo-merck-3d-print/.

Outlier Case	What's Novel: Wow!	Why Potentially Strategic: So What?	How to Amplify Impact: Oomph!!!
Genomera	Using virtual social media technology for scientific, biological experimentation. Founders look to become the "Facebook of Genomics."	The incredible turnaround time from research design to data generation allow for multiple iterations and parallel experiments.	Increase speed and diversity of scientific experiments combined with falling costs of genetic testing will bring personalized medicine closer to reality and break the bottleneck of the health research pipeline.
Robin Hood Minor Asset Management	The alternative fund, or the "wild side of finance" uses a "parasite algorithm" to replicate best performing trades in a stock market. Considers engaging in synthetic finance. The fund allocates a percentage to the coop's revenue to chosen artistic and societal projects.	The fund uses democratic organizational structures to represent the coop members' voices while automating investment decisions to an algorithm. Uses a strategy termed "minor" to act differently.	Experimentation in financial markets by non-financial institutions paves the way for potential democratization of a largely closed industry. Allows access to returns on capital to those excluded. Develops radical new frameworks for thinking about access to opportunities in a society.
Nor1	Nor1 monetizes unsold inventory and matches it with travelers who are willing to pay a reduced price for it upon check-in. Nor1 offers room and service "upgrades" to customers on a standby basis, via upselling.	The Company has patented PRiME®: a real-time, data-driven pricing and merchandising engine.	Upgrading via upselling provides incremental revenue to the hotels, effectively handles overbooking situations, and paves the way for higher customer loyalty. To the customers it ensures higher satisfaction.

Outlier Case	What's Novel: Wow!	Why Potentially Strategic: So What?	How to Amplify Impact: Oomph!!!
B&O	B&O Play, the 3-year old brand from B&O, is helping the company to move from the high-end luxury market to one that caters to the young smartphone generation.[6] Designs and manufactures innovative, high-grade, modern consumer electronics, since 1925.	The 90-year old company stays in tune with the needs of the market and technology advancements by relentlessly engaging strategy, organizational design, and innovation process.	Continuous resilience and willingness to innovate through strategic renewal helps to fill in the gap between the current core capabilities and the evolving base of competitive advantage.

---

[6]http://www.telegraph.co.uk/technology/news/11593787/BandO-Play-a-grown-up-audio-brand-for-the-smartphone-generation.html

Authors

Liisa Välikangas is Professor of Innovation Management at Aalto University and Hanken School of Economics in Helsinki. She is on the board of various private and public organizations, including the Finnish Funding Agency for Innovation and Robin Hood Minor Asset Management. She has been affiliated with Stanford University, London Business School, Keio University in Japan, and IMD in Switzerland, and worked for Strategos, a strategic management consultancy, and SRI International in Silicon Valley. Her research on innovation, strategy, and resilience has been published in _Harvard Business Review_, _MIT Sloan Management Review_, and _Wall Street Journal_, among other leading journals, and presented to various executive audiences. She is the author of _The Resilient Organization, How Adaptive Cultures Thrive Even When Strategy Fails_ (McGraw-Hill, 2010). Liisa lives in Finland and California.

Michael Gibbert's first encounter with strategic novelty and outliers was as an apprentice to a professional chef in a two-Michelin-star kitchen in Wiesbaden, Germany, in a (failed) attempt to get the third star. Intrigued by the theoretical underpinnings of novelty and outliers, he turned to the academe of business management, reading for a Masters at Stellenbosch, South Africa, and a PhD at St. Gallen University, Switzerland. After several research and teaching stints at INSEAD, Yale, and Bocconi, he joined the faculty at the Università della Svizzera italiana, in Lugano,

Switzerland, where he is a professor of marketing. The author of several books and influential articles, his quest for strategic novelty happily received more accolades on the academic (compared to the culinary) front. He lives, cooks, and teaches in southern Switzerland.

Lakshmi B. Nair is a PhD student at Università della Svizzera italiana, Switzerland. She explores the methodological sophistication of research, with a predominant focus on qualitative methodology. Her work so far encompasses studies on rigor, transparency, and impact of research methodology. Before embracing the academic way of life, she was a banker (HDFC Bank Ltd.), an MBA (First Class, Mahatma Gandhi University), and a BSW (Rank Holder at Kerala state level, Mahatma Gandhi University). When she is not following outliers, she follows her other passions: cooking, reading, dancing, traveling, and talking (not necessarily in that order).

Markus Paukku is a postdoctoral fellow at Stanford University. Based in San Francisco, Markus studies novel organizational and business models in emerging markets and nascent industries. Currently he is investigating the reimagination of higher education through digital technology and online learning. Markus received his PhD from the Aalto University School of Business and has degrees from McGill University and the Helsinki School of Economics. His research has been published in *International Business Review* and is regularly presented at international academic conferences such as the Strategic Management Society.

Inês Peixoto is a doctoral candidate at Aalto University School of Business in Helsinki, Finland. Along with looking into the strategies of outliers, Inês has a keen research interest in how nascent markets emerge and evolve, in particular the role of ambiguity and uncertainty in market rules and the transformative potential of innovative strategies. Currently, she is examining the European biofuels market, having presented her work in international conferences and seminars, including Strategic Management Society (SMS) and Society for the Advancement of Socio-Economics (SASE). Originally from Lisbon in Portugal, Inês has degrees in environmental engineering and in management from Universidade Nova de Lisboa. When she is not peering into the novel, she enjoys exploring the old in music records, second-hand books, and film.

Contributors

Akseli Virtanen is a theorist of new political finance, born in Finland and currently based in Santa Cruz, California. He is a co-founder of Robin Hood Minor Asset Management Cooperative, an activist hedge fund, which bends powers of finance to the production of the common and creation of new economic space. The financial services of the merry men and women of Sherwood are here again: only this time they log into the brains of the bankers at Wall Street to share their means of production with those who don't normally have access to financial capital. Akseli is the author of *Arbitrary Power: A Contribution Towards a Critique of Biopolitical Economy* (n-1 Edições, forthcoming 2015).

Alice Taylor is the founder and CEO of MakieLab, a toys-and-games company in London and the creator of Makies, the world's first 3D printed toy at retail. Alice was recently honored with two of the Hospital Club 100 prizes (Creative Entrepreneur category and Games/Tech category), and won the Rising Star Inventor of the Year at the Chicago Toy and Game Fair 2014. Previous to MakieLab, Alice was Commissioning Editor for Education at Channel 4, where she commissioned multiple award-winning games and media for kids and teens, winning awards that included two BAFTAs. Pre Channel 4, Alice was VP Digital Media at BBC Worldwide in Los Angeles.

Andrea Carugati is Associate Professor, Department of Management, Aarhus University, Denmark where he leads the Information System Research Group. Andrea's research focuses on the strategic impact of technology on IT-driven organizational change, and on the deployment of information technology in organizations. Andrea has published, among others, in the European Journal of Information Systems, Database for Advances in Information Systems, European Management Review, European Management Journal, at the International Conference on Information Systems, EGOS, and at the European Conference on Information Systems.

Eri Gentry is President and co-founder of BioCurious, the first "hackerspace for biotech," home to the 3D DIY BioPrinter printer project, and one of FastCompany's Top 10 Most Innovative Companies in Education. She is a researcher and resident Biofuturist at the Institute for the Future, co-author of the book *Maker Pro*, and past CEO and co-founder of Livly, a research company on a mission to end killer diseases. She was named a White House Champion of Change for Citizen Science and one of Techonomy's Top Ten for 2013.

Eric Nowak is a Professor at the Swiss Finance Institute (SFI) and the University of Lugano (USI). His research on corporate governance, private equity, and IPOs was published in leading international journals including the *Journal of Finance*, *Journal of Business Venturing*, and *Business History*. Eric studied at the Universities of St. Gallen (HSG), Bocconi, and Chicago. He holds a PhD in finance from HSG and obtained his venia legendi in Betriebswirtschaftslehre from the *Goethe University* of Frankfurt. From 2010 to 2011 he served as the Rock Center for Corporate Governance Visiting Scholar at Stanford University. He was the Swiss investigator for the EC Research Network Regional Comparative Advantage and Knowledge Based Entrepreneurship (RICAFE II). Eric has a wide range of practical experience and knowledge in entrepreneurship from start-up activities. Among the start-ups he has co-founded, he is in supervisory board of aktionaersforum AG, an online shareholder communication company, and member of the scientific board of CEPRES GmbH, a web-interfaced private equity data provider. He also is the founder, owner, and Chairman of the board of Swiss Rating Agency SA, Lugano, a USI-incubated start-up active in credit risk analytics. Furthermore, he has worked on numerous consulting projects and in arbitration proceedings particularly for companies in the areas of private equity and event-driven hedge funds. Many of Eric's former students have successfully founded companies under his guidance, among them Indian Energy Ltd. which did an IPO on the London Stock Exchange, CEPRES GmbH which was acquired by Deutsche Bank, and 2iqResearch which has been financed by the Swiss VC *Next Generation Finance AG*.

Giacomo Cattaneo is PhD fellow at the Department of Management, Aarhus University, Denmark, and Research Associate at the Chair of Entrepreneurship, ETH Zurich, Switzerland. He holds an MSc in Management, Technology, and Economics from ETH Zurich, Switzerland. Giacomo's research focuses on the relationship between the processes of strategic renewal and innovation to explain why companies struggle in the face of volatile and dynamic environments.

Harikesh Nair is a Professor of Marketing at Stanford GSB. His research is in the area of marketing analytics. His work brings together applied economic theory and econometric tools with marketing data to better understand consumer behavior and to improve the strategic marketing decisions of firms. His recent research covers pricing, workplace analytics, quantitative incentive design, social media and social interactions, advertising, network effects, diffusion of technologies, and empirical industrial organization, especially in contexts in which marketing activities have dynamic implications for the behavior of consumers and firms. His research has been published in leading marketing journals including *Journal of Marketing Research*, *Management Science*, *Marketing Science*, and *Quantitative Marketing and Economics*, and written up in popular-press outlets like *CNBC*, *The Economist*, *Financial Times*, *US News*, and *The Wall Street Journal*. His research has been recognized with awards from the Quantitative Marketing and Economics Journal, the American Marketing Association Foundation, the Swiss Academy of Marketing Science, and the U.S. Council for University Transportation Centers. Harikesh received his PhD in Business from the Graduate School of Business at the University of Chicago. Prior to that, he received his MS in Transportation Engineering from the University of Texas at Austin, and his B.Tech in Engineering from the Indian Institute of Technology (IIT) at Madras, India. He has been at Stanford since 2005, and teaches classes on Data and Decisions, Pricing and

Monetization in the Stanford MBA program; on empirical analysis of dynamic decision contexts in the GSB PhD program; and on Marketing and Pricing in the GSB executive education and custom education programs. Harikesh serves as an associate editor at Management Science and Quantitative Marketing and Economics. At the GSB, Harikesh was the Fletcher Jones Faculty Scholar from 2007 to 2008, the Spence Faculty Scholar from 2011 to 2012 and the Louise and Claude Rosenberg Faculty Scholar from 2009 to 2010 and 2012 to 2013. In 2014, *Poets&Quants*, a magazine focused on Business schools, voted him one of the 40 Most Outstanding B-School Profs Under 40 in the World.

Heraldo Negri de Oliveira is a Brazilian biologist and partner and a co-founder of BUG Agentes Biológicos where he is also the Director of Production. Prior to BUG, Heraldo worked at the Department of Entomology of Luiz de Queiroz College of Agriculture at the University of São Paulo (USP/ESALQ), Brazil. He also has an MBA in Agribusiness by USP/ESALQ. Heraldo has authored dozens of scientific papers and books in the area of biological control.

Lars Frederiksen is Professor (MSO) at Department of Management, Aarhus University, Denmark where he leads the Innovation Management Group. He was awarded his PhD from Copenhagen Business School, Denmark and hereafter worked for more than 4 years at Imperial College Business School, London. Lars specializes in the management of innovation and technology with particular emphasis on innovation strategies, knowledge creation and search, user innovation in communities, and innovation in project-based organizations. More recently Lars ventured into studying mobility of entrepreneurs and entrepreneurial teams. Empirically, Lars focuses on industries such as software, roads and water, engineering consulting, and entertainment (i.e., music and films). Lars' work appears in journals including *Organization Science, Academy of Management Journal, Journal of Product Innovation Management*, among others.

Liis Männamaa is an Implementation Manager with Nor1 developing the relationship with the main property contacts and supporting the implementation process of Nor1's products into new and existing portfolio of hotels. Having experience in working with tourism and hospitality companies in various countries in Europe, she enjoys communicating with global hotel chains and analyzing the properties to recommend pricing strategies that maximize hotel room revenue. Liis received her Master's degree in Economics and Communication, Major in International Tourism Management at Universita della Svizzera italiana in Lugano, Switzerland, and cannot imagine her life without traveling and experiencing new cultures around the world.

Mario Bellinzona oversees all activities for Nor1 in the EMEA region, supporting the company's growing client base and partner marketing initiatives with a dedicated European Account Revenue Management, Support Analysis, and Business Development Team out of Nor1's regional office in Frankfurt, Germany. Before joining Nor1 he held positions at Trust International as VP Global Sales and Marketing, Sr. Manager Strategic Initiatives, and Key Account Manager. Prior to Trust International he was Product Manager for electronic corporate booking solutions and Management Information Systems at Amadeus Germany, a provider of global travel technology and distribution solutions. He holds a Bachelor's in Economics and Business Management with focus on Travel and Hospitality from the Department of Cooperative Studies, Berlin School of Economics and Law.

Michael Renard has more than 29 years of recognized, revenue-generating experience in commercial operation, business development, and sales and marketing for the life science industry. With Beckman Coulter, he held various positions in program management, business operations, and business development. He most recently was the Vice President of Marketing for North America commercial operations where he was responsible for achieving $2 billion in revenue across 11 major product lines. Before Beckman Coulter, he was Vice President and General Manager in a development-stage incubator division of Sanofi, Inc. and director of corporate accounts at Kallestad Diagnostics. Michael holds an MBA from Rockhurst University and a BA in Biology and Chemistry from St. Olaf College.

Milena Mend studied psychology and communication science at the University of Zurich (CH) before she started the Masters in Management, Organization, and Culture at the University of St. Gallen. She is particularly interested in how organizations evolve, establish, and disappear and how innovations change human working life.

Nicolai J. Foss is Professor of Strategy and Organization at the Copenhagen Business School, and holds part-time professorial positions at Warwick Business School and Norwegian School of Economics. His main research interests are the resource-based view, organizational economics and design, and strategic entrepreneurship. Nicolai's work has been published in the main journals in management research. He is a member of the Academia Europaea.

Nozomi Umenai is director of marketing communications at Gengo, Inc., a global people-powered translation platform that enables everyone to read and publish across languages. Prior to Gengo, Nozomi was part of Tokyo-based PR agency BILCOM's international department, where she was responsible for controlling and developing the public image of international clients such as Facebook and Four Seasons Hotels and Resorts. Nozomi then went on to join Wantedly, a social recruiting platform, where she worked as an internal PR representative helping plan and raise awareness to a Japanese audience. Nozomi holds a Bachelor of Arts in both Anthropology and Sociology, as well as a Masters in Visual Culture from New York University. Nozomi currently resides in Tokyo, Japan, and is fluent in both Japanese and English.

Pekka Salokannel is an international award-winning Industrial Designer from Finland whose passion lies in 3D printed product design. Upon graduating from Lahti Institute of Design, Pekka worked as a designer in Golla. In 2012 he joined Tinkercad, where he was responsible for educational content, and also worked together closely with Makerbot, Mozilla Festival, and 3D Printshow. In 2013 he founded Fabrigate, offering consultation, design, and educational services with clients such as Shapeways, Cubify, and Twikit. Pekka is an ambassador for 3D printing and has been a guest speaker, giving lectures and workshops in U.K., China, Russia, and Finland. He has his own brand Colors of Birch, a 3D printed eyewear and jewelry fashion brand which has been exhibited at Paris Fashion Week, Amsterdam, and Beijing. He is currently developing the brand Kokosom as one of the co-founders of this 3D printed custom eyewear company.

Tito Jankowski is one of six co-founders of BioCurious, a community biotech lab in Sunnyvale, California. He is a proponent of open source hardware, biotech hackerspaces, and synthetic biology. His work has been covered by the *New York Times*, *Wired*, *Nature*, and *GQ France*, and in *Biopunk: Kitchen-Counter Scientists Hack the Software of Life* (Marcus Wohlsen), *Makers: The New Industrial Revolution* (Chris Anderson), and "Maker Pro" by Maker Media. Contact him at tito@biocurious.org.

Tomi Laamanen is Chaired Professor of Strategic Management, Director of the Institute of Management, and Director of the PhD Program of Strategy of the University of St. Gallen. Before that Tomi was Professor of Strategic Management and Director of the Institute of Strategy at Aalto University (1997–2011). Tomi holds two D.Sc. degrees; one in Strategy and one in Finance. His research focuses on strategic management with a special emphasis on mergers and acquisitions, management cognition, strategy process, capability dynamics, and management's cognition. Tomi is Associate Editor of the *Strategic Management Journal* and member of the *Editorial Boards of Academy of Management Journal, Academy of Management Discovery*, and *Journal of Management*. At the moment, Tomi chairs the Strategic Management SIG of Euram, the Strategy-as-Practice (SAP) division of the Academy of Management, and co-chairs the Strategy Research Foundation (SRF) of the Strategic Management Society and the Strategic Management Society Special Conference in St. Gallen, 2015. In addition, Tomi has actively worked with a number of firms in different roles as Chairman, Member of the Board, or consultant.

References

Abrahamson, E. 1991. Managerial fads and fashions: The diffusion and rejection of innovations. *The Academy of Management Review* 16 (3): 586–612.

Aguinis, H., Gottfredson, R.K., and Joo, V. 2013. Best-practice recommendations for defining, identifying, and handling outliers. *Organizational Research Methods* 16 (2): 270–301.

Alexy, O., George, G., and Salter, A. J. 2013. "Cui Bono? The Selective Revealing of Knowledge and Its Implications for Innovative Activity." *Academy of Management Review* 38 (2): 270–291.

Andriani, P., and McKelvey, B. 2009. Perspective—From Gaussian to Paretian thinking: Causes and implications of power laws in organizations. *Organization Science* 20 (6): 1053–1071.

Augier, M., March, J. G., and Marshall, A. W. 2015. Perspective—The flaring of intellectual outliers: An organizational interpretation of the generation of novelty in the RAND Corporation. *Organization Science, Articles in Advance*.

Bang & Olufsen. 2011. Bang & Olufsen launches new strategy to boost top-line growth. Press release, August 2011. http://www.bang-olufsen.com. Accessed April 24, 2015.

Birkinshaw, J, Hamel, G., and Mol, M. 2008. Management innovation. *Academy of Management Review* 33 (4): 825–845.

Bogers, M., and West, J. 2012. Managing distributed innovation: Strategic utilization of open and user innovation. *Creativity and Innovation Management* 21 (1): 61–75.

Carlile, P, and Lakhami, K. 2011. "Innovation and the Challenge of Novelty: The Novelty-Confirmation-Transformation Cycle in Software and Science," Working Paper No 11-096, Harvard Business School.

Carroll, L. 1920. *Alice's Adventures in Wonderland*. New York: Macmillan.

Chan Kim, W., and Mauborgne, R. 2004. Blue ocean strategy. *Harvard Business Review* 82 (10): 76–85.

Chesbrough, H. 2003. *Open Innovation*. Boston, MA: Harvard Business School Press.

Chua, D. C. K., Leong, K. F., and Lim, S. 2010. *Rapid Prototyping: Principles and Applications*. 3d ed. Singapore: Stallion Press.

Collins, J. C. 2001. *Good to Great: Why Some Companies Make the Leap—and Others Don't*. London: Random House.

Daft, R. L., and Lewin, A. Y. 1990. Can organization studies begin to break out of the normal science straitjacket? An editorial essay. *Organization Science* 1 (1): 1–9.

Davies, S. 2015. TaskRabbit plans for an odd-job revolution. *Financial Times*. http://www.ft.com. Accessed February 18, 2015.

Deleuze, G., and Guattari, F. 1975. *Kafka: Toward a Minor Literature*. Trans. Dana Polan. Theory and History of Literature 30. Minneapolis and London: University of Minnesota.

Eisenhardt, K. M., and Graebner, M. E. 2007. Theory building from cases: Opportunities and challenges. *Academy of Management Journal* 50 (1): 25–32.

Ernst, R., and Kamrad, B. 2000. Evaluation of supply chain structures through modularization and postponement. *European Journal of Operational Research* 124 (3): 495–510.

Fagerberg, J., and Srholec, M. 2008. National innovation systems, capabilities and economic development. *Research Policy* 37 (9): 1417–1435.

Felin, T., and Foss, N. 2004. Organizational routines: A sceptical look. DRUID Working Paper No 04-13. ISBN 87-7873-163-1.

Fleming, L., and Sorenson, O. 2003. Navigating the technology landscape of innovation. *MIT Sloan Management Review* 44 (2): 15–23.

Foss, N. J., and Saebi, T. 2015. *Business Model Innovation: The Organizational Dimension*. Cambridge: Cambridge University Press.

Fuentelsaz, L., Gomez, J., and Palomas, S. 2012. Production technologies and financial performance: The effect of uneven diffusion among competitors. *Research Policy* 41 (2): 401–413.

Gibbert, M., Hoegl, M., and Välikangas, L. 2007. In praise of resource constraints. *MIT Sloan Management Review* 48 (3): 15–17.

Gibbert, M., Nair, L. B., Weiss, M., and Hoegl, M. 2014. Oops, I've got an outlier in my data—what now? Using the deviant case method for theory building. 74th Annual Meeting of the Academy of Management in Philadelphia.

Gino, F., and Staats, B. 2012. The Microwork solution. *Harvard Business Review (online)*. https://hbr.org/2012/12/the-microwork-solution/ar/1. Accessed December 19, 2014.

Gladwell, M. 2008. *Outliers: The Story of Success*. London: Hachette.

Hajek, A. 2004. *Natural Enemies: An Introduction to Biological Control*. Cambridge, UK: Cambridge University Press.

Hamel, G., and Välikangas, L. 2003. The quest for resilience. *Harvard Business Review* 81 (9): 52–65.

Hawkins, D. M. 1980. *Identification of Outliers*. London: Chapman, Hall. Mahoney, J. and Goetz, G. 2006. A tale of two cultures: Contrasting qualitative and quantitative research. *Political Analysis* 14: 227–249.

Hill, C. W. L., and Rothaermel, F. T. 2003. The performance of incumbent firms in the face of radical technological innovation. *Academy of Management Review* 28 (2): 257–274.

Hsuan, J. 1999. Impacts of supplier–buyer relationships on modularization in new product development. *European Journal of Purchasing & Supply Management* 5 (3): 197–209.

Jarvenpaa, S., and Välikangas, L. 2014. Opportunity creation in innovation networks: interactive revealing practices. *California Management Review* 57 (1): 67–87.

Katila, R., and Ahuja, G. 2002. Something old, something new: A longitudinal study of search behavior and new product introduction. *Academy of Management Journal* 45 (6): 1183–1194.

Krause-Jensen, Jakob. 2010. *The Flexible Firm: The Design of Culture at Bang & Olufsen*. New York: Berghahn Books.

Levitt, S. D. 2008. "From Good to Great. . . to Below Average." Freakonomics, 28/7/2008. http://freakonomics.com. Accessed April 23, 2015.

Lieberson, S. 1992. Einstein, renoir, and greeley: Some thoughts about evidence in sociology. *American Sociological Review* 57 (1): 1–15.

Lovink, G. (ed.). 2015. *Money Lab Reader*. Amsterdam: INC Publications 2015 (*forthcoming*).

Lyytinen, K., and Damsgaard, J. 2001. What's wrong with the diffusion of innovation theory? http://finntrack.co.uk/. Accessed July 15, 2015.

March, J. G., Sproull, L. S., and Tamuz, M. 1991. Learning from samples of one or fewer. *Organization Science* 2 (1): 1–13.

Massini, S., Lewin, A., and Greve, H. 2005. Innovators and imitators: Organizational reference groups and adoption of organizational routines. *Research Policy* 34 (10): 1550–1569.

McGrath, R. 2012. How the growth outliers do it. *Harvard Business Review* 90 (1): 110–116.

McKelvey, B., and Andriani, P. 2005. Why Gaussian statistics are mostly wrong for strategic organization. *Strategic Organization* 3 (2): 219–228.

Miller, D. 1990. *The Icarus Paradox*. New York: Harper Business.

Murray, F., and O'Mahoney, S. 2007. Exploring the foundations of cumulative innovation: Implications for organization science. *Organization Science* 18 (6): 1006–1021.

Owen-Smith, J., and Powell, W. W. 2003. The expanding role of university patenting in the life sciences: Assessing the importance of experience and connectivity. *Research Policy* 32 (9): 1695–1711.

Padgett, J., and Powell, W. 2012. *The Emergence of Organizations and Markets*. Princeton, NJ: Princeton University Press.

Pascale, R., Sternin, J., and Sternin, M. 2010. *The Power of Positive Deviance*. Boston, MA: Harvard Business Press.

Paukku, M., and Välikangas, L. 2012. Outlier organizations and systemic transitions: Towards a research agenda. Conference Paper—*Strategic Management Society 32nd Annual Conference*.

Roper, S., Du, J., and Love, J. H. 2008. Modelling the innovation value chain. *Research Policy* 37: 6 (7): 961–977.

Rosenzweig, P. 2007. *The Halo Effect*. New York: The Free Press.

Scheffler, I. 2010. *In Praise of the Cognitive Emotions (Routledge Revivals): And Other Essays in the Philosophy of Education*. London: Routledge.

Schumpeter, J. 1994/1942. *Capitalism, Socialism and Democracy*. London: Routledge.

Siggelkow, N. 2007. Persuasion with case studies. *Academy of Management Journal* 50: 20–24.

Simon, H. A. 1947. *Administrative Behavior: A Study of Decision-Making Processes in Administrative Organization*. New York: MacMillan.

Stahl, A. E., and Feigenson, L. 2015. Observing the unexpected enhances infants' learning and exploration. *Science* 348 (6230): 91–94.

Strati, A. 1992. An aesthetic understanding of organizational life. *The Academy of Management Review* 17 (3): 568–581.

Strauss, A., and Corbin, J. M. 1990. *Basics of Qualitative Research: Grounded Theory Procedures and Techniques*. London: Sage Publications, Inc.

Upton, G., and Cook, I. 2006 *Oxford Dictionary of Statistics*. Oxford: Oxford University Press.

US Department of Commerce. 2012. National Institute of Standards and Technology. /SEMATECH e-Handbook of Statistical Methods. http://www.itl.nist.gov. Accessed July 15, 2015.

Välikangas, L. 2007. Rigidity, exploratory patience, and the ecological resilience of organizations. *Scandinavian Journal of Management* 23 (2): 206–213.

Välikangas, L. 2010. *The Resilient Organization: How Adaptive Cultures Thrive Even When Strategy Fails*. New York: McGraw-Hill.

Välikangas, L., and Sevón, G. 2010. Of managers, ideas and jesters, and the role of information technology. *Journal of Strategic Information Systems* 19: 145–153.

von Hippel, E. 2005. *Democratizing Innovation*. Boston, MA: MIT Press.

Yin, R. K. 2003. *Case Study Research: Design and Methods*. 3d ed. Thousand Oaks, CA: Sage.

Index

Note: In the index, *b* refers to information in boxes, *f* refers to figures, *n* refers to footnotes, and *t* refers to tables.